MAKEBA: MY STORY

MAKEBA
MY STORY

BY MIRIAM MAKEBA
WITH JAMES HALL

NAL BOOKS

NEW AMERICAN LIBRARY

NEW YORK AND SCARBOROUGH, ONTARIO

Permissions and Acknowledgments

"Alone," from *The Weary Blues* by Langston Hughes, reprinted by permission
of Alfred A. Knopf, Inc., a division of Random House, Inc.

Lines from "Come on-a My House," reprinted by permission of Bagdasarian Enterprises.

Portions of "Blues in the Night" by Harold Arlen and John Mercer.
© 1941 Warner Bros. Inc. (Renewed) All rights reserved. Used by permission.

"(Sittin' on) the Dock of the Bay," lyrics and music by Otis Redding
and Steve Cropper, copyright © 1968 and 1975 East/Memphis Music Corp.,
copyright assigned to Irving Music, Inc. (BMI), 1982. All rights
reserved. International copyright secured.

Ms. Makeba and Mr. Hall also wish to thank Carole Hall, Jay Levey,
and Hamilton Cloud of Imaginary Entertainment; Bart Andrews and Sherry Robb
of Andrews and Robb.

NAL TRADEMARK REG.U.S. PAT.OFF. AND FOREIGN COUNTRIES
REGISTERED TRADEMARK—MARCA REGISTRADA
HECHO EN CHICAGO, U.S.A.

SIGNET, SIGNET CLASSIC, MENTOR, ONYX, PLUME, MERIDIAN
and NAL BOOKS are published *in the United States* by NAL PENGUIN INC.,
1633 Broadway, New York, New York 10019,
in Canada by The New American Library of Canada Limited.
81 Mack Avenue, Scarborough, Ontario M1L 1M8

Library of Congress Cataloging-in-Publication Data

Makeba, Miriam.
Makeba.

1. Makeba, Miriam.   2. Singers—South Africa—
Biography.   I. Hall, James.   II. Title.
ML420.M16A3 1987   784.5'0092'4 [B]   87-18496
ISBN 0-453-00561-6

Designed by Barbara Huntley

First Printing, January, 1988

2   3   4   5   6   7   8   9

PRINTED IN THE UNITED STATES OF AMERICA

PROLOGUE

I LOOK AT AN ANT AND I SEE myself: a native South African, endowed by nature with a strength much greater than my size so I might cope with the weight of a racism that crushes my spirit. I look at a bird and I see myself: a native South African, soaring above the injustices of apartheid on wings of pride, the pride of a beautiful people. I look at a stream and I see myself: a native South African, flowing irresistibly over hard obstacles until they become smooth and, one day, disappear—flowing from an origin that has been forgotten toward an end that will never be.

If given a choice, I would have certainly selected to be what I am: one of the oppressed instead of one of the oppressors. But, in truth, I had no choice. And in a sad world where so many are victims, I can take pride that I am also a fighter. My life, my career, every song I sing and every appearance I make, are bound up with the plight of my people. I have been denied my home. We have been denied our land. I have watched my family diminish as relatives are killed by soldiers. We have seen our best blood spilled in Sharpeville, Soweto, Crossroads. I am in exile on the outside. We are in exile on the inside.

But there are three things I was born with in this world, and there are three things I will have until the day I die: hope, determination, and song. These things I also hold in common with my people. If you believe, as I do, that every man and woman is an object of wonder and joy in the heart of the Superior Being, then it is not too much to expect that some day all wrongs will be righted, and justice will prevail. We all want the same thing: a decent life, peace, love. This is not politics; it seems to me that this is common sense. I have never been to a

1

university, but I do have common sense. I got it from my mother's breast.

My mother. She was an extraordinary woman. And though she died in 1960, she is still a very real part of my life. What is 1960? A date. A number. It has no meaning in my culture. In the West the past is like a dead animal. It is a carcass picked at by the flies that call themselves historians and biographers. But in my culture the past lives. My people feel this way in part because death does not separate us from our ancestors. The spirits of our ancestors are ever-present. We make sacrifices to them and ask for their advice and guidance. They answer us in dreams or through a medium like the medicine men and women we call *isangoma*.

When a Westerner is born, he or she enters a stream of time that is always flowing. When a point in life is passed, it is finished. When a Westerner dies, he leaves the stream, which flows on without him. But for us, birth plunges us into a pool in which the waters of past, present, and future swirl around together. Things happen and are done with, but they are not dead. After we splash about a bit in this life, our mortal beings leave the pool, but our spirits remain.

I close my eyes and the past surrounds me. It is today. The faces—so many!—are alive. I respectfully greet my grandmother once more. I laugh with my playmates at school. I suffer again my eleven automobile accidents. (I know I should stop keeping count at this point, but I still do.) I exult at the pleasure and hope of my wedding nights. I curtsy to Emperor Haile Selassie, with his pet lions, to President Kennedy, with his serious but warm eyes, to Mr. Belafonte, my Big Brother who brought me to America, and to Paul Simon, the American pop star who brings me back to his country after so many years. I feel the warmth of the studio lights, so bright, and the warmth of my African sun, so much brighter. I see the cheering audiences who from the stage look like heads of cork bobbing on a dark sea. I am thankful to have such a living past. It gives me strength. And courage is what I, and all of us, must have, always.

I look at the past and I see myself.

1

I KICK MY MOTHER AND cause her great pain. But she forgives me my tantrum this one time only. She is all alone in the house. I am nowhere to be seen, yet. My mother's name is Christina, and she is a trained nurse. She knows what to do when the labor pains begin. She boils the water. She prepares her *icansi*, her mat made of rush. Beside her as she lies down are some scissors, some strips of clean cloth, and a bowlful of water. There is no doctor. Doctors are for white people. They are a rare luxury.

It is late Friday afternoon, and the air is crisp with the approach of winter. My father is out looking for work in the great concrete sprawl that is Johannesburg. The room is still. My mother does not cry out when she feels her flesh part. She has had five children before. Three of them have lived beyond infancy. But this pregnancy has been difficult. For her. For me.

In a moment I am in the world. My mother cuts the cord that joins us. Then she looks at me, and she is alarmed. I am a scrawny baby. My head is huge. She slaps me and I cry out. This reassures her. Tears come to her eyes. I made it. We made it. There are those who said neither of us would survive the ordeal. I wail and wail! The dog barks outside. The neighbors come. I may be scrawny, but have I got a voice!

Exhausted, my mother passes out, and I grow silent. My grandmother, a woman of great power and compassion, picks me up and sees that I am very sick. She looks at my unconscious mother, shakes her head, and mutters, *"Uzenzile."*

"You have no one to blame," she is saying, "but yourself." My mother has been warned that another child could endanger her life. *"Uzenzile"* is a common expression. When a child is told not to play with matches, but she does anyway and she burns herself, she is told, *"Uzenzile."*

My father returns. His name is Caswell Makeba. He is a good man, and kind. But life is very hard during this Depression, and, indeed, it is never to be easy for us. This is no time for me to arrive. But my father greets me with great wonder. He is my mother's second husband, and I am his first and only child. He grows frightened when he holds me. I am so thin, and terribly ill. My sliver of a body convulses, and I gag on the air that I breathe. My skin is hot and I cannot eat. I am in such pain that it is painful for others to look at me.

For two days, my father prays for me to die.

My mother loses weight. She had a picture taken of herself with her sister a few months before. She was pregnant with me at the time, but even so she is shown to be a big woman. Now she is a pale shadow. With the help of my grandmother, she pulls through. So do I. The relief in the house is so great that when my grandmother again chastens my mother by saying *"Uzenzile,"* there is humor in her tone. "This is your own fault!"

"Uzenzile," my mother repeats. She thinks of the word and of the warnings she has ignored. She plays with the word. "I will name my daughter Zenzi."

It is the custom for a child's African name to comment on the events surrounding his or her birth. My mother, Christina, was born the day her father was commandeered into the British army during the Anglo-Boer War. Her African name, Nomkomndelo, literally means "the child was born the day the father was commandeered." My mother is a member of the Swazi tribe. My father, Caswell, whose African name is Mpambane, is a Xhosa. Since I am his daughter, I am Xhosa, too. But in South Africa tribal differences are not important. We are all the same people. It was the British who first divided us. To be a tribalist is to be a racist. In South Africa the real differences are between blacks and whites and Coloreds. I will find this out.

Before long I am given an official document by the white

people who control our lives. It is called a birth certificate. The paper states that I arrived on the Fourth of March, Nineteen Hundred and Thirty-two. There were no such papers in my mother's time, and no one, not even she, knows her exact age. But from her name we know she was born during the Boer War, around the turn of the century.

▼▼▼▼▼

I must tell you how things happened for us, the original South Africans, so you will known how the evil of today came to be.

Our Great White Masters, the descendants of the English and the Dutch settlers, have historically hated each other. We probably have this hatred to thank for our survival, because when the English and Dutch were not busy killing each other, they were hunting us down, the Africans.

In the 1600s the Dutch came to our beautiful seacoasts on the southern tip of the great African continent. They carried those bell-shaped rifles that look so quaint in the paintings of the Pilgrims at the first American Thanksgiving. But the Dutch in South Africa had no desire to live in peace or to give thanksgiving with the native Africans. They used their blunderbusses to chase the Zulus, Sothos, Xhosas, Swazis, and other tribesmen off our land. The British came, and they called both the Dutch and the French Huguenots, who had also come, "Boers," which is the Dutch word for peasant. The Dutch and Huguenots called themselves Afrikaners. The English spoke English, but the Afrikaners spoke Afrikaans, which is a mongrel Dutch with some German. Afrikaans has a guttural and ugly sound. It would later be very effective to use when the authorities ordered native families from our homes or commanded soldiers to fire into unarmed crowds. It is the language of genocide, and, in fact, it sounds like the German the Nazis speak in Hollywood movies.

We, the Africans, had developed a just and complex tribal life before the Europeans came. Our ancient laws and traditions, like our art and architecture, grew from our profound closeness to our land. We had grown crops on our great plains and built village huts beside our riverbanks thousands of years before man entered the Western Hemisphere. There were tribal wars, but we lived in harmony with the land for so long we had no reason to think this harmony would not last forever. Ours was a marriage, a love affair—the land would nurture us, and we would honor the land.

But the land was too rich and too good. The powerful and greedy invaders saw this at once. Came each new period in history, our land provided the natural resource that was needed: diamonds and gold for the Crowned Heads during the Reign of Monarchs, coal during the Industrial Revolution, oil during the Automobile Era, uranium for the Atomic Age. For these riches the European settlers fought one another. We Africans were not consulted or even paid attention to. We were pushed aside, robbed of our land. When we protested we were massacred. A handful of whites took power, and with their boots they pressed the faces of an entire people to the dirt. Three hundred years have passed, but the weight of oppression is still on our backs. It has not grown lighter. The taste of dirt, flavored with our tears and our blood, is still bitter.

▼▼▼▼▼

Tribal ways have become mixed with Western ways by the years of my infancy. We worship our ancestors with sacrifices, but we wear suits and drive cars. Johannesburg is now a great modern city. But it is a white man's city. The native Africans live in isolated ghettos. There are black lawyers and doctors, but they have only other blacks as clients and patients. We are the servants of whites. Our wages assure us that we stay in poverty. We cannot vote, and a British colonial government of which we are no part decides our fate. Soldiers and policemen and a network of informers watch over us to make sure we do not engage in interracial relations or break any of the many laws that restrict our movements and our lives. Once a free people, we are now captives. The white businessmen who employ Africans for poverty wages, the white housewives who employ African domestics as virtual slave laborers, the white clergy who seek to banish our tribal religions, the administrators who enforce the laws that keep us down, they are like an occupational army.

We try to cope. One of the racist laws says that blacks cannot drink. Africans are not "civilized" enough to drink. If a black is caught with alcohol, he goes to jail. But there is an African beer called *umqombothi*. It is brewed in secret from cornmeal and malt. My mother makes it to sell to the neighborhood. Sixpence a pint for one jar of the heavy dark brew. The income helps.

When I am eighteen days old, the police raid our house. They discover the *umqombothi*. My mother is taken away, and I am in her arms. She is told she must pay an eighteen-pound fine or go to jail for six months. My father cannot scrape up eighteen pounds. It is impossible. He stands bleakly at the jailhouse door and watches his wife and baby daughter go away from him for half a year. All because of some beer brewed from cornmeal. I am crying, not because of his pain, which I cannot understand, but because of the red scarfs all the women wear in prison. They frighten me. Whenever I see a red scarf I start to bawl. It takes a while for me to get over this.

"Once in jail, you have to go back at least three times," my mother tells me. She will repeat this when I am older. And she will be right. I will be going to jail a lot in my life.

When my mother was a girl, she lived on a farm, where her parents, brothers, and sisters all worked for an Afrikaner farmer. She learned to speak Afrikaans. This comes in handy now in jail. My mother becomes a translator between the Afrikaner prison matrons and the African prisoners. The Afrikaners cannot speak the tribal languages. We, however, are multilingual from an early age. Xhosa, the language with the enchanting clicking sounds, Zulu, and Sotho in particular are spoken by just about everyone. My mother is also very good with her hands. To help out my father, she does embroidery for people who place orders with her. Her reputation for knitting grows throughout the prison. Soon the warden's wife brings her husband's socks to my mother to darn. This becomes a privilege: The woman has my mother leave our cell and go to the warden's office to work. She tells my mother to bring me along. I lie on the floor and keep quiet. I am a perfect baby, for a felon.

When my mother and I are freed, my father takes us north, to the city of Melspruit. This is in the eastern Transvaal, one of the four South African states. The capital city of Pretoria is located here. The other three states are in the south: the Cape of Good Hope (good hope for whom?); the Orange Free State (another strange name if one is black); and Natal. My father has a job with Shell Oil. He does administrative work. My mother still has to go to work in someone's kitchen to make ends meet. She is forced to leave her other three children with my grandmother in Pretoria.

And so I, a toddler, stay alone in the small brick house when my parents are away at work. Gradually, as my senses bring things into focus, my world begins to open up. Something enters my life that will become my first memory. (The things I have mentioned were later told to me.) It is a dog. His name is Timmy. He stays with me all day. He is small and cute, with white speckles over his black fur coat. But let anyone get near me and he starts to bark and growl like a killer. No one can touch me when he is here.

There is another animal who will also leave a deep impression: a cat. I am almost five, now. I like to spend my time out in the flower garden. My parents love flowers. The house is completely surrounded by tulips, lilies, roses, carnations, violets, gardenias, birds of paradise, and poinsettias. It is lovely and colorful, and I enjoy spending my day here in the garden. Grapevines grow on the trellis that covers the walkway that runs from the back of the house to the kitchen. The kitchen is a little building that is detached from the house because it gets very hot in there. The grapevines on the trellis make a shadow on the ground, and in the swirling patterns I see the moving shadow of a cat. This cat is usually given little scraps of discarded meat by a woman who is a relative. She sits now at a little table outside the kitchen. But she must be in a bad mood this day, because she ignores the cat. He looks down at her from the grapevine. She just continues to work. Suddenly, the cat jumps down at her. His claws catch her on the neck. She stands up and clutches her throat. I cry out. Blood pours out of a cut vein. People rush to help her, but it is too late. She dies. The greedy cat has killed her.

I will be afraid of cats from this day on. They will know it, too, and never let me alone.

Timmy gets run over by a car. I cry and cry and cannot be consoled. But when another, more important death strikes, I am more bewildered than sad. I do not understand. Nobody tells me why or how the terrible thing happened. I am only told that my father will not be coming home anymore. (Later in life, I learn that he died with yellow eyes, and I guess that jaundice or hepatitis might have taken him.) There is a funeral and grief, but I will not remember these things. I will only remember the sudden turmoil. The house in Melspruit vanishes. It becomes a memory. And so, in the confusion, does my father. I am too young to have known him as anything more than a presence. I am five years old going on six. My life is thrown into confusion. I am frightened.

In my culture, there is no such thing as a single woman alone with children. There is no such thing as "alone" at all. There is the family. My mother takes me immediately to my grandmother's compound in the Pretoria neighborhood of Riverside. Then she continues by train for thirty minutes to Johannesburg, where she must work as a domestic. I am by myself. But I am not alone.

My grandmother has twenty-one grandchildren. They all live in the compound. I am the youngest. I am reunited with my brother and sisters from my mother's first marriage: my sisters, Hilda and Mizpah, and my brother, Joseph. I see that Mizpah and Joseph have lighter skin than I. Hilda and I are dark like my mother. Joseph gives me the nickname Keri, from *knobkierrie*. A *knobkierrie* is a weapon the African warriors carry, a long stick with a round knob at the top. Joseph says because I am very skinny and have a big head, I look like a *knobkierrie*. I like him. We will feel close all our lives.

Many families live in my grandmother's compound. People build their mud houses here with bricks made from dried dirt. The floors are dirt, too. They pay my grandmother two pounds a month for rent. She is not a rich woman, though. We all work very hard.

"No little girl is supposed to sleep until sunrise," my mother told me. And, indeed, I am up every morning at five o'clock to do my chores. I have already swept the yard by the time the older people get up. There is no running water, so, while my sisters make the fire, I go down the hill to the well. I drop in the bucket, and crank it back up with the chain. After I fill my four-gallon tin, I place it on my head and trudge the quarter kilometer uphill to where my grandmother lives. I learn to walk without holding on to the pail. This is an accomplishment, and it makes me feel grown-up. The water I bring is used for washing, cooking, drinking, everything. I must make the trip to the well four or five times. African children really work hard.

My sisters have made a charcoal fire from the coal that is dug from the ground and shipped overseas for industrial use. It is smoky, but my grandmother is lucky: She has an iron stove with a chimney. Other families in the compound have to make stoves by poking air holes in the bottoms of four-gallon tins like the one I use to carry water. We have to be inventive in our poverty. We learn to make floor polish from candle wax. We stuff our mattresses with the soft brown coy that grows like wool on the shell of the coconut.

There are many fruits to be had: apples, apricots, plums, and peaches. But our staple food is cornmeal. Every day: cornmeal medium-rare, cornmeal well-done, always cornmeal. Rice is a luxury, something we eat once a week on Sundays. We make custard with it on Saturday night. There is no refrigeration, or even electricity, but it is cold in the Transvaal, so we cover the custard and put it under the floor until Sunday afternoon's big meal of rice, chicken, and custard. Spinach with peanuts is a favorite. We eat different squashes and weeds, which grow wild. In America, these are called "greens." The pumpkin plant leaves, when they're young, make very nice greens. Also potato leaves. We eat the pumpkin, too.

There are so many cousins that we are divided into groups: the older boys and girls eat together, and then the younger boys and girls. We gather around a big bowl of cornmeal with fried tomatoes and onions and, if we are lucky, meat sauce, and we dig in. In addition to my cousins, other children come and join us. In Africa one does not measure food. A woman cooks all she can because she never knows who is going to show up. When we have, we cook for everyone. When we don't have, well, we do without.

At night I go to sleep in the arms of my cousins. We sleep several to an *icansi*, the mat made from rush. It is easy to feel safe against the night when I am surrounded by these big girls. But the night holds many dangers.

The darkness is shattered by a loud banging on the door. I wake up, confused. My cousins are frightened. One screams when the door flies open with a crash. Flashlights go on, blinding us. We chatter to each other in our native tongue, except for one English word: "police." The Africans have no word for police. The concept is foreign to us. There were no police in Africa before the white man came. Now, the white policemen in their brown uniforms force their way inside. "Pass!" they shout. "Pass!" I press myself against the wall with my cousins, and as

I shiver in my bedclothes I stare at these men. The only white people I have ever seen have been the policemen who enter our ghetto. These men are Afrikaners. The English do not like to be policemen.

"Pass!" They are checking for passbooks, and looking for illegal residents. An African's passbook determines where he or she will live. If we travel, we must get permission from the Ministry. We cannot go across town without a permit. A black without a valid passbook goes to jail. With time, I will get used to the police breaking in during the middle of the night to check up on us, to keep us off-balance. It is their way of keeping us down.

One of my uncles does not produce his passbook quickly enough to satisfy one young policeman, who is almost a boy. The youth curses my uncle and slaps him. My cousin, who is my uncle's son, begins to cry. He loves his father and looks up to him. Now he has to watch his father be humiliated by this pimply, foul-mouthed child with a gun. My uncle has to take the humiliation. We all do, else we go to jail, where the police will beat us or do anything they want. Sometimes people are taken away and are never seen again. No one dares ask questions. We know. So, my uncle swallows the insults, and his son watches, and learns, and remembers. I watch, too. I am learning a lot about the way the world is for us.

By day we try to guard ourselves as best we can. The children at play or doing chores in the compound keep an informal watch. As an excuse for a raid, the police will often come looking for illegal beer. As soon as some police are spotted, a signal is given and word is quickly passed. Relatives or visitors with invalid passbooks skip out. Baseboards are quickly removed from the bottom of walls. Whiskey bottles and jars of beer are stored inside. When the police enter, everything has returned to normal. Constant harassment is an important tool for the authorities so they can keep us preoccupied and subjugated. But our own vigilance and resistance gives us back our dignity. What other people have to live like this? It must be the Jews in Germany, and the people of the European countries that are now being occupied by the Nazis.

▼▼▼▼▼

So the long years begin to pass, and I am with my big family and my twenty-one cousins. I learn things, like how to crochet. I wear little woolen caps like the other girls. When it's not so cool we wear colorful scarfs on our heads. My older cousins look out for me. They bring me things: candy, and sometimes toys, things that mean a lot to a little girl. My grandmother, whom I call Gau-gau, which means "granny," likes to spoil me because I am the youngest. She gives me special treats. Sometimes she lets me sleep with her. One of my cousins brings me a hula-hoop. It will be twenty years before these things become a fad in America. I love my hula-hoop, and I get good at it. When you are lucky enough to have one you have to show your friends, and you don't stop all day. (Later in life, when I am on stage singing, some of my movements recall the fun I used to have: the undulations of my hips look like I'm spinning a hula-hoop in slow motion.) After a while, the authorities ban all hula-hoops. It seems some kids are spinning from morning to night until they injure themselves. One of my girl cousins tells me that some kids have even died!

But I am spending less time with the older girls. They don't want me around when they discuss their boyfriends. I'm too little. They tell me to get lost. I skip rope and play hopscotch with the girls my age. We make rag dolls. But I like the boys better. My brother Joseph and his friends like me, too. I begin to spend lots of time with them.

Our neighborhood is one large extended family. Every adult is every child's parent, and every child is every adult's son or daughter. What this means to me is that if I do something wrong, any adult has the right to spank me, to discipline me, to tell me to cut it out. And if I am foolish enough to go home and complain to my grandmother that "Gilbert's mother" or "Mrs. So-and-So" spanked me, she will demand to know why and then she will spank me again! She assumes the adult is always right. This is awful for a child; it's double punishment! Later I will grow to appreciate a culture in which every adult takes responsibility for the children of the community and has their moral development at heart.

Like every little girl, I get into trouble. A few miles down the road are the white people's fruit orchards. Some of my cousins and I decide to sneak in and steal some fruit. We know that if they catch us they will whip us. But we are hungry, and the adventure has a special allure. There is some barbed wire we have to crawl through. I scratch myself. But no one is around when we enter the orchard. We pick fruit up off the ground. We don't take any off the trees. A Boer farmer comes and we run for it. But men with sticks surround us. We're afraid they will beat us, but they don't. What they do is force us to eat all the fruit that is in our pockets. They shout at us to finish it all. We eat and eat until we are sick. I feel green, like the apple in my hand. After this day I will not care much for fruit.

At the end of each weekday, while the dinners are cooking on the stoves, the fathers come home to the compound from their jobs. All the children run to them, shouting "Ba-ba! Ba-ba!" (Daddy! Daddy!) I run, too, as happy as the others. I, too, shout "Ba-ba! Ba-ba!" But all around me the other children are being picked up by their daddies, and I realize, it's not *my* Ba-ba. I don't have a Ba-ba. This makes me very sad. I miss my mother terribly. I have a mother, but she is not here. She is in Johannesburg cooking for the white people.

Because I am a small child, the authorities give me permission to visit my mother. The government does not want too many black people in the cities. A husband is not permitted to visit his wife if she works in the city but he does not. If the reverse is the case, and the husband works in the city but the wife does not, the man must return to the native areas outside town for a conjugal visit. If the rules are broken, the people get fired from their jobs. My mother does not have to face a separation from her husband, because she does not remarry. She is afraid her children might not like a new father. Besides, she is busy. I take the black people's train from Pretoria to Johannesburg, holding on to my bottle of raspberry soda with both hands and staring out the window at the flat brown winter countryside. This is not tropical Africa. It gets cold in South Africa, and snows in some areas. Tarzan would not recognize this place. If he wanted to see a lion or a monkey, he would have to do what we do and go to the zoo.

In a little while I am in my mother's arms. I stay in the little room they give her in the back of the big white house. I watch her as she prepares the elaborate European meals for the family, from the soup to dessert. She can bake anything, like wedding cakes and all the sugary things we can never afford to have at home. My mother gives me cookies and candies to eat, but I don't like them very much. Too sweet.

About once a month my mother visits me at my grandmother's compound. These are always happy times for me. There is usually music in the house, and dancing. We dance on special occasions or simply when we are happy and feel like it. My mother has a wonderful voice, and she is a good musician. She plays many traditional instruments: the mouth organ, the thumb piano, and the drums. My mother performs the traditional dances. She is always shining because she is *good*. On Sundays all the children and the neighbors get together in the courtyard and we dance and sing, eat and drink. The occasion is sometimes a wedding, but usually it is a commemoration of the dead. This is not a wake. It is a remembrance celebration. A year after a relative has died, a cow or goat is sacrificed in the person's memory. It is a serious occasion, but also a happy one. We talk to our ancestors at these times. We ask them to prepare the way for us, because they have gone ahead and they are closer to the Superior Being.

My people have learned to mix the religious practices of our tribes with our Christianity. I have been baptized a Protestant. I go to Sunday school, often on the same day my family makes sacrifice to a dead relative. When the Europeans came, they said we were nonbelievers. They denied the validity of our ancient religions. The Boers called us *kaffirs*, which means pagan. To call a South African tribesman a *kaffir* is to insult him in the worst way imaginable. It is like calling an American black a "nigger."

Although we do not abandon our ancient ways, we accept Christianity. I like church because I am in the Sunday school choir. During the services we sing hymns like "Nearer My God to Thee" and "Rock of Ages" in Afrikaans and English. There are also Xhosa hymns, Sotho hymns, and Zulu hymns. I wear a white blouse and a navy blue skirt, with little red ribbons in my hair like the other girls. This is a new experience for me, singing before people. I am excited. The spirit really moves inside of me. I am small, but I sing right out. It's fun.

When I return home, I stop for a moment beside the wide field across the street from my grandmother's compound. During the early part of the day, boys and men play soccer here. But later the Bapedi come. These are tribesmen from the northern Transvaal. They are in Johannesburg working at jobs. I hear their drums and watch them dance. The Bapedi are very musical people. Their music is very intricate. I watch the women dance. Their lively movements are fascinating. The Bapedi shout and laugh and act very happy. This is strange, because these people are even worse off than we are. Is it the music that makes them act like they don't have a care in the world, I wonder? It must be. Already I have discovered that music is a type of magic. Music can do all sorts of things. It can make sad people happy. It can make dull people sit up and pay attention. I know what it does to me. Music gets deep inside me and starts to shake things up. I begin to squirm. My lips turn into a smile and my hands begin to clap against one another. My body moves. It is as if I am possessed. The Bapedi stomp and sing out in the field, and there I am, on the edge, singing with them, apart from them but sharing their joy. Who can keep us down as long as we have our music?

▼▼▼▼▼

2

▲▲▲▲▲

I WALK HOME FROM SCHOOL
with two girlfriends. The journey is five miles. It's hard making
this walk day after day. This afternoon there is another problem:
The skies are low and black, and raindrops, big and wet, begin
to pelt us. My friends and I begin to run. There is thunder and
lightning. We run faster. A bright flash lights up the ground.
The thunder sounds like a bomb. My companion and I look
back. Our girlfriend is not there. We see orange flames on the
ground. A black thing is burning. We rush back. The remains of
my friend's clothes are afire on a body that has been charred
black. Her eyes are empty sockets and her tongue sticks gro-
tesquely out of her mouth. For a moment I stand and stare in
horror and disbelief. Then I turn and run. Some boys have come
upon the scene, but I pass them without stopping.

I run all the way home. I have never known such fear. When I
get to my grandmother's mud-brick house, the door is closed. I
do not slow down or even notice. I knock the door down! I am
going so fast that the door on its old hinges falls down when I
strike it. Below me, lying on a mat on the floor, is my older sister
Mizpah. She is covered with blood. Sweaty strands of hair fall
over her face as she looks at me, too exhausted to speak. I am so
terrified I cannot talk or even scream. A woman I do not know is
here. A squirming, newborn baby is in her arms. The woman is
a midwife. My sister has just given birth. The world has lost a
life and has gained a life almost at the same moment. I have

witnessed both. But the shocks are too great. Beside myself, I collapse. The boys who also witnessed the tragedy on the road appear and explain the reason for my delirium.

When clouds gather outside my window in the morning, I fear a rainstorm. My grandmother pampers me by letting me stay home from school when I tell her I have a headache. But there is something I have discovered at the all-black school that makes me overcome my terror of lightning. It is the senior chorus.

When she was in school, my sister Mizpah was a member, and I used to sneak into the school's little square auditorium after classes to listen. I liked the way the boys and girls were lined up on the stage, where the flag of the South African colony is posted on one side and the Union Jack is on the other. Whenever the teachers caught me peeking out from behind the seats, they threw me out. I was easy to find because I always sang along. Mizpah told me I shouldn't embarrass her, but I could not keep away. This senior chorus is much finer than the church choir that I was in. Listening to them, I got so stirred up inside that I had to sing along.

The teacher who leads the chorus is named Mr. Molefe. He is very dark, and his large hands cut through the air as he conducts the music. It was a scary moment for me when those hands stopped conducting, and Mr. Molefe turned and searched the auditorium to find the little voice that was singing behind him.

"You, there, little girl! What is your name?"

"Zenzi." My voice is very soft and shy when I am not singing.

"You look too young to be a senior."

"No, sir. I'm not even a junior."

There was some tittering from the big girls. My sister gave me a dirty look. I guess she was thinking to whoop me.

Mr. Molefe smiled at me. "How would you like to join us?"

I did not know what he meant. "Huh?"

"How would you like to sing with us? You can't seem to keep quiet down there. You might as well be on stage."

I couldn't believe it. I got up and stood on the stage where he placed me. I looked like a skinny, big-headed midget surrounded by the big girls with their long legs and full chests.

Now Mr. Molefe uses me as a surprise attraction. A novelty.

During rehearsals he tells me I really sing well. All I know is I enjoy it. We go to competitions with other schools. We perform songs written by South African composers. They are in the tribal languages, and some are frankly seditious to the white rule. But since whites do not speak our tongue, we get away with it.

As a black child, just attending school is almost an act of sedition. Education is considered "bad" for us, or, at best, unnecessary. The natives have been assigned the roles of servants to our colonial masters. We are not taught geometry because we will not be given a chance to use it. We are not taught geology. The less we know about the outside world the better. We are to live in isolation.

There is a child's book called *Black Beauty*. It is banned. The authorities do not read the book, so they do not know that it is about a horse. They think it is about racial pride!

What we are taught is the culture and history of England. Of our own tribal histories, there is nothing. Of the arts and accomplishments of our own people, not a word. We learn of Winston Churchill. I am told that he is a great statesmen, and I believe that he is: for England, if not for us. I am told that Franklin Roosevelt is a great statesmen. For America, we know he is, but not for us. The teachers talk a lot about Hitler. They say that if he ever gets to us he is going to make lamp shades out of our skin. I don't know why he is mad at us, because he is at war with England, and South Africa is just a colony, and, besides, what do we natives have to do with the colonial government here? But I do not want to have a lamp shade made from my skin.

We also hear of Mahatma Gandhi. He is making trouble for the British in India, but never to mind that, we are to study his message of pacifism. The authorities want us to be nonviolent, too.

I do not understand the war. I am only seven when it begins, and it is very far away. I'll be a teenager when it is over. My people have no rights in a country that has been taken from us, but we are still forced to die for it. My uncles are drafted into the army. Many of my friends' fathers leave. A long time passes, and some return to tell of fighting in North Africa. They return sick with malaria. At least they are alive. Two of my uncles never return. Their bodies are not shipped home for burial. We never see them again. The authorities do not let us live in dignity, and they do not let us die with dignity. No one can say that the British are not consistent.

It is illegal for a black to own a shortwave radio. We might hear things from the outside world that we should not, like how other people in totalitarian states are rising up against their oppressors. If you can afford one, you can have a regular radio, and listen all day to syrupy white-people's music and censored newscasts. There are two sets of newspapers: the ones for the whites and the ones for us. The authorities control the content of the black press, although natives staff the editorial positions. There are collaborators throughout black South Africa: rich people who grow fat off the sufferings of their brothers, and the strong men who are betrayed by a lack of opportunity and must find work in the police forces. And there are the spies and informers. Informers are discovered all the time amongst us. If they are lucky, they are beaten. If they are not lucky, they die.

I open up a black newspaper and look at the fantasy inside. Nothing is connected with real life. There are stories about witches casting spells on people. Every crime committed by a black is played up. The advertisements tell us that we are ugly, and the only way to obtain true beauty is to try to become as much like a white as possible. We are encouraged to conk our hair to make it straight. The ads for chemicals to bleach our skin fill a page.

The whites have to justify their rape of our land, and so they claim that we are inferior. We are not worthy of God's gifts. It says so in their Bible. They lay claim to our land and our lives and then, to add insult to injury, they patronize us. They say we are ignorant children. Our salvation and welfare are—alas!—"the white man's burden."

And after a while a terrible thing happens. For many of my people, the message begins to sink in. Day after day we are treated like dirt and told we are inferior. It is drummed into our heads. First, your self-respect disappears. You begin to hate everything that is black. The white culture is full of references to things that are black and evil. We are told not to let a black cat cross our path. With the war, there has come a thing called the black market, where money is traded illegally. But what black person ever heard of money before the white man came?

When you begin to hate yourself, you look at someone who is in your own image and you don't have any love for him, either. The streets in our township at night erupt with violent fights. Young people stab each other, kill each other. "Why do you look at me like that?" a boy will shout, and then, stab! I see a knife fight almost every day. The authorities do nothing. They encourage this division among us. On weekends and at Christmastime the ghetto becomes a slaughterhouse. People kill each other, and the authorities say, "Oh, it's just holiday drunkenness." This way the authorities don't have to do anything. If someone wants to kill you, they just wait until a holiday, because they know they won't be prosecuted. Kill a dog or a bird in a protected area and you go to jail. Kill a white man and you hang. But kill a black man, it's all right.

I, too, fall victim to envy. You would have to be blind not to see that everything that is better or even good goes to the whites. You cannot help but think: I wish I was white so I might live well and not suffer the way I do. But if I am envious of white people as a little girl, I am only envious of the way they live. I do not want to *be* white. I will never bleach my skin, although I am dark. I will not straighten my hair. As time passes I begin to discover something about myself: I am not bad-looking. As my body grows, my head becomes more proportional. My mother says that I am pretty. Mothers are supposed to say that. But there are boys, certain boys, who also say I am cute. By the time I am a teenager I begin to believe them.

I don't have many girlfriends. Most of my friends, my best friends, are boys. I feel at ease with boys. They don't gossip like girls do. We go out to the field and fly kites. We talk about everything. They tell me about their girlfriends. I do have some girlfriends, and I get together with them every Sunday to play jazz records from America. We meet at somebody's house, make food, and sit for hours listening to Ella Fitzgerald and Billie Holliday on the wind-up record player. I like them a lot, these great jazz singers. My big brother, Joseph, gives me his records to bring. He is very musical himself. He plays soprano saxophone and piano. Joseph encourages me to sing. He taught me American songs before I even knew the language. When his friends come over he has me sing for them. Sometimes I don't even know what I am saying, but I put all I have into it.

. . . a man is a two-face:
a worrisome thing
who'll leave you to sing
the blues in the night!

Joseph is proud of me. His friends applaud.

When I am with boys whom I like I grow aware for the first time of how poor I am. When I was younger I didn't care if I had to go to school without shoes. But now I am embarrassed because the other girls have shoes and I don't. My mother buys me a pair, but I have to save these for Sunday to go to church. These are difficult days for my mother. Her work is not getting easier. I try not to complain. My older sister Hilda, who is my favorite, helps me. Usually I wear hand-me-down clothes. Hilda makes me some new dresses of my very own.

The World War comes to an end. Nothing changes for us, except that my uncles who are still alive come home. All the black war veterans have been promised pensions. The promises are not kept. Instead, each man is given ten pounds—and a bicycle. They have fought and died to make the world safe from an evil that wanted to enslave everyone. Those of my people who survived now return to a land where we are little more than slaves ourselves. And things are about to get worse.

For myself, as a teenage girl, it is a time of great personal change. I am becoming a young woman. There are ceremonies in our culture when a child comes of age. My boyfriends turn sixteen and they leave to go to the hills. For three months they are away from their parents and homes as they undergo the circumcision rites that will make them men. The elders teach them how to defend themselves with *intonga* sticks. There is other training. And then the boys are circumcised. At that age they can really feel the pain. But this is the idea: to learn to endure pain, to become a man.

Girls have their own rites. When a young girl becomes a woman at the time of her first period, she is put in the same house as other women of her age and condition. For three months the elders come and give instruction on lovemaking, and they teach the skills and graces a woman must know. But by my time, this tradition is observed less and less by girls. Who has the three months to spare? My mother, older sisters, and grandmother teach me what I have to know. Besides, I am now enrolled in the Kilnerton Training Institution.

This is the senior high school. I still sing in the chorus. I have grown up in this chorus. I am no longer a novelty, but one of the ensemble. We stand rigid with our hands clasped over our chests when we perform, four rows of singers. As I grow older, I advance up row by row. Every Christmas, we sing Handel's *Messiah*. "Hallelujah! Hallelujah!" But we also perform very profound songs written in the tribal languages that talk about our way of life as it is. These songs are to educate the people. We Africans have always been able to communicate with each other through singing. If something happens today, tomorrow somebody will write a song about it. Positive or negative: If it happened, there is a song. Some are played on the radio until the government finds out what they mean, and then they are banned. But we sing them amongst ourselves. Our songs mean more to us than the official media of the press and radio. The government realizes this. When the monetary system is changed from the pound to the rand, native artists are hired to explain to our people what the new money means.

One profound song we sing is "Today's Times," in Sotho. It was composed, like many of our songs, by our chorus director, Mr. Joseph Mutuba. Mr. Mutuba becomes a very important person in my life. He thinks I am a good singer, and he encourages me in every way. He forms a trio with myself and two other girls so we can gain experience performing. With Mr. Mutuba at the piano, we sing to raise funds for our school at community centers, churches, and at other schools. My partners and I make look-alike dresses. For the first time I learn stage movements. We move slowly and gracefully, using the entire body. Not everyone in our audiences knows Zulu or Sotho, so I have to make them understand with my gestures and facial expressions. Music has always affected me, but now I learn to project my emotions. Under Mr. Mutuba's direction, I also learn to do more than make pretty sounds with my singing voice. I begin to communicate. I am becoming a performer.

A big event is about to happen, and we in the chorus are thrown into a heavy schedule of rehearsals. The King of England is going to pay a visit to South Africa. His daughter, Princess Elizabeth, will celebrate her twenty-first birthday here. My friends and I debate whether she will look like the princess in the storybooks. Will she and her father wear crowns? Will they ride in a coach?

And the most important question: Will they see *me*? It seems that Mr. Mutuba has decided to give me a solo spot when we sing to King George. The chorus and I work and work. Finally, the big day arrives. This will be my first command performance. I am nervous and excited.

The radio tells us that King George has been ill, and he has come to Africa for our sunshine. He doesn't get it. Instead, it rains this morning. I stand outside, in front of the chorus on a raised platform. We get sopping wet. Before me is a microphone. I have never sung into one before. I am terrified that the lightning will strike it and kill me. My grandmother, my brother and sisters, relatives, and other guests are among the crowd standing beneath umbrellas and watching us. The King's car is supposed to pull up in front. We wait and wait. I hate the rain. I hate getting wet. I'm so wet and cold I wonder how I am going to sing.

At last the motorcade is sighted. Mr. Mutuba gives the signal and we start to sing. I raise my voice as the cars come into view. I follow them with my eyes. They do not stop. They do not even slow down. The long black cars just drive right by. I think I see a man in a window waving at us. But I can't even tell if he is wearing a crown.

What a gyp.

Perhaps it is better that King George did not hear my song. Mr. Mutuba composed it, and gave it the title "What a Sad Life for a Black Man." The lyrics are in the vernacular, and the white people cannot understand. The song is very powerful. It attacks the bitterness and the divisiveness within our black nation that has been brought on because we are a colonized people. It ends:

> *Wake up my people!*
> *Let us get together*
> *Because the fault is within us*

We sing this song at all the competitions for years. Then some smart aleck goes and tells the authorities what it means, and it is banned.

On weekends, I go with the other students to the school basketball games. This day we are playing Maravastad, our crosstown rival. I look down at the unfamiliar boys playing from the other school. They run around in their shorts. I think my thoughts. I pick one out. He is good-looking, tall, and very well built.

To my surprise, I spot him outside when the Maravastad team is headed for their bus. He sees me, too. He must be feeling cocky since their team won, because he comes right on up to me.

"Hello!" He is so much taller than me! He is older, too. His muscles seem to come right out of his jacket. I smile shyly. I don't know what to say.

"I love you," he says. South African boys always say they love you the first time they set eyes on you.

Suddenly sassy, I know what to say next. It's like a game. "What do you mean you love me? Where do you love me from?"

He says, "So long." His team bus is leaving and he runs off to catch it. I don't even know his name. I feel something inside that is confusing and wonderful, like a strange and exotic orchid opening up within me. Its perfume will stay with me and disturb my sleep for nights.

A few weeks pass, and it becomes our school's turn to go to Maravastad for the rematch. I have been waiting for this. During the game I spot the boy on the court. He is as cute as I remember. I gather my courage, and afterward I seek him out.

He remembers me, and he seems pleased to see me. I know this is true from his smile. It is like the sunrise, and it fills me with light. The boy's name is James Kubay. They call him Gooli, and so will I. He is nineteen years old and he is still in school. He asks me if he can take me home. I tell him that I live on the other side of town. It is nineteen miles away. He tells me that he doesn't mind the bus trip.

It will be a trip that he will take many times. I have had boy friends before, but never a boyfriend. It is so new and exciting, and he is so good-looking and strong that I fall right into love. My older sisters tease me. I tell them that they are jealous. I am so deeply and sincerely in love that perhaps they really are.

Gooli takes me to the movies. It is a theater for blacks. We sit

in the balcony, and his great big hand holds mine. The movies
we see come from Hollywood. We can identify with the American blacks in them because they are servants like we are. But
they are lucky ones because of where they live, and every
African wants to go to America, because it is the land of opportunity. The official press will not tell us these things, but we
learn that black people can make something of themselves in
America. Although it is very hard to do, it is not impossible like
it is here. We hear of blacks who have achieved this and that:
Marcus Garvey and Booker T. Washington. Right up on the
screen we see Lena Horne, Duke Ellington, and Ella Fitzgerald. I
rest my cheek on Gooli's broad shoulder and dream what the life
of a big American singer must be like.

▼▼▼▼▼

A few months after King George's visit, a national election is
held in South Africa. My people have no part in this election,
but it will decide our fate. We will look back on the fall of 1947 as
a time when things went from bad to worse.

The Afrikaners have always been a majority within the white
minority. But the English have always held the political power.
This is because Britain won the Boer War many years before.
The English became the administrators and the Afrikaners became the farmers, policemen, and supervisors of the blacks.
After World War II, the candidate of the Afrikaner's Nationalist
party, Dr. Milan, began to charge up the Boers. "We are oppressed, yet we are the majority," he tells them. "We were the
first to get here and this is our land." His words apply more to
us than to the Boers, but the Boers rise up and elect the Nationalist party ticket.

It is in this year, 1947, that a new word enters our language:
apartheid. It will become one of the most hated words the world
has ever known. The Boers are going to create the type of
country they always wanted, and to do this they must make us,
the natives, invisible. The word *apartheid* is Afrikaans: *apart*,
which means "apart" as it does in English, and *heid*, meaning
"hood." "Aparthood." It is what Mr. Orwell in England would
call "newspeak" in a book he publishes around this time called
1984.

In *1984*, Mr. Orwell writes of a totalitarian state that oppresses
its people by rewriting history and convincing everyone that

black is white, wrong is right, and war is peace. But, oh, Mr. Orwell, do not look to the future for such a place. Look to today. Look at South Africa.

To justify the way they have stolen our land from us, the Afrikaners suddenly declare that the country was never ours in the first place. In fact, we never existed. When the first Dutch settlers arrived in the 1600s at the Cape of Good Hope, there were no natives to meet them. We are now told that our ancestors migrated down from the northern Transvaal after the white settlers had already established themselves.

This rewriting of history makes us laugh and cry. We laugh, because we ask who it was the Dutch thought they were fighting during all those battles when they were slaughtering us? And we cry because we know a government that can make up a lie like this can lie about anything.

But the government is rewriting history for a reason. We are told that since we were not native to this region, it is improper to refer to us as natives. We are now "Bantu." The Native Affairs Department in Pretoria now becomes the Department of Bantu Affairs. What, we ask, is a Bantu? We are told: All Africans from the Congo in Central Africa all the way south are now considered "Bantu People." Tribes that have nothing in common are now lumped together. The British once liked to exploit tribal differences; the new authorities find it better to take away our identities.

Men come to each African house and install plastic radio speakers. There are no dials on these radios because there is only one station: the official station. We can only turn the volume up or down. All day and all night there is bland music and propaganda news broadcasts. The announcers tell us Africans how well off we are in this country, and how bad things are up north. There is never any news of the outside world. Announcements are made telling us what we can and cannot do. The broadcast system is called Ready Fusion, and it is different from something Mr. Orwell might invent only because we have to pay for it. We don't believe a word of the propaganda, but we listen. It is important to keep up on all the new acts that are being passed to control us.

The separation of races is now being enforced by the Immorality Act, which makes interracial relations illegal. But the new official policy of apartheid calls for many more steps to distance us from the whites. The Group Areas Act is passed to segregate all housing for Africans. The law will lay the groundwork for the forced relocation of thousands of people into barren wastelands called "homelands"—a horror that as of now we cannot even imagine. We are too busy coping with another law: the Bantu Education Act.

It's all over for the separate but more-or-less equal education that I have experienced under the old regime. The Boers want us as ignorant as possible. Schools for blacks are closed down and teachers are fired. Class time is cut back. The curriculum is redesigned. The new system assures that the Africans will remain ignorant, and good for nothing but servant jobs and menial work.

I am almost all the way through the educational system before it changes. I do not see what happens next. With life more unsettled than before for Africans, things get harder for my family. My mother moves from job to job, and to help make ends meet I must leave school to go to work. I am now sixteen. My love for Gooli has not lessened. No matter what happens, we vow to go on seeing each other.

▼▼▼▼▼

Now that I am going out into the white world, I must be careful how I act. I do not know any white people, but I have learned how to speak to them. If a man or woman addresses me, I must answer, *"Ja, baas,"* which is Afrikaans for "Yes, boss." Always to a policeman I must say, *"Ja, baas,"* or else I may end up somewhere! If a white child addresses me, I must say, *"Ja, klein baas,"* which is "Yes, little boss." I must be very careful if I want to survive.

I go and take a job in Wavely, a suburb at the foot of the mountains near Pretoria. I work for a Greek family, taking care of their child, washing their clothes, and cleaning their house. The little boy becomes very attached to me. We play games together, and he doesn't seem to care that I am black. We get along fine. I am comfortable with my first job. The husband is kind to me, and Gooli can come visit me here. I receive my first monthly pay and send it home.

The second month the woman does not pay me. She says she is short of cash, and she asks me to wait until the third month. I agree. But when the time again comes to be paid, the woman refuses. She looks at me sternly when I ask her why.

"You'll get nothing out of me, thief."

I am astonished. "Thief? Me?"

"That's right. You stole a watch."

I protest that this is impossible. I never even go into the masters' room. But the more I plead, the nastier this woman gets. She picks up the phone and calls the police.

Two officers arrive, and they search my room. I stand to one side, afraid. The little boy is just as nervous. He knows something is wrong, and he is worried for me. He clings to my skirt. The police lift up the pillow off my bed and there it is: the missing watch.

I break down and cry. I have seen the wife give her husband dirty looks when he smiles and is kind to me, but I never thought she could do this. The little boy cries, too. He holds on to my skirt and begs them not to take me away.

I look up and there is the husband. He is speaking to the police. One of the policemen holds the watch and shakes his head with disbelief. "Look," he tells the husband, "these people know how to steal. She would never leave this in such an obvious place."

"Of course," the other policeman says, "we know the pattern, here." It seems that this woman has fired three previous maids. To keep from paying the wages she owes, she accuses them of stealing. She knows that whites can do anything they like to a black.

But the husband also knows his wife's ways. He knows how good I am to his son. And he feels sorry for me. When the police ask him if his wife is lying, he coolly tells them that yes, she is.

The woman storms out. "Oh!" she says to me. "*Kaffir!*"

I am still crying, but this time out of relief. The police ask me, "Do you want to stay here?"

I am sorry for the husband and the little boy, whom I am fond of, but I am too scared. "No! I'm going home. I don't even care if she never pays me."

But the husband gives me my wages for the two months. I also take this money home, and before long I am again employed. Another Pretoria family; another job as a nanny. This time I look after two children, a boy and a girl. In the backyard away from the big house there is a small room for me. I keep my little suitcase there and my few things, as well as my prized possession: my one and only photograph of my father. Sometimes at night I take it out and look at it and try to recall what he was like. He died when I was so young. Already his image is hazy, and it is like trying to grasp smoke to remember him.

After a few weeks I am told that the family is going on vacation and I am to come along. We go by car to the seashore near Durban. The beach is wide and beautiful. It is for white people only. If blacks want to swim, they go to the city pool. While I am at the beach I stay close to the family. The wife has brought along two four-gallon tins. She gives them to me.

"Fill these up."

"With what, mistress?" I ask.

She looks at me as if I am too dumb to live. "With seashells, of course. I need them for my handicrafts."

For three months I pick up shells. Big ones, little ones, pretty ones. One afternoon I am told to stay behind when the family leaves. The end of the trip is getting near, and the wife wants her tins filled to the top.

I am left alone. People look at me, a black girl there on their beach, but I tell myself that I am a white family's servant just doing my job. Durban is tropical, and the sun sets slowly this summer day. People leave and I don't even notice them go. Suddenly, there are two Afrikaner policemen coming toward me. I wonder what kind of trouble I am in.

The police don't waste a minute. "You're under arrest for loitering."

I am scared, and I try to explain. "But I'm working. I'm gathering seashells for my mistress."

For a moment I think they are going to hit me. "Who told you to speak?"

They take me to the police station. I go meekly, but I drag along the eight gallons of seashells. I am afraid that if I lose them my story will also be lost. The policemen do not tell the sergeant that I was loitering. What they tell him instead means prison for sure.

"She was waiting to prostitute herself."

One crime committed by a black is the same as another to them. We are all guilty in their eyes. I beg them, "Oh, please,

please! Take me to my employers. I'll show you where they live. They'll explain."

They make me leave the shells at the station. The mistress is very angry when the policemen bring me, and she starts to scold me.

"Good for nothing! Can't you do anything right?"

She slaps me. I start to cry. "But you told me to stay behind and pick up shells."

She goes to the station to get the shells, and when she comes back she scolds me some more. Plans are made for the family's return trip to Pretoria. It is decided that they will go by car and I will travel by train with the mistress's stupid shells.

It is a black people's train, of course, and I travel third class. The two heavy cans of shells are a burden. I put them down on an empty space at the entrance of the next car, then I return to my seat and try to sleep sitting up. An announcement is made at a stop to tell us that the train will be changing cars and we should stay where we are.

I look out the window and I see the car behind moving backward. "Oh, no!" I am here, and the tins full of shells are there. This is big trouble for me. I get up, go to the door, open it, and jump down to the tracks. I run to the other car about fifty yards away. When I arrive I reach up and pull down the cans. Shells spill all over the track ties. I stoop and start to pick them up. A whistle blows. The train ahead begins to move away from me. I lift the cans and try to run, but they are heavy. The train is picking up speed, leaving me behind. I don't have a penny to my name. I say, "Good-bye, shells, Zenzi's going home!"

I drop the cans and race to catch up with the train. I make it back to Pretoria. My employers are to pay me my wages for the summer when I return. But I don't go back. The woman can have me arrested for losing her property. I have to give up my earnings and also leave behind my little suitcase and belongings. And I have lost my father's only photograph. This is the worst hurt of all.

I go back home and decide to get work taking in laundry. There are many bachelors from other African countries and from Europe who have come to work in South Africa under contract. We collect their clothes on Monday and return them, washed and ironed, on Friday. This brings in a little money. My mother is living in my grandmother's compound now. She is ill with an infected foot that doesn't seem to want to get better.

Gooli still makes the nineteen-mile bus trip to see me. We go to the movies and watch our favorites: Humphrey Bogart and Richard Widmark. This day we do something different after the show. Gooli knows a place where we can go and kiss. We dare not kiss in the theater. I am too shy. We just hold hands.

Gooli has a friend who is older. This friend has a room of his own away from the main house where the rest of his family lives. I have known Gooli for a long time, and it does not take much convincing to get me to go with him. When we arrive we are all alone. Gooli turns off the light and he starts to do things to me that I have never felt before. I don't like it. I am frightened. I have no idea what is happening to me. But Gooli is forceful and determined. He is so strong and full of passion that I let him have his way.

At seventeen, it is the first time that I make love.

And I get pregnant.

3

WE FEAR THAT MY MOTHER
may become crippled. The swelling in her feet gets worse. She
can no longer wear shoes. My mother has always been a good
dancer and tennis player. My father taught her the game. Now
she can barely move. We take her to several hospitals. The white
doctors cannot tell us what is the matter. But we do not expect
them to tell us. We think we know. To find out, we call upon
one of our tribal doctors, an *isangoma*.

An *isangoma* is a person possessed by the spirits of our dead
ancestors, and it is these spirits who give the doctor his or her
medical skills. It must be understood that in our culture, spirit
worship is not a passive thing. The spirit world is actively
involved in the world of the living. We pray to our ancestors and
ask for their guidance. Animals are slaughtered in ceremonies to
their honor. In our dreams we receive answers, or sometimes
through an *isangoma* when he or she is in a trance and communi-
cating with the other side. But more than this, certain spirits,
called *amadlozi*, take possession of special individuals who can,
with training, becoming *isangoma*. The spirits guide the *isangoma*
in telling people what is wrong and in prescribing cures. *Amadlozi*
want to help the living. But to do this they need the cooperation
of the person they possess. He or she must abandon their
ordinary life and go through difficult training with the elders
called *ukuthwasa*. The training may last for years, and it is so
hard that people have died. No one wants to be possessed by

amadlozi; it is frightening. And *ukuthwasa* is frightening. The alternative, though, is worse: insanity and sometimes death. The *amadlozi* are mischievous if their will is not heeded. People who have been told that they have *amadlozi* but who do not go through *ukuthwasa* suffer depression, illness, and financial problems. These problems get worse and worse if the spirits are ignored.

My mother has certain psychic powers that, frankly, make my life miserable. It is hard for a teenage girl if her mother knows everything she does. I come home and my mother asks where I've been. I make up something, like I have been studying with my girlfriends instead of listening to jazz records with them. My mother gives me her knowing look. In fact, she does know. It just drives you *crazy*.

So, when the *isangoma* comes and tells my mother that *amadlozi* are within her, no one is surprised. Because the spirits are making her sick, we urge my mother to go through *ukuthwasa* at once. It is a hard decision for her. Recently, the authorities have been cracking down on the *isangomas*. Some are arrested. Some disappear. The whites do not understand our practices. They feel threatened, because the medicine of the *isangoma* works. Secretly, the white people come to our doctors to be cured. This is a very dangerous thing to the authorities. Apartheid will only work if everything associated with blacks is worthless.

Since my mother is a member of the Swazi tribe, she leaves South Africa and goes to Swaziland to undergo *ukuthwasa*. Swaziland is a small round country that touches Mozambique but is almost completely surrounded by Natal Province. Swaziland is also a British "protectorate." I do not know how long my mother will be away, or what will happen to her. But we all know that she must do this.

My mother is not around, then, when I discover that I am pregnant.

The shock hits me hard. I am sick with worry. Again and again I ask myself: "What am I going to do?" My girlfriends get pregnant all the time. None of us knows about birth control. The girls drop out of school and have their babies. Some have abortions, but this is always dangerous. Many die because they try to perform the operation on themselves.

How am I going to tell my family? They might throw me out

of the house. My eldest sister, Hilda, knows by looking at me that something is wrong. I tell her that I am pregnant. She cries. And then I cry. She is scared for me. My grandmother is shocked when she learns. At the house it is as if a wake is going on. Everyone wonders what is going to happen to me.

I worry about Gooli. He has graduated from school, and he is about to join the police academy. I am seventeen and he is four years older than me. At twenty-one, he is now an adult. There is an expression among my people: "He died wearing a hat." In the story, a child who is curious about his father asks his mother whatever happened to him. The last time the woman saw him was when she told the man that she was pregnant with his child: He grabbed his hat and ran out the door. The mother now answers her child: "Your father died wearing a hat."

I wonder if I will have to tell this to my child.

Gooli is surprised. But then he is happy. He really is a man. He recognizes the child as his, and he tells his parents that he wants to marry me. His mother is not happy, but Gooli is determined. I write to my mother and she returns from Swaziland to meet him. He comes to her in my grandmother's compound. In his slow, deep voice he asks for my hand in marriage. He honors custom, and pays her a dowry. The traditional dowry is ten cows. We are city people, so the practice is to pay the worth of ten cows in cash. This is a great deal of money for Gooli. The dowry is not meant to be my "value." It is a way of thanking my parents for having me so I can be his wife and do all the things I am supposed to do.

Quickly, a church wedding is arranged for us because Gooli must go down to the Cape for his training, and my mother must return to Swaziland to continue with hers. I stay in my grandmother's compound, where the six or seven people who usually share our three rooms keep me from being lonely. But I have lots of time to think about the baby inside of me. Softly, I hum to him or her. I have not really sung since I had to leave school and my beloved chorus. But I guess I will not have many chances to sing from now on, anyway. I am now a man's wife, and I am going to be a child's mother. I will have my own house and family. In my mind I see it, and it is lovely. I cannot ask for anything more. The year is 1950, and life is getting worse for my people with each passing month, each new apartheid law. But I am full of happiness and fond hopes. What I see ahead is so clear and warm and so secure: Gooli, myself, and our child. The future is very, very bright.

▼▼▼▼▼

Every month or so I see Gooli when he is permitted to return home for a visit. We arrange where we will live when the baby comes. By custom, newlyweds live in the house of the groom's parents. I am ready for this, but I am nervous. I have to say good-bye to my family. And Gooli's mother does not like me. She is a very chichi type of woman. Her clothes are expensive and exquisite. Gooli's parents, the Kubays, own a lot of property, including some homes around town that they rent out. For the time being, the government still allows blacks to own property. Mrs. Kubay looks down on me because I am poor. It disgusts her to think that a poor girl could take the love of her son. But I have won his love, and I will try very hard to win hers, too.

Gooli's father is a nice man. He likes me. But he is very ill. He spends much of his time in bed. We don't know what his sickness is. The white doctors will not tell blacks what is the matter with us. They treat us, but we are not permitted to ask questions. The white doctors act as if our illnesses are none of our business.

By his symptoms, we think we can tell what Mr. Kubay is suffering from. But the knowledge is frightening. Gooli's father has cancer.

Gooli's police training will keep him in Cape Town for three months. The baby is due around Christmastime. My husband will be given special permission to come home once he hears that the baby has been born. On the thirteenth of December I feel labor pains. I am taken to the Catholic hospital. The nuns who are the nurses here are both black and white women. They are kind to me as time passes, because the baby does not come at once. A day goes by, and then another. I am in pain all of the time. The nuns force me to eat. A third and fourth day come and go, and I am still in labor. My sisters visit me. They are worried. They tell me that our mother is coming back from Swaziland for the holiday and to also see the baby.

But the baby just doesn't want to come. I am weak from the pain. Finally, after I have been in labor for one week, the doctors decide to perform a caesarian. I am taken to the operating room. The nuns shave my stomach. But just before the knife falls to cut me open, I feel the baby coming. The delivery is successful, but I do not see the outcome. I pass out from exhaustion.

I sleep for a whole day and a whole night. On the next day I awaken and I finally see my child. She is a girl. Her skin is light like her father's; lighter than mine. She is not like I was: She is a beautiful-looking baby. My mother is here to share this moment with me. We laugh and cry and talk about the baby's name. I decide to call my child Bongi, which means in our language "we thank thee." Every time I call her name, I will be thanking the Superior Being and my ancestors for giving me this beautiful daughter out of my suffering.

The hospital keeps me for five days. My relatives and in-laws come to see the baby. On the third day after Bongi's birth, Gooli arrives. He is proud to be a father, and very happy. He adores our little girl. The academy gives him only twenty-four hours for his visit, and he spends it holding the baby and caressing me. I am miserable when he leaves.

The hospital releases me on the twenty-fifth of December. I have never had a worse Christmas Day. My left breast is giving me terrible pain. I think it is because I have too much milk. I feed Bongi with the other, healthy breast. I cannot sleep at night because of the throbbing ache. In the morning my left breast has swollen horribly. My two sisters are trained nurses. Hilda takes a look and she is shocked. "It looks like a cow's udder!"

She takes me to the Pretoria General Hospital. It is closer than the Catholic hospital. I am told that I have an abscess in my left breast. They cut into it and the wound drains through a tube. When this is done, the tube is removed and the incision closes. They tell me to go home.

The pain returns, worse than before. I am truly frightened now. When I go back to the hospital, the white doctor gives me a paper to sign. I ask him what is going to happen to me.

"We're going to cut it off," he tells me.

"My breast?" I am horrified. But just by asking this question I am offending the doctor. He has not the time or patience for a black who will not jump when he commands.

"Do you want to die?" he says.

My terror overcomes my shyness, and meekly I ask, "There must be some other way?"

He snatches back the papers. "Get out." I do not move fast enough. "I said, get out and go home!"

"All right," I say. "I would rather die with two breasts."

The doctor cannot believe that I don't agree to the mastectomy. He yells at me as I try to leave. "You're a married woman. Why do you need your boobs?" I flee from his voice. "Saving them for some other man? You *kaffirs* are all alike."

My mother takes over. She is learning many of the African remedies at *ukuthwasa*. She tells me that she will be away at training for a long time. The elders are having difficulty placing all of the spirits that are within her. There are so many. While she is there in Swaziland she is learning all there is to know to be a medicine woman.

A flat cactus is cut open by my mother and the pieces are warmed on charcoal. She gently applies these to either side of my abscessed breast. They feel good. As I lie still, I begin to doze off. Just before sleep takes me, I feel wetness on my side and on the sheets beneath me. I sit up, the cactus compress falls off, and a jet of liquid shoots out from the hospital incision that has reopened. I call my sister Hilda.

"Please, squeeze it out!"

But she is scared. She won't go near it. Some nurse she is! I take my hands and press them to my breast and squeeze and squeeze. Pus, blood, and water drain out. It is such a relief, like a great weight being taken off me. So, I think, my mother is truly becoming an *isangoma*. She has cured me.

▼▼▼▼▼

Life with Gooli in the house of his family is very hard. The mother does not like me at all. She is Colored, which is what we call people of mixed race. Her father was Italian and her mother was a Shangan tribeswoman. Mr. Kubay is a Shangan also. Gooli is their only son, although he has two older sisters and three younger ones.

Mr. Kubay's illness gets worse. I am sorry for him, and for myself, since he is the only one in the house who seems to truly like me. Often he calls for me, and he asks me to sit by him.

I cannot spend too much time with my father-in-law in this way, because I am kept far too busy. I have to take care of Bongi and keep house, of course, but when I wake up at four in the morning it is not to do these things. I work for Mrs. Kubay. The sisters and I work very hard to make and serve alcoholic beverages. Mrs. Kubay has the whole thing very well organized. She makes a lot of money, for what it is. We brew gallons and gallons of beer. There are many customers who come by day and night to buy a pint for a shilling. I am kept running up and down all the time. All the money I give to my mother-in-law. She gives me nothing in return, except criticism.

But I work very, very hard. I am young and strong, and I don't need much sleep. My house is spotless. All of Bongi's needs are taken care of. Mrs. Kubay really has no reason to complain, because I serve her well. When she is nasty or sarcastic, I keep quiet. My people grow up knowing that you respect your elders. You never talk back. If you feel they are wrong you keep quiet. If you ever talk back to your parents when they are angry, they will just spank you. Later, when they calm down, you go back and say, "I know you thought I did this and not that, but . . ."

But there is never a good time for me to approach Mrs. Kubay. And there is another, bigger problem that is beginning to worry me. It is Gooli's jealousy. I am surprised by his first outburst, but I have no time to feel flattered that he is jealous because he becomes angry and violent. One of his friends comes one day, and he helps me hide the beer when we learn the police are in the neighborhood. Gooli sees us coming up from the cellar together. When things return to normal after the raid, he demands to know what I was doing. I explain. He is not satisfied. He accuses me of being a flirt and he orders me to our room with a look in his eye as if he is going to strike me. I am so upset I run away.

Gooli confronts me often. When his friends come by for beer, he gets upset if I even notice them. "Why did you look at him like that?"

I do not even know what he is talking about. "Look at *who* like what?"

"You looked at Ronnie like you were *interested*."

I am confused and frightened by the way he is acting. I cannot believe that he thinks I am doing what he is saying. He just seems to want to get angry with me, and to accuse me of something. There is no one I can talk to there. My sister Mizpah comes to visit often, but she likes Gooli and she tells me to be patient with him.

I work and work. Mrs. Kubay's business keeps me busy day and night, and still I have the house to clean, Bongi to take care of, cooking to do, the washing and everything else. I am not given a household allowance, or, of course, any of the beer profits. Gooli's mother does all the shopping. When I need clothes for myself or something for the baby I have to go to her. Sometimes she brings me the things I need. Sometimes she does not.

Gooli's father dies, and I lose a friend. The many hours I spent at his side in the quiet room where he lay were the only peaceful ones I have known in this house. I have been here for a year, now. The news comes that my elder sister, Hilda, is very ill. I receive permission to go home to visit her. Again, the white doctors do not tell us what the illness is, and, again, we think it is cancer. She is pregnant but she is losing a lot of weight. My mother has completed her *ukuthwasa*. She has returned from Swaziland after two years of hard training, and she is readjusting to normal life. She looks after Hilda, but my sister is too far gone. When the baby arrives, Hilda is too weak. The ordeal of childbirth kills her. The baby struggles on for eighteen days, and then he, the poor, poor thing, he dies, too. There is little happiness in either of my houses: the old or the new.

Gooli is acting like a policeman on the job and off. He looks handsome in his khaki uniform when he goes off to work in the morning: tall and stern. Our Maravastad district in Pretoria is his precinct. Black policemen have a difficult time. They are not issued guns, only sticks and handcuffs. And they are not permitted to arrest any white man. If a black policeman catches a white man in the act of committing a crime, the black policeman must wait until a white policeman arrives. But what is sad and shocking is the cruelty with which black policemen treat their fellow Africans. They beat and harass their own people without mercy. They must do this, we know, to show that they are impartial, and to gain the approval of their white masters. Being a policeman is one of the few positions of responsibility given a black man in our country. But it is hard trying to belong to something that you can never really belong to. It is hard trying to prove that you are different from your own people. Gooli must know in his heart that he is being exploited, and maybe it is this feeling that is changing him and making him bitter.

I have never seen Gooli on the job. But from the way he acts at home with me, his wife whom he is supposed to love, I do not doubt that when the time comes for him to get rough with his own people, he will do it. He has started to beat me. His family does nothing. When Gooli's friends come over, he no longer shouts at me, he just locks me in our room. At first I cry, like I did when the beatings started. But then I think that at least I can take a break from all the hard work and spend some time with my Bongi. She is so happy when we are together. She crawls, now, and makes her first words. I get down on the floor and encourage her. She is such a beautiful little baby that I think, truly, I am blessed.

It comes time for me to put Bongi to bed. I tuck her in and turn off the light. I look down at my baby in the dimness and I sing to her a lullaby that my mother sang to me when I was a girl.

Hush, now, my beloved
Hush, now, my pride

I kiss my daughter on her soft, light-brown cheek.

Hush, now, love of my heart

▼▼▼▼▼

Bongi is one year ten months old. I'm now twenty. Gooli and I have been married for two years. His temper is worse. The way he treats me is so bad that his friends begin to feel sorry for me. I am really suffering.

One night, one of my husband's friends comes to me. I guess he can no longer stand to one side without trying to help me.

He tells me, "I just left Gooli in my house"

"Oh?"

"He's with some nurse."

"Oh!"

My stomach aches with fear. But I have to find out.

My baby is a problem. No one in the family will ever help me in any way, even to look after Bongi for an hour. Besides, where am I to tell them that I am going? I must take her with me. In

Africa, we women tie our small children to our backs with blankets. I strap Bongi to me in this way, and I set out for this man's house.

When I arrive, the door is closed. I open it. I see Gooli in the darkness. I see the woman he is with. The fear in my stomach turns to acid; it begins to rise in my throat like vomit. I turn and run away in shock. Gooli's friend did not know who the nurse was. But I do. It is my sister, Mizpah.

I think of all the Sundays that she came to visit me, and how Gooli would always walk her to the bus stop. I wonder how many other women he has had, while he has been accusing me of flirting to cover up his own guilt. Out of breath, I arrive back at our room and slam the door. I cannot see because of my tears. The door flies open with a terrific burst. Gooli comes through, and I cry out. He looks as if he is going to kill me. His great fist strikes me on my cheek. I fall back. My blanket comes loose and my baby drops and hits the floor on her head. I scream. Gooli comes after me. He throws me down and starts to beat me. His hands hit my ribs and stomach again and again. I hear the blows land, and Bongi crying with pain. Gooli stands over me and he kicks me. He shouts that I am a spy and a sneak. I scream and scream.

When he is done with me, he leaves. I crawl to my baby. She is bleeding from the nose and mouth. I pick her up and run out into the night. The family stands there, looking at me in silence. They have heard my screams. They wonder what I have done to be beaten. Whatever it was, they think I deserved what I got.

I do not know what to do. With my baby in my arms I run to the police station. I forget: This is where Gooli works. I realize this once I enter. I am terrified that they will call my husband to come and pick me up. But when I beg them not to, and they see how hurt the baby and I are, they call a taxi to take me to the hospital. Bongi and I are treated and released. The relief I feel that my baby is not seriously hurt is a moment of happiness in this nightmare. I do not have any money, but I hire a taxi to take me home. The trip to my grandmother's compound is nineteen miles. My mother is there. She pays the taxi and hugs me. She doesn't say anything at all; she just holds me. I hold Bongi. Ever since I was six years old, my mother has been away from me. She has had to go away to work at white people's homes. But she is back, now. She is *isangoma*. And we will be together now for as long as I am here in South Africa.

I come to live in my grandmother's compound once more. My mother does not want me to go back to Gooli. I'm scared myself. I have really been beaten. My husband does not come and get me. For several days I must rest. My rib cage is swollen. During this time I get to know the woman my mother has become. She is someone completely different from the woman I used to know. Once my mother was a very fashionable dresser. She always wore the latest styles. Now such things do not appeal to her. She still cannot wear shoes. Every time she puts on shoes her feet swell up. This is because there is a spirit within her that does not want to wear shoes, so she cannot.

My mother is still a large woman, but her face is worn and lined from the ordeal of *ukuthwasa*. It has been discovered that many *amadlozi* inhabit her. She seems to always be waiting for them to come out and take possession of her. She seems to be quietly listening for her spirits. I still love my mother very much. When she needs someone to help her when the *amadlozi* do come, I am the one.

When I return home now and something is wrong, my mother knows it right away. She knows what kinds of African medicines to give for certain illnesses. This knowledge of herbs and roots was part of her training. People come to her for advice or treatment: people who are ill or who have problems. They know she can "see." Sometimes my mother can cure them right away. Other times she has to consult the *izintlhola*, or bones. This is another skill she learned. My mother sits on the ground with the bones of a goat in her cupped hands. Sometimes these are shells, or even stones, but they are always twenty-one in number. My mother concentrates very hard. The spirits will communicate through her with these bones. The *izintlhola* slip through her fingers and make patterns on the ground. According to the way the bones fall, they explain exactly what needs to be done. From them, my mother prescribes a remedy or performs a cure.

Sometimes the rolling of the bones is not good enough for the *amadlozi*. They prefer to communicate more directly. The will of these spirits is great. This is why my mother cannot wear shoes. This is why *amadlozi* ruin or kill some men and women who will not go through *ukuthwasa* and give them their freedom. And so, because these spirits really are show-offs, they sometimes take complete possession of my mother. She becomes them.

It begins when my mother grows very quiet. She may be sitting by herself, or she may feel something from someone who has entered the compound, perhaps seeking her help. Now she goes into a trance. I must attend to her at these times. In a short while, the spirit announces itself. My mother is no longer my mother. She is the *amadlozi* who has come forth from within her. She speaks in their voices. If the *amadlozi* is a man, a man's voice comes from her. Through my mother they sing, dance, and tell tales. They also let the sufferer know what is ailing him. All the spirits want to be clothed in a certain way. One will want a blue dress, another a set of beads. This is my job as dresser, to clothe my mother in the manner the spirit fancies. If it is an *amadlozi* that I already know from past visits, I go to the trunk right away and bring out the necessary dress or robe. My mother never takes snuff, but there is one spirit who always desires this, so I must provide it. Besides some water from time to time, they don't seem interested in eating or drinking.

I get to know the spirits when they come. My favorite is Mahlavezulu. He was once a very young, athletic man, and very strong. He has a lot of charisma. When she becomes him, my mother puts an *ibeshu*, or loincloth, over her skirt. She puts on the traditional bracelets over her upper arms that African men wear to make themselves look regal. Because he was a warrior, Mahlavezulu will sometimes want a shield, a spear, and a *knobkiri* stick. I have to find these things for him. I like Mahlavezulu very much. He always has beautiful songs that he sings. And his dances are very intricate. He talks about himself. When he was on this earth he was a very good swimmer. He helped people across some of the longest and widest rivers in Africa. He put them on his back, and they held on while he swam.

Some spirits give me trouble because they speak in a language that I cannot understand. There are a group of *amadlozi*, both men and women, who are called *abandzawe*. No one can understand a word they say until we find an old lady from a remote area in the Northern Transvaal who can identify their tribe. The *abandzawe* are a lively people. They dance and sing and really wear out my poor mother's body.

When the *amadlozi* leave, after giving certain directions where we can go in the hills and find the herbs needed for medicine, my mother goes back into a trance. Sometimes it takes her a long time to come out of it. When she does she is her old self. She doesn't remember a thing that has happened.

For a long time after I found Mizpah with Gooli, my sister has been afraid to come home. I know that she was attracted to my husband and she did not think. But I do not discuss it with her. I am hurt and angry, yes, but she is my sister and we will be sisters for the rest of our lives. My mother thinks it is good for me to get away. She says it is best for her to raise Bongi for a while. I do not want to leave my daughter, but there are not many choices I have. Arrangements are made for me to live with an aunt in Johannesburg and then with the aunt's daughter, my older cousin Sonti Ngwenya.

Cousin Sonti's husband is very well off. He owns a fleet of taxicabs. Now that I am living with them, I spend the days washing the taxis. I do this with Cousin Sonti's son, Zweli. Zweli is seventeen, and I am two years older than he is. He is good-looking and cocky. His mother spoils him to death by buying him expensive clothes. He likes to go to the American shops and buy fancy suits and Florsheim shoes. He sits polishing those shoes all the time.

"Hey, Zweli!" I say, washing a taxi with my big brown sponge. "Come here and help me."

But he's polishing and polishing those shoes. "Can't! I got a *date*." He winks at me like he is some big man. He knows he is one of the best-dressed guys in town.

One day Zweli asks me to the rehearsal of his new band, which he calls the Cuban Brothers. The name is a fantasy, because no one is from Cuba. None of us have even met a Cuban. From the movies, though, we know they look like Cesar Romero and Carmen Miranda. Also, none of the Cuban Brothers are real brothers with anybody else in the band. This doesn't bother Zweli. He is full of plans. He says he knows the man who is the manager of the Donaldson Center, a community center where the band can make its debut.

"You can sing for us," he tells me. Everybody in the family knows that I can sing. They have heard me perform during my seven years with the school chorus.

Zweli doesn't have to ask me twice. Before, I never wanted to sing around my in-laws' house. I was too sad. But now I want to sing my lungs out, and forget all my troubles. The Cuban Brothers have practiced several Big Band hit songs. I get to know these, and soon I join the rehearsals. Zweli has a spunky little group: a drummer, a piano player, some brass, and some boys, including Zweli, who back me up when I sing. We have fun together. Soon we will begin performing before the public. Nobody knows what is in store for us, or for me. Certainly, I do not.

W<small>E</small> ARE HAPPY AMATEURS. Whenever there is a community sing, or a fund-raising activity for the church, or an amateur contest, the Cuban Brothers are there. I am the band's female vocalist. Like the others, I do not get paid. It's just fun for me. I like my friends in the group, these young boys. It seems as if my nightmare marriage to Gooli was from some other time, and I am starting over with this new life of mine. Of course, I am only twenty years old.

I guess I am as tall as I ever will be, which is five feet three inches. This is not very tall, is it? And I am very shy, too. I am just this way by nature.

Except when I sing. Then, watch out! *"Come on-a my house I give you candy!"* The hit songs from America make their way over to us. We include some in the Cuban Brothers' perform-ances, along with ballads and dance tunes in all the tribal languages. We are getting to be known in our township of Orlando East. People come to the Donaldson Community Center to hear us. They dance. We have a good time.

But it is difficult for a young woman to be on stage. Many people in our society look at it as something bad. The old thing that women are not supposed to go on stage and show them-selves takes some time to die. I have heard the neighbors gossip: "So-and-so's daughter is a whore because she is on stage." I can imagine what they are saying about *me*: "She left her husband to show herself on stage! Why isn't she at home raising her child, instead of having her mother do it so she can sing?"

But my mother has made up her mind when it comes to my singing. She encourages me to do it because it is what my father would have wanted if he had lived. My father was a very musical man. He played piano and composed music. My mother would sing and he would accompany her. My mother tells me that my father wanted me to study music. It was his one real hope for me. Now that I am singing with my nephew Zweli's band, my mother thinks it is fine.

But I am not to be a female Cuban Brother for long. Some men show up at the Donaldson Center during one of our shows. Maybe they have heard of us. Maybe they just came by chance. But here they are, and one of them is a singer named Nathan Mdlhedlhe. Mr. Mdlhedlhe is the leader of one of the country's most popular bands: the Manhattan Brothers.

Everyone has heard of the Manhattan Brothers. We listen to them on the radio. They put out records, and they tour all over the country. When I finish singing with the band and Mr. Mdlhedlhe comes up to introduce himself, I can't believe it.

As I do whenever I meet someone who is older or someone I should respect, I curtsy to him. This is the way I have been brought up.

"I really enjoyed your show, Miss Makeba," he says. He is a tall and large man, very commanding. A thin mustache of the debonair "Manhattan" style runs above his lip. His suit, I notice, is a nice one.

I thank him for his compliment, although I think he is just being polite. Surely an amateur band like ours is beneath his notice.

But he seems sincere when he says, "You have a lovely voice. It's the voice of a nightingale."

I must look very surprised and embarrassed, because he smiles down at me. "I'm sincere. And I want you to come audition for us. The Manhattan Brothers need a female vocalist."

If I could manage to speak, I might argue. I would say that he surely does not mean *me*; that the Manhattan Brothers can choose among any female singers in the country as their vocalist; that I have never sung professionally before in my life . . .

Zweli and the others are too amazed to complain that they

might lose me. It's only an audition, I tell myself and everyone else. It's so farfetched.

Yes, it is farfetched. Very far. But somehow, I don't know how, I fetch it. The men listen to me sing. In addition to Nathan Mdlhedlhe and the musicians, there are the singers Joe Mogotsi, Rufus Khoza, and Ronnie Majola. They like the way I look, the sound of my voice, and the way I behave on stage. I listen to their compliments in a daze. And when they tell me I am hired, I really think I am dreaming. How did this happen? One day I am singing with an amateur band with Zweli, and the next moment I am to be with one of the biggest groups in the country. Life has not been easy for me, and it never made much sense to dream of things that are too impossible. I never wasted my time dreaming of living a life in show business, or of doing what I like to do more than anything else in the world, which is singing. But now, all of these are coming true as if it is, well, a dream!

They tell me that the job does not pay a lot of money. The travel is hard. But if they pay me a shilling it will be more than I have ever earned before as a singer. And the travel I think of as an adventure. All I can answer is: "When do you want me to I start?"

"The first thing you'll need is a name," Nathan tells me. Even though he is the leader of the group, he won't allow me to call him Mr. Mdlhedlhe. "Miriam Makeba sounds better than Zenzi Makeba. We'll use your English name."

New handbills and posters are made for the Manhattan Brothers. They say: "And Introducing Miriam Makeba, Our Own *Nut Brown Baby*."

Rehearsals begin at Nathan's house. I learn right away that with four men singing behind me—Nathan, Ronnie, Joe, and Rufus—I have to be *loud*. There will be times when I won't have a microphone to help me. On their own, the men sing American songs by the Ink Spots and the Mills Brothers. When we are together we sing native African tunes as well as popular songs in English. Because we are black, however, we are not permitted to record songs in the English language. Six musicians make up the band: a sax, trumpet, straight-up bass, piano, and the drummers. I listen carefully to what everyone tells me. The men are older than I by at least ten years, and they know a lot about show business. I am very eager to learn. Everyone is kind to me, and encouraging.

My older cousin, Peggy Phango, is also a big help. She takes me to the movies, and we talk. Peggy is a good singer and actress. She was just in a movie that was made here in South Africa called *Cry, the Beloved Country*. The story is about South Africa. The great old actor Canada Lee is the star, and also a young man by the name of Sidney Poitier.

Peggy is full of advice. She teaches me all about clothes and how to match colors. During the performances I am to wear Western-style outfits: the stiff petticoats that flare out. Sometimes I wear tight, strapless evening dresses. I am very tiny, but my proportions are good, and with Peggy's help, I can even look glamorous.

She tries to pluck my eyebrows, but it is too painful. "Please," I beg her, "leave me alone." Makeup does not agree with me, either. I don't like it. My mother says, "Don't put all those things on your face. They don't look right on you." Of course, there is nothing non-African about makeup. In the old days, people had different colors of clay that they used to make designs on their bodies and faces. The Egyptian women used makeup three thousand years ago. But today, ladies' makeup is manufactured by white companies for whites. It does not suit the color of our skin. A black girl looks as if she is wearing a mask. Her face is a different shade from her neck.

I am to be paid five pounds per show. This is not much money, but it is a living if we give five performances a week. The shows, held in concert halls in the black townships, are long. We sing for four hours, from eight in the evening until midnight. The audience sits in chairs, which are removed for dancing afterward. The musicians then play until five in the morning. But I do not stay to dance. I'm too tired. Also, if we are in the Pretoria area, I rush home to my mother's so I can be with Bongi. She is a beautiful three-year-old; thin like me, but already growing tall like her father. My separation from Gooli is permanent, now. Soon we will be getting a divorce.

A journalist from the big African newspaper *The Bantu World* comes to one of our shows. The next day someone gives me the paper and there is my first review. The Manhattan Brothers gather around to see if their hunch about me was correct. I am too nervous to read, so I give the paper to someone else. The reviewer writes that I "sing like a nightingale."

"What did I tell you!" Nathan says. Everybody whoops it up and is very happy.

"Oh, my!" I say. I am proud, but very embarrassed by the attention.

Now when Nathan introduces me during the shows, I am no longer the "Nut Brown Baby." I'm "the nightingale."

In South Africa, there is a new dance every week. The couples like to show off before the bandstand. But they are not the only ones who are showing off. Gangsters come to the clubs. I have been warned that these are very rough places. There are fights, shootings, stabbings. Some of our shows end in riots. It's very dangerous. The gangsters do whatever they want. Blacks are not supposed to drink, but these men come in, sit in front, and pull out their bottles. They put these before them on the table. Then they take out their guns and put these in front of them on the table, too. We are all supposed to look, and we can't help ourselves: We do. They are like actors, these gangsters, although they do not play. In South Africa, movies are taken very seriously, and there is a movie in the cinemas now in which Richard Widmark plays a hoodlum. They call him Styles, and he dresses up in a hat, a belted jacket, and those Florsheim shoes. The black gangsters go out and dress just like him. In the movie, Richard Widmark eats an apple after each of his crimes. So, all the African hoodlums have gone out and gotten apples, too! I see them right there on the tables between the bottles and the guns.

I am singing in Alexander Township. The club is known to be very, very rough. I look down from the stage and I see all these gangsters in front. They sit back with their feet up on the tables and they look at me. I can tell they want me as their gangster moll. I'm nervous. A girl may like them or not like them, it does not matter, because if they think they want her, they take her. I sing one of the Manhattan Brothers' most popular songs: "Saduva." When I am finished, the gangsters make me sing it again. Nathan and the boys play the number once more, because we know these men mean business. But the gangsters are not satisfied. They make me sing "Saduva" again, and then another time. It becomes a game to them. I am scared to death.

All the musicians can see the guns on the table. The gangsters can start shooting up the place anytime they want. I am forced to sing "Saduva" over and over, until I have sung it twenty times. I am about to collapse from nervous exhaustion. Nathan steps forward and says the show is over. He is very brave. I hurry off stage, and with another singer who is there, Susan Rabashan, we leave through a side exit.

We are in the alley when the gangsters come out and spot us. I think they are probably drunk and might try to do something to us right there. Susan and I run to the street to try to get a taxi. The men chase us. A car comes with other men inside. They signal for us to jump in. We do, and we find ourselves in the company of a rival gang. Susan is truly scared, but, fortunately, among these men I recognize a distant cousin. Sipho is his name. I know that even though these men belong to a gang, I am once again safe in the embrace of my extended family. I thank Sipho for rescuing us. His friends are amused and maybe disappointed that they can't have their way with us, but, really, Sipho would just have to kill them if they tried anything. So they take us home.

Home, at the end of 1953, is my very first house. Blacks are not allowed to own property anymore. We can only lease. I can't afford to buy a house, anyway, and I rent a little place in Mofolo. Mofolo is one of the black Southwestern Townships of Johannesburg. Because of apartheid, all of the Africans are being herded into these townships that the government is building. My house in Mofolo is a gray prefab one just like all the others. It has four rooms: a kitchen, a living room, and two bedrooms. The bathroom is outside. The yards are not big, but the people of each house make nice little flower gardens in front. In the backyards there are vegetable gardens, and sometimes chicken coops. We shop in clean, modern stores that are run by blacks but owned by whites.

My mother comes to live with me. For the first time in her life, she no longer has to work. I can support her. And Bongi comes, too. My house is truly a home. I am not so busy with the Manhattan Brothers that I cannot appreciate this happiness. I watch my daughter run down the block, a happy little four-year-old, past all the gray houses with the little trees tied to the lawns with strings. The land is flat, and as far as the eye can see there are gray houses. Where the gray of Mofolo ends, the white houses of White City township begin. My brother Joseph lives in the Dube Township, two train stops away. Other family members have been relocated here. We make the best of these settlements. Having relatives around helps. We are all in the same boat. But this is nothing new for Africans.

▼▼▼▼▼

The Manhattan Brothers are recording stars for Gallotone Records. I join them in the studio many times to make 78 rpm recordings. We are paid for these sessions, and that is all. I receive two pounds ten shillings for a day's work. We don't know anything about royalties, and Gallotone is not offering. Even if we compose songs that are published, we are not paid royalties. There is a musicians' union in South Africa, but we are not permitted to join because we are black. Some of the groups decide to try to organize one of our own. It will be a difficult task, and even if we get all the black singers to sign on, there is no guarantee that we will be recognized by the record companies.

Work begins when we rent a three-story building in downtown Johannesburg. We call it the Artists' Union Center. There are meeting rooms here, and places for us to rehearse. Classes are offered for children who want to be musicians. Everyone volunteers to make the Center work. Some of us pose for advertisements for a piano manufacturer, and the company gives us a piano that we need. Not only professionals, but others who love music come and teach the young people.

At Gallotone one day, I am asked to make a record on my own.

"With the Manhattan Brothers backing me?" I ask.

"No," they tell me. "You'll be solo on this one. It'll be a Miriam Makeba record."

My very first record! The song is originally a Xhosa tune: "*Lakutshuna Ilangu.*" Mankhewekwe Dvushe wrote the beautiful love song, which is about a lonely man who sits before the setting sun. He does not see his lover, and he is asking what has happened to her. He says, "*I will come looking for you everywhere/in the hospitals, in the jails/until I find you/Because as the sun goes down, I can't stop thinking of you.*" Hospitals and jails: The Africans know what this means. Whenever one of us is missing for a time and we don't come home, the first place the family looks is the hospital or the jail.

The song sells very well. I am asked to record other records on my own, but this one was my "breakthrough." They play my record on the radio. The song travels overseas. In America, a songwriter likes it and writes some English lyrics. Gallotone asks if I will rerecord the song. I wonder how I can do this, since it is forbidden for a black person to sing on a record in the English language. But the company knows a hit when they see one, and they insist. I guess color barriers are broken this way. I go back into the studio, and once again I record the beautiful song that now goes by the strange title, "You Tell Such Lovely Lies."

What has happened to my wonderful Xhosa song? The American version has nothing to do with the original. The new lyrics are terrible: *"You tell such lovely lies with your two lovely eyes/ When I leave your embrace, another takes my place."* Everyone who hears the Xhosa version and the American version is disappointed. They are nothing alike. But the new one sells well.

People begin to recognize me on the street. Some say, "How do you do, Miss Makeba?" Some even thank me for a performance. But this is all. In my culture, no one wants to be impolite or pushy. In the West, show business people are always asked to sign their names on pieces of paper. It seems that their admirers find some magic in these signatures; they can say they now own a piece of the celebrity and a part of their idol's glamor. Someone tells me it's like the Aztec Indians who ate the hearts of mighty warriors killed in battle so they could obtain their enemy's strength. These Westerners are very superstitious people.

▼▼▼▼▼

Just because we are performers does not mean that life is easier for the Manhattan Brothers or myself. Nothing can change the fact that we are still black. The apartheid laws bind us just as tightly. In fact, life is even more difficult for us because we have to travel, eat at restaurants, and stay at hotels all the time. Nathan makes sure that all our papers are in order. Still, this does not guarantee that we will not be harassed.

One night we are traveling from Pretoria to Johannesburg. Our bus passes the International Airport, and a moment later we are stopped by the police. Two young men order us out. The policemen search the car, looking for anything from alcohol to weapons. Guns and knives are illegal for a black to possess, of course.

The policemen are irritated that they cannot find anything. Nathan steps forward and says, "Here are our night passes."

Nathan has made a bad mistake. He has spoken to the policemen in English. There are no English policemen, only Afrikaners, and they hate the English. We hold our breaths.

The young policeman is stern. "Can't you speak Afrikaans?"

Nathan apologizes. He explains who we are and says we are returning from a performance. It is sad to see this tall, proud, and handsome man forced to humble himself before two blond pimple-heads in uniform.

"You say you are a singing group?" one of the policeman asks in a sarcastic manner. I wonder what is going to happen, since he can do anything he pleases with us.

"Okay, then," he says, "sing."

And they make us sing. The Manhattan Brothers, one of the country's top groups, is forced to stand beside the road in the middle of nowhere, in the middle of the night, and serenade two arrogant white kids who are probably police because they're too dumb to be anything else. Nothing is more humiliating than this.

The police are enjoying their play. They finally wave us away when they are bored with us. We are stopped twice more that night before we make it back home. At least we do not have to perform again.

Many times we are stopped so the police can inspect our night passes. Even though we always take the precaution of having these, a policeman in a bad mood sometimes says, "We're going to lock you up." It's useless to protest, unless you want to get beaten. I end up in jail a lot. It is really bad when it happens on a Friday night. The courts are not in session until Monday. We must spend the weekend in jail. Our Saturday night performances have to be canceled, and we all lose the income. When Monday comes, we stand before the magistrate. Depending on his mood, we must pay a fine or face a jail sentence.

There are times when each African wonders how much longer we can stand living the way we do, as subhumans. The whites do not want to treat us like human beings because it is easier to keep us down if they think we are animals. But we know we are human beings. We know we are as good as anybody. We also know that something has got to happen. There is only so much anger, resentment, pain, and fear that can build up in a person before there is an explosion.

One night we perform at a place where some men are meeting to try to keep that explosion from happening. They want change, but change through nonviolent means. I recognize the group's flag when I enter the hall. Its three colors are black, green, and gold. The black represents the African people. The green is for our fertile country. And the gold represents our land's great mineral wealth. Black, green, and gold: the colors of Africa, and the colors of the African National Congress. Over forty years ago the ANC was founded by the same type of black lawyers and educators who are meeting this day. After the Manhattan Brothers perform, we are introduced to them. I am very shy. Politics is something I know nothing about. I curtsy and do not look the men directly in the face when we shake hands. There is a bearded young man with a kind, round face to whom I show the same respect. His name is Nelson Mandela, and he says he enjoys my singing. I thank him and quickly leave, because everyone is busy with something called the Freedom Charter. In this document these men are about to declare: "South Africa belongs to all who live in it, black and white." This is revolutionary. I fear the government is going to shoot them all.

▼▼▼▼▼

The fame of the Manhattan Brothers spreads beyond the country's borders. Nathan arranges for us to tour Swaziland, Lesotho, and the Portuguese colony of Lourenço Marques. Lesotho is our first stop; an easy trip because the little British protectorate is completely surrounded, like a dot, by South Africa. In Lesotho, blacks are permitted to drink all the alcohol they want. This doesn't mean much to me, because I don't drink. I guess all that beer I had to make for my mother-in-law made me dislike the stuff. But the musicians have a real good time after the show. We drive back to the South African border, and the bus is loaded down with bottles.

Of course, the customs police won't let us in with the loot. "You can't come in here with that. Either you leave it here and go inside, or else back you go."

No one wants to part with a single bottle. The band piles back into the bus, we drive back into Lesotho for a mile, and then everyone sits down on the ground and starts to drink up everything they bought. I can only stand by and watch what happens. Plenty does. The Manhattan Brothers get *so* stoned! Somebody starts a fight, and I have never seen a fight last so long. The musicians, the singers, everybody is in it. Some try to step in and stop the fight and they get a punch. They punch back and now they are a part of it. I am going from group to group, trying to get out of the way, but saying, "How are we going to get home?" Nobody pays me any mind.

We spend the night here in this field, in the middle of nowhere. Everyone is either too stoned or too bruised to continue. I sit in the bus that night curled up in a blanket. The boys straggle in the next morning, all these puffed-up faces and black eyes. Everyone laughs about it, but it will be a funny-looking group at tonight's performance.

The longest tour that we make starts in the countries of Southern and Northern Rhodesia and ends up in the Belgian Congo. This is the type of Africa the West likes to think of when someone mentions our continent: dense jungle, wild animals, miles and miles of unspoiled forests. But we are not tourists, we are traveling professionals, and the going is very rough. We travel by train and car. Many nights we have to sleep along the side of the road in our car when the driver is tired. The windows are always tightly rolled up, because we are strangers here and we are never certain whether we are in a game park or not. In the darkness I hear the monkeys chatter and a lion roar. Lions eat at night. The men tell me not to be nervous, but even to them a lion is no joke.

By day we pass the herds of giraffes and springboks, the elephants and gazelles. And then, just where the forests of Rhodesia are the thickest and the monkeys are the noisiest, the car turns a corner and there I am: ten feet high, smiling from a great big billboard with a bottle of Coca-Cola in my hand. I have seen this picture all over South Africa. But here? The advertising men never told me it would go this far. They came to see me at the recording company and offered me 150 pounds. I was not going to turn down that much money. My daughter Bongi saw these billboards around town, and, very excited, she came home to tell me how happy she is to have a famous mother. I had to smile, because I was down on my hands and knees at the time scrubbing the kitchen floor.

This is the way I like my life, though. And there is excitement and adventure in my days that I never dreamed of. This day, for instance, we take a break from our tour of Rhodesia and go to the famous Victoria Falls. We make our way down to the bottom, which is a very difficult journey. I have never seen anything like this great waterfall. The ground shakes beneath our feet. The sheer, vertical drop of white water reaches all the way up into the sky. We just stand, look, and listen. The Superior Being is always with us, but there are places where he really lets you know it.

Nathan, Ronnie, Rufus, I, and the others write our names on the rocks beneath Victoria Falls. I wonder how long our names will last. It doesn't matter. Our lives are so short compared to the falls, which will go on and on. But for now, here is little Miriam Makeba, writing her name on a rock. I am twenty-two years old. If you want, you can buy my records. You can hear me on the radio or see me give a show with the Manhattan Brothers. And I'll look right back at you from the pages of a magazine or from a billboard with a bottle of Coca-Cola in my hand!

Who would have ever imagined that any of this could happen so fast, and all at once? I forgive myself if I enjoy it, because there is too much danger and oppression in my country to think that any of it will last.

5

I AWAKEN TO FIND MYSELF in the worst nightmare of my life. I will not be free from its horror for two days.

My collarbone feels as if it is on fire. The air is hot and steamy. The van that I am in is on its side, and I am crumpled against the passenger's window. When I fell asleep I must have slumped down on the driver, and the steering wheel must have struck my collarbone. I do not remember the accident, but I know I must get out: quickly, before the car catches fire.

I stand and squeeze my way past the steering column, then out the window above me. I am that skinny. It is about four in the morning, and dark outside. The van is on a slope. When I drop down to the ground, I collapse. My hip is also hurt. I hear someone groan. Matthew Mbatha, the driver, is below. He has been thrown out. His face is bloody. It was Matthew who volunteered to drive some of us back to Johannesburg when the Manhattan Brothers wanted to stay behind and go to a party after our Durban concert. We are one of the acts in a show called *Township Jazz*. Matthew is a musician from another group. I remember there were more of us in his van, people who did not want to go to the party, like me, and wanted to start the eight-hour journey to Johannesburg early.

Everyone has been thrown clear of the wreck. I see Victor Mkhize, the famous comedian. He is unconscious, and hurt very badly. There is another young man, a musician, who is bleeding from the head. He and two other teenage musicians are in shock. I think: Where are the children?

Four young boys are also in the show. They are part of a penny-whistle group. They lie scattered across the slope with our torn and battered luggage. Cuts and scratches cover their small, scared faces. But they are just shaken up, and not seriously hurt. Then I see the other car. My heart leaps into my throat: It is a family of whites. There is a husband and wife, the husband's brother, and two children. The husband and one of the children are dead. The brother will lose a leg.

We are in the middle of the country, twenty-eight miles from a town called Volksrust. We wait until dawn for the police to arrive. We are in too much shock to speak to each other. When the police appear they are furious that a car of natives has had an accident with a car of white people. They put the dead man and boy in their cars, and load the rest of the whites into the ambulance that comes. I have a mohair blanket from Scotland that I like very much. I curl it around me. It is winter, and we are cold. A policeman pulls my blanket off me and puts it over one of the dead bodies.

"Please," I say, "it's very special . . ."

"Shut up!"

I shut up, of course. The ambulance leaves. The police go away. No one has paid the slightest attention to our injuries. We wait for hours. The police come back, but not to help us. Whatever the facts were, to them we are guilty of the fatal accident. One of the policemen pulls out his gun and points it at us. "You killed white people! I could shoot every one of you!" We kneel, cringing, before him. I cover my eyes. We don't know if he will shoot or not.

He goes away. The police want us to leave, and they don't care how we do it. But the car is smashed. Matthew's face has swollen as big and round as a basketball. Victor Mkhize is still unconscious, the young man is in terrible pain, and the children cry with fright and cold. I am really hurting, myself, and scared.

It is early afternoon when two young Swiss men drive by in their Volvo. They see me waving. "Hey! You're Miriam Makeba!" I can't believe my good luck: They saw our show in Durban.

"Please, take me to town," I beg. Because I am the only older person who is not seriously hurt, I leave the others beside the road.

In Volksrust we go to the hospital. I explain that there has been an accident, and some injured people have been lying unattended along the side of the road for ten hours. But it is a white hospital, and they won't listen. I am ordered to a native hospital. The two Swiss men are not permitted to enter the segregated black area without permits. They give me money to take a taxi. I thank them sincerely.

When I arrive at the native hospital, I find a small infirmary. My hip is giving me great pain. My neck is swollen. But I cannot rest. The infirmary is too poor to have an ambulance. With some directions, I go off to rent a little truck. The man is black, but he does not trust me because I am from the big city, Johannesburg, and he thinks I might cheat him. I beg his sons to help me. They convince their father by saying they will come with me. I have to pay nineteen pounds in cash, but I get the truck. We drive back to the scene of the accident.

Nobody is here. Our van lies on its side, and the other car has gone. The musicians in our group, the four children, Victor, and Matthew have disappeared. It is now late in the afternoon. Because it is the dead of winter, the day is already ending. I drive with the two young men around the countryside, searching for anyone who might know what has happened. We go for miles without passing a house. Finally, I see some people walking along with a lantern. Yes, they heard of the accident. They know that some young children are at the train station. I ask directions, and we go off to find not a station but a little roofless platform beside some tracks where the trains pick up passengers. The four little boys are there, shivering in the dark, hungry and scared. They tell me the Swiss gentlemen returned to the accident and took away the three injured men. After this, the police returned, chased away the two remaining teenage musicians, and brought the boys to this desolate place. Whatever luggage the children could carry in their arms they salvaged from the wreck. We load this into the truck, and we all go into town. The children have not eaten all day. I take them to some people's house, and the family gives them food. It is late at night, now, and I am worried about Matthew, Victor, and the young man.

Luckily, I see the Volvo of our Swiss friends. I ask them to which hospital they took the injured. They say, "The first one we came to."

This would be the white people's hospital, I know, so our men will have to be moved. I cannot do this alone. With the sons of the truck's owners, I set off for the long trip to Johannesburg to find the Manhattan Brothers. When we arrive it is early morning. Nathan tells me that they passed the site of the wreck the previous morning, but no one saw anything because it was still dark. We go immediately to Gallotone Records to get some cars. Twenty-four hours have passed since the accident. I am finally taken to a hospital to be treated, and after this I do not want to go back to Volksrust. The long car trip frightens me. But Nathan needs me to point out the hospital.

It is almost afternoon when we return to find our friends near death. Not only did the white hospital not admit them, which I had assumed, but the authorities also refused to give them *any type of medical treatment at all.* An injured dog would have been shown more compassion. Instead, Matthew, Victor, and the young musician were placed in a back room. The authorities assumed they would either be picked up, or they would die. It did not matter to the people in charge.

At the native infirmary, the men are given some treatment, but their injuries require that we take them to Baragwanth, the big hospital that serves the black townships of Johannesburg. It is late at night when we arrive. Matthew is treated, and he survives. The doctors operate on the young man for a ruptured bladder. His pain, like Matthew's, is at an end. But Victor dies on the operating table. He would have lived if he had been attended to when the accident first happened, *almost two days ago.*

Victor Mkhize, one of our most beloved comedians, is dead because he is black. All of us might have died because the authorities would rather threaten us like the policeman with his gun at the side of the road than lift a finger to help us. They would prefer us dead. There are too many of us. The land is no longer ours. Are we so stupid, our masters want to know, that we do not realize we are less than dirt beneath their feet? We are not human beings, we are scum. Why don't we just die? It disgusts them that we do not. It makes them angry and upset, because they now have to find ways to do it themselves.

I have just looked genocide in the face. Hate-filled, murderous eyes were glaring at me, a black South African. Exhausted from my injuries, I pass out. This time, I and some of the others have survived. But for how long? How long?

▼▼▼▼▼

Bongi is crying as she runs to me. She has just started school under the Bantu Education Act. My generation was the last to receive even minimal schooling. Under the new act, black children will learn to read a little and write a little, but no more. They are being prepared to be servants and manual laborers. Many of the children where I live who have been in school for years still do not speak proper English. The whites in South Africa complain that we are their intellectual inferiors, and they cannot even talk to us because we know nothing. But whose fault is this?

Bongi is not crying now over of the handicaps she will face because of her education.

"They called me *boesman*! They called me *boesman*!"

It hurts me to hear this. "*Boesman*" is an evil name the black Africans give light-skinned, mixed-raced people. Lighter skins are looked down upon by these people, and to call someone a *boesman* is like calling an American black a "nigger." Bongi is black, but she is not as dark as I am. She is light like her father.

I cannot fight my daughter's battles for her, so I say to her, "Go back and tell those children that, yes, you are light, but you are beautiful."

Already, Bongi knows she is a pretty little girl, and this is not going to change because of some mean children. Her smile lights up, and she runs back into the yard. "So what if I'm light?" I hear her say. "I'm beautiful!"

But if some blacks look down upon mulattoes, the government considers them superior to us. In our country, the authorities have made a third race: the Coloreds. According to the Immorality Act, no white can have any intimacy with a black, and vice versa. But even so, two million Coloreds have appeared. It just goes to show that you cannot keep people from doing what they want.

If a black mother gives birth to a Colored child, she is permitted to keep the child, although the boy or girl will be sent to Colored schools. At the age of eighteen, the young person must decide whether he or she wants to live as a Colored or as an African. Because of the Group Areas Act, blacks, whites, Coloreds, and Indians—that sizable colony from India who have been here for many years—all live in separate neighborhoods. The authorities determine who is to live where by simply looking at a person's skin. If a black's skin is bright, he may be classified Colored. And in this way, many Coloreds "pass" as whites. The young Colored man or woman at age eighteen must decide to give up his or her family for good and enter the Colored world—where he or she will be rewarded by the System with clerical jobs and other privileges denied blacks—or else be classified as an African and face the hardships and discriminations that are our way of life. The choice to never see one's family again is difficult, but few choose to be black.

The Indians also feel superior to us. It is unheard of for a young Indian man to go out with a black girl and talk about marriage. Like the whites and the Chinese, the Indians usually impregnate black girls, give them some money, and then leave them.

There is quite a lot of talk, then, and even some scandal about Sonny and me.

Sonny Pillay is the first famous South African Indian—he is a well-known singer—who openly goes out with a black woman like me. He is one of the main performers in our new touring show, *African Jazz and Variety*. Thirty-six artists are on the program of the popular review. The great South African singer Dorothy Masuka, who was one of my idols when I was young, has top billing. Sonny is right below her, and then the rest of the names are listed on down until "Miriam Makeba, and Others." Although I am listed last, at least they now put me above the "Others." The Manhattan Brothers are not a part of this revue. I am working away from them for a while.

It is 1956, and I am twenty-four years old when *African Jazz and Variety* begins a tour that will last eighteen months. The troupe travels from city to city, playing to white audiences and, once a week when my people are permitted into the theater, to black audiences. This is always on Thursday, when the domestics are given the night off. The Manhattan Brothers and I still find time to record for Gallotone. The company has also decided to create a new singing group called the Skylarks with me as the lead. Three other girls sing with me. I record songs with the Skylarks on the side, and we even have some hits.

It is funny how we dream up songs. We go up to the roof at Gallotone and start improvising. Someone comes up with a melody, and someone else thinks of some lyrics. The next thing you know, we are running downstairs and bursting into a recording room. "Please, we have to put this down before we forget it! Right away!"

The producers see us working like this, and after a while they give us a tape recorder.

It is a busy time. But love has never cared about my schedule. It just barges in whenever it wants. There is nothing I can do, especially if the man is Sonny Pillay.

Sonny is very handsome, with dark, straight hair, and brown eyes that are full of warmth and love and humor. Eyes don't lie, and I can tell by his that he wants me very much, as much as I want him. Because Sonny is famous, and I am getting to be known, we become an "item." This means that our private lives suddenly become everybody's business. My friends say, "You can't go out with an Indian!" I think that maybe they are afraid that I will get hurt. But I tell them, "I'm going out with an Indian who is not ashamed to be going out with me." Bongi likes him, and my mother is not shocked in any way. She has always liked my friends, no matter what color they are. As long as they are polite and have good manners, she doesn't care.

It is difficult to find time to be together, but somehow Sonny and I manage. He introduces me to the movies of Elvis Presley. Here is a white American who moves and sings almost like we do. My friends and I like Elvis, until we read in the paper that he has said that he does not care for black women to write him fan mail because we aren't good enough to wipe his shoes. We know that most of what we read in the official papers are lies—the authorities probably heard that black women like this white singer and they are trying to discourage it—but since we are never really sure what the reality is outside of our lives, we are a little disappointed.

The producer of *African Jazz and Variety*, Mr. Alfred Herbert, is the first white man I get to know. His mother is Sarah Silvia, one of the major figures in the Jewish theater. Mr. Herbert is always full of energy and good cheer. He has to be an optimist, because there are so many problems trying to do a black review. With the help of his mother, Mrs. Silvia, he manages to book us into the Town Hall in Johannesburg. No blacks have ever sung here.

Traveling is still a problem for us. It is hard to find a restaurant. We are not permitted to eat with white people, of course, and the places for the Africans are not very good. I buy myself an enameled hot plate, a spoon, a fork, and a knife. At the stores I buy baked beans and sausages and eat them from the can in my room. Sometimes we have people invite us to their homes, and then we eat good food.

Mr. Herbert gets us the necessary permissions to travel. We go by bus, car, or the natives' train. On our way to Cape Town, the police stop us. A bus full of Africans to them is like a red flag in front of a bull. They make a search, and to our horror they discover a gun. This is trouble. No one claims it, and we are all taken to jail.

I am not permitted to call home. My mother does not know where I am. I am very worried that Bongi might get scared, because I make it a habit of calling her every day, no matter where I am. Sometimes I think I am practically working for the phone company. My worry becomes panic when the judge orders us to be held in jail until the matter with the gun is cleared up. A day passes, and then another. I am traveling with six men, and no other women. I sit alone in a woman's cell and cry. I want my mother and my little girl. I want to be held in Sonny's arms. But I am away from them all for an entire week. Finally, Mr. Herbert tracks us down. He convinces the gun's owner, an Indian musician, to claim his property and promises he will get him a lawyer. We are released, but it has been the most time I have been in jail since I was six-month-old baby.

Even though traveling has its dangers, Bongi comes with me during her summer vacation. She is six, now, and for three months we are together. I am very happy. She is my only child, and I think I may be spoiling her, but I can't help it. Whatever I can I give her, and sometimes that is bad for a parent to do. But I feel guilty because I am away from her so much, traveling around the country.

Bongi likes the musicians as much as they like her. She writes a poem and reads it for us on the bus. One of the musicians puts it to music, I add some lyrics, and we have a song that we sing as we drive along. It's a silly little song, with the Zulu name "Sahamba." But when I get back to Gallotone, I record it. Bongi's poem becomes a hit!

Dorothy Masuka, the woman whose name tops the list of artists in *African Jazz*, has become my best friend. It is unusual for me to have a close friend who is a woman. I have always liked the company of boys, and then men. And then to have one of the singing idols of my youth as a friend is really unusual. Dorothy and I are always singing: backstage at the shows, on the train, or at Gallotone, where we begin to record together. She is smart and fast. Dorothy also composes beautiful melodies. Always, she is thinking of a new one. When one pops into her head, she comes to me and says, "Hey, Miriam! Take this part." I hum it, and she improvises by humming another part. It is too bad that we cannot record together, but we have contracts with different record companies. Still, we have fun together.

▼▼▼▼▼

A filmmaker from America comes to the Town Hall to see *African Jazz and Variety*. He needs a singer for a documentary he is doing about a black's life in South Afrika. There are thirty-six cast members in our revue, but Lionel Rogosin says he thinks that I am the most original artist in the show. He asks me to play myself in a nightclub scene. All I have to do is sing two songs.

The idea of being in a movie excites me. But Mr. Rogosin's documentary offers as many dangers as it does opportunities. The authorities do not approve of his "true-life" story. So, the filming is being done in secret. If Mr. Rogosin is booted out of the country, he can go back to America and make another movie. But the other black cast members and I would be in real trouble.

Mr. Rogosin is very persuasive. "Miriam," he tells me, "no one can expect a talent like yours to stay cooped up in South Africa forever. People all over the world will see and hear you sing in my film. And they'll see you in person, if you let me take you with me when it comes time to do the promotion."

A chance to leave South Africa! To see Europe, and maybe America! I accept the part in the film, and Mr. Rogosin encourages me to apply for a passport right away. I do so, because for a black to get permission to leave the country takes a long, long time.

For the title of his documentary, Mr. Rogosin chooses the name of the anthem of the African National Congress: *Come Back, Africa*. The story is about a man named Zachariah, who lives in one of the African villages in the country. Zachariah gets a contract to come to Johannesburg to work in a gold mine. But he has bad luck, he keeps getting into trouble with the authorities. He forgets to call the white man *"baas,"* and he gets fired from one job after another. After a while he gets angry and goes out of control, which can only mean tragedy for a black.

My one and only scene takes place in a *shebeen*, which is a little club where blacks, who are not permitted to drink, are illegally served alcohol. A group of journalists are discussing politics. I come in, and they recognize me. "Hey, Miriam! Sing us a song." I sing a song, but they won't let me go. "Sing us another!" I do, and that is the last anyone will see of me in *Come Back, Africa*.

To fool the authorities, the filming is done in the middle of the night. We show up at the nightclub set at one o'clock in the morning. Things go well, and I get to see how movies are made. Then I go home, and Mr. Rogosin says that he will be keeping me informed about the film.

The long *African Jazz and Variety* tour is coming to an end. We have a few more trips, and one takes us to Durban, where Sonny's family lives.

"I don't want you to stay in a hotel," he tells me. He wants me to come to his house.

"But we're not even married," I say. I really am nervous. The gossip about Sonny, the Indian, and me, the African, is painful. I would rather stay in a cheap African hotel than face Sonny's family. I ask him, "What about your mother?"

"She'll have to get used to it."

Sonny really does love me, and I love him. We go to his parents' house. I stay in my room, and Sonny stays in his. But the family is cool toward me, and very cautious. They look at me very closely, and the uncles do not try to hide the fact that they are not happy with their nephew's ways. But Sonny is strong, and he imposes the situation on them. I think, "Oh, oh. Another family where nobody likes me." But the days pass quickly with all the work of putting on the show, and before long we are back in Johannesburg.

Rehearsals are about to begin for a black jazz opera, which promises to be very controversial. The story is a true one, about the life of the great African boxer Ezekiel Dlhmini. Dlhmini was a great, strong man who knocked down everyone he fought. The people gave him the nickname "King Kong," after the mighty creature from the movie. But his life was full of frustration, and it ended tragically because the authorities would not let him continue his fighting. They would not let him travel overseas, where his true competition was. This is because some years before another great African champion, Jake Tule, who was also undefeated at home, went to England and killed the first man he fought. When Tule came home he had a hero's welcome. The authorities were upset: This black man kills a white, and his people treat him like a hero. They were not going to let that happen again. So later, Dlhmini was not permitted to go abroad. His great talent was forced to rust. He took to drink. Then one day "King Kong" kills his girlfriend because he thinks she is cheating behind his back with his best friend. He goes to jail, where, somehow, he dies by drowning in a pond of water. Everyone wants to know: How did this great strong man, six foot four, drown in a little pond of water, even in chains? We all suspect some foul play by the authorities. It is from these suspicions that a white man, Mr. Harry Bloom, writes the book to the jazz opera *King Kong*.

The producer and the director of the show is another white man, Mr. Leon Gluckman. Like Mr. Bloom, and Mr. Alfred Herbert, who produced *African Jazz and Variety*, Mr. Gluckman is Jewish. So is the music arranger and even the stage crew. The Jewish people more or less run the theater in South Africa. It is also a fact that the Jews are more likely to help Africans from time to time. In the theater, we do not have to call the director *"baas"* because he is white. (We call him "boss" because he's the director!) We are all collaborators in an exciting production. Everyone respects everyone else's talents. This is as it should be, since there is a lot of talent in this show.

I have many friends in the cast. The lead role, the boxer Dlhmini whom everyone calls "King Kong," is given to tall, handsome Nathan Mdlhedlhe, the leader of the Manhattan Brothers. Dlhmini's best friend, Lucky, is played by another Manhattan Brother, Joe Mogotsi. I play the boxer's girlfriend, Joyce. She is known as the "Queen of the 'Back of the Moon,' " which is a *shebeen*, an illegal bar for blacks. It is a lively part for a twenty-six-year-old to play. Joyce dresses nicely, sings some of the show's best tunes, and in the end she gets to die in the niftiest strangulation scene since Othello killed Desdemona. Joyce is like Desdemona because she dies when her lover thinks she betrayed him.

In the orchestra is a young man named Hugh Masekela. Hughie and I have been friends for years, ever since he was a fourteen-year-old student at the Huddleston Boys' School and I was a twenty-one-year-old singer with the Manhattan Brothers. The head of Hughie's school, a priest named Huddleston, was a missionary who would travel all over the world to raise funds for the boys. In America he met some jazz musicians, and he asked them to donate some instruments. They did, and Father Huddleston brought these home and offered them to any boy who was interested. Hughie took the trumpet, and when he looked at the bell he saw the name Louis Armstrong etched into the brass. Hughie and five other boys formed the Huddleston Jazz Band, and the act was good enough to perform at some of the same places that booked the Manhattan Brothers. I got to know Hughie, and kept track of him over the years. He played and played, and now he is a young man of twenty in the orchestra of *King Kong.* But his parents are not being nice. Because they want him to be a medical doctor, and Hughie wants to be a musician, they just don't care about him anymore. This is very sad, because everyone can see that Hughie has talent. I encourage him every chance I get, and sometimes a little encouragement goes a long way.

There is another young person in the cast who is a friend of mine, and her name is Letta M'Bulu. I met her when she was thirteen and she won a talent show put on by the black musicians' union. Though she was a little girl and I was much older, we liked each other, and I started giving her records to listen to. Now, in *King Kong,* she is playing the part of the little schoolgirl, and she is showing everyone what a fine voice she has.

The day that *King Kong* opens in February of 1959, the box office tells us that the show is sold out for six months. At the final dress rehearsal we are all very excited. There is a definite spring in my step when I cross the stage during a scene. This is my first show, my first time in the theater, and I am as excited as anybody.

There is a crack on the stage floor. One tiny crack in the whole large area. Everyone steps right over it. But I am wearing high heels. My shoe catches, and I sprain my ankle. In five minutes my foot is swollen.

Mr. Gluckman, our producer, doesn't know what to do. No one ever thought of an understudy. A doctor comes and injects something into my foot. The pain goes away, but my shoe won't fit. Someone goes out and buys me another, larger pair. I wear one regular shoe and one larger shoe during the opening night performance. Nobody notices, not even my mother. This is the first time she has seen me perform. And it will be her last.

My mother has never seen a play before. The big scene at the end comes when I am being strangled by the boxer. A scream fills the theater. But it is not mine. It is my mother! She thinks that I am really being killed. She screams, "My child! My child!" My sister-in-law, the wife of my brother Joseph, has brought her, and she is so embarrassed when she calms my mother down and explains what is happening.

My mother's work as an *isangoma* continues no matter what I do, of course. People come to the house to be treated by her, and to consult with the spirits through her. I still attend to my mother when she is in a trance. I must take care of the needs of the *amadlozi*. An old spirit friend comes to visit when I am present. He is Mahlavezulu, the great warrior. This day he speaks about me. I am very interested because this spirit has always been my favorite.

The voice comes through my mother. It is stern and firm. "You will leave South Africa. You will go on a long journey, and you will never come back."

I do not know what to make of this. I do not have any plans for a trip. *King Kong* is a great success and I am happy to be a part of it. One of the songs I sing in the show, "Back of the Moon," is a hit. And I am making money: seventy-five pounds a week. There are plans for a tour, but this will not take us out of the country.

But you do not just forget about something that is said to you by an *amadlozi*.

The audiences who come to see *King Kong* are integrated. Mr. Gluckman has found a clever way to get around the apartheid laws. The performances are held at the auditorium of the University of Witwatersrand. Since both black and white students attend this university, the authorities cannot tell who are students and faculty in our audiences and who are people from the outside. So people like my mother are seated next to white people who might have been her employers.

At the university where the performances are held, the other leads and I are put up in the dormitories of the medical school. The students are away on vacation. Sonny comes to visit me in my little dorm room. It is as if we are two students.

There is no easy way, Sonny tells me, to say what he has to say, but he is going to England to pursue his career. I cry. I am upset and angry: Why does he have to go to England? But I know. We are all prisoners in this country, Indians as well as blacks. (Even the whites are the prisoners in the glass house they have built. They are prisoners of their illusion that this is their country and that all other people are their inferiors. They cannot escape the cage of their illusion, because on the outside they would be lost.)

Even though he is an Indian, Sonny receives his passport right away. Because I am black, I have not received mine after a year. I am still waiting. Mr. Rogosin writes me that the film *Come Back, Africa,* is completed. He plans to enter it in the Venice Film Festival. If he is successful, he wants me to come to the premiere. It is a dream that makes me feel sad instead of hopeful. Escape from this country is so hard.

Sonny leaves. He tells me he will come back. Because I love him, I have to believe him.

And, even though I don't know it yet, I am carrying his baby.

▼▼▼▼▼

I am downtown, walking in front of the General Hospital. *King Kong* has been in Johannesburg for six months, and we have only four more performances before the show goes on the road. The sun is very bright, and I suddenly feel dizzy and faint. The sidewalk spins beneath me. It gets larger as I pass out, falling.

When I awaken there are only two performances left of *King Kong* in Johannesburg. I have been unconscious for two days, and close to death. My eyes open on the sight of my mother.

I try to speak. I try to say, "I want water." My lips move, but my voice is too weak to make sound.

"You're at Nokuphila," my mother tells me. This is the black hospital fifteen miles out of town in the Western Native Township. I fainted right outside the General Hospital, but because I am black I could not be admitted. I was brought here.

The doctor who operated on me comes and tells me that I had an in-tube pregnancy that burst, as an appendix bursts. I am lucky to be alive. When he leaves I tell my mother that I did not know I was pregnant. She knows that Sonny is the father, and she asks me if we plan to get married. I have thought about this before, but I am too tired to think about it now.

Abigale Kubeka has taken my part in the show. Auditions were held very hastily when they learned that I was sick. Little Letta M'Bulu sang very well, but she is too young to play Joyce convincingly. Abigale Kubeka was in my group, the Skylarks, at Gallotone Records. She sang tenor. Her voice is so low that, in the show, the orchestra has to transpose their music. This causes some problems for them. My semiprivate hospital room fills up with flowers, fruit, and friends, including Mr. Gluckman, the producer. He tells me that I absolutely have to be in the show when it opens in Cape Town. People are lining up down there to buy tickets. I am not well, but I say I will try.

The show moves to the Cape, but I must stay behind to get better. After a few days, Mr. Gluckman comes to say that *King Kong* will not open without me. I pack my bag, and we go to the airport. I have never been on an airplane before. I sit beside Mr. Gluckman, and I am scared to death. It is not that I am afraid to fly. I do not even have time to worry about this. I am scared because I am the only African on the plane. I have never had any contact with white people in a situation like this. I have always been a servant or an employee of people like Mr. Gluckman. Trains and buses are segregated in South Africa, of course, and none of the white passengers have ever had to travel with a black person before. They look at me, and they are not happy. I do not even look out the window, not even in curiosity, because I am so tense.

When we get to Cape Town, we go straight to the hall. Everyone is so happy to see me that I feel better right away. They are in mid-rehearsal, and the orchestra applauds me because now they can go back to their old, familiar way of playing for my voice.

Sonny has written a song that I record called "Oh, So Alone." The song expresses how I feel without him. He writes me from England that he is getting work. I write back that I think of him, and I am, oh, so alone.

And, suddenly, I am, oh, so frantic! Lionel Rogosin writes that two years after he finished filming, *Come Back, Africa* is being screened for a few critics, and they are very enthusiastic. They all ask who the girl is in the cabaret scene. Mr. Rogosin insists that I join him at the Venice Film Festival. He is in communication with Ian Bernhardt, an official with the musicians' union, about my passport and tickets.

But the film is still controversial, and my departure from South Africa has to be kept quiet. All the work is done with as little fuss as possible. Gallotone does not give out a press release, and the papers do not write that I am going away. Anything might happen. Only my mother knows I am leaving. My departure is scheduled for the end of August, after *King Kong* finishes its run.

August in South Africa is wintertime. The day is cold and cloudy when I take Bongi for a walk and tell her that I am going away. Bongi is a tall, playful girl of eight, now, and she is excited that I am going to see some of the wide world. The passport Mr. Bernhardt was able to get for me says that I must be back in a few months. Bongi tells me all of the things she wants me to bring her from Europe, and I promise that I will try.

Before I leave, I slip into Gallotone to record two songs. One, in English, was written for me by the talented African song-writer Gibson Kente. There is much emotion inside when I sing his words. They touch my heart on the eve of my first, great journey.

> *Good-bye, mother*
> *Good-bye, father*
> *And to you, my little baby*
> *Though I'm leaving,*
> *My heart remains with you . . .*

I do not know what is in store for me. My nervousness and excitement are all tangled up. But I am thrilled to be going, even for only a few months. Mahlavezulu, the spirit who spoke through my mother, said that when I leave, I will not be coming back. But my daughter is here, whom I won't give up, and I love my mother too much. If someone were to tell me that I would never be returning, and I knew this for certain, I would never go away.

But I am going away, and the second song I record, in Zulu, speaks to my people. It is called "Iphi Ndlhela"—"I Ask You to Show Me the Way."

> *Stay well, my people*
> *I am leaving*
> *I am going to the land of the white man*
> *I ask you to be with me*
> *To show me the way*
> *We will meet and see one another*
> *Upon my return*

Upon my return. It is my promise.

▼▼▼▼▼

The plane comes and takes me safely out of the country. The two songs are released. They become hits. It is only now that my people realize that I am gone.

6

I TRAVEL ALONE AND ON South African Airways no white person will sit next to me. I am the only black on the plane. The people look at me with surprise and then they just pass right by. We have left Johannesburg, on our way to Amsterdam, and I have three seats all to myself.

And I have a window! The propellers of two of the big plane's engines spin on the wing so fast they become invisible, and I can look through them and see the clouds over the brown winter land. The villages along the crooked rivers pass below, and the cities that are segregated into different areas for each race. From so high, where all man-made things look so small and insignificant, the idea that a land so vast can be chained by apartheid laws seems ridiculous. Even the idea of countries seems silly, because from the air no borders can be seen when we leave South Africa, flying north. I sit glued to the window. Mountain ranges pass below, rivers and plains. The land gets greener. We fly over Central Africa, and then the jungles. Now we come back to earth to refill the fuel tanks in Nigeria.

The plane taxis across the runway. I look out and my eyes nearly pop out of my head. There is a man on the tarmac directing the plane. He is *black*. "Oh, wow!" I say. "I guess I'm out of South Africa." No blacks are permitted to work in aviation at home.

When we take off again it is late. I'm sleepy. The hostess comes by and asks if I want my seat made into a bed. I thank her, and while she does this I take my little travel bag and go to the lavatory. I brush my teeth and wash my face. And now I take off my dress. In my little bag I have my nightgown. It seems natural to me that if I am going to sleep I should change into my nightgown. When I come out of the lavatory, people stare at me. I think it is because I am black. I go to my seat and sleep comfortably all the way to Amsterdam.

When we land in Holland, we are taken to a restaurant in the airport, and we are told that while the plane is being prepared for the trip to London, we will be served a continental breakfast. I think, "Wow, a *continental* breakfast!" I figure we will be given food from all over Europe: hot chocolate from Switzerland, French pastries, Danish cheeses, and tea from England. But the restaurant makes me nervous. There sure aren't any like *me* in Amsterdam. If I sit at a table next to white people, will I get arrested? At the very *beginning* of my trip? But I really want this continental breakfast, so I risk sitting down. The hostess comes by and gives me coffee. Then bread, jam, and butter. I wait for the continental breakfast, but nothing more comes. I think, "Is this all? Coffee, bread, and jam?" I was expecting something out of this world. At least I experience what it is like to sit down in a restaurant like anybody else. It is a strange feeling, this freedom, and I will have to get used to it.

When it is winter at home, Europe is enjoying its summer. But when we land in England, the weather is cold and foggy. I look out the bus window and I can't see a thing. It's so gloomy. Disappointed, I think, "Man, this is London?" I am here for two nights before continuing to France. I suppose I should rest, but the excitement of traveling sends me out into the streets to look around. But in London I cannot tell one place from another. Every place looks alike to me.

The sun is shining when the plane lands in Paris, and I look forward to the train trip so I can see some of the countryside on my way to Aix-en-Provence, where I am to meet Mr. Rogosin and his wife. The train station in Paris is crowded with people. I am confused. I put down my bags, and when I turn around the suitcase with all my shoes is gone. Someone has stolen every pair of shoes I have except for the ones I am wearing. And these start to hurt my feet when I have to stand up all day in the passageway between the train cars. The train has been over-

booked, and there is no seat for me. I am tired and scared. I
begin to have doubts about the trip. No one has really told me
what I am to do. What if they don't like my singing in the film
and they laugh? I feel sick and hot at the thought. This is a great
adventure for me, but I do feel out of place the way everyone
keeps staring at me: this little black girl who can't speak French.
There is no window in the vestibule, and so I can't see anything.
I'm hungry, and my feet hurt. I wish my mother was here to talk
to me. I want my Bongi. Tears come, and I cannot help it.

At Aix-en-Provence I limp off the train, so tired I want to fall
down. Someone shouts my name. Lionel Rogosin is running
toward me.

"Miriam! The new star!"

He is bursting with excitement. "Everyone in Venice is clam-
oring for you. And I just came back from the States, where I
showed *Come Back, Africa* to some people I thought might do you
some good. Hold on to your pulse, little one, and guess who
wants you for his show? Steve Allen!"

I smile politely. Who?

"*The Steve Allen Show*, out of L.A.! He's up against Ed Sullivan
on Sunday nights."

When I do not respond, Mr. Rogosin frowns. "Of course, you
don't get Ed Sullivan in South Africa."

"Are you talking about television?" I ask. The authorities do
not permit television in South Africa at all. They feel it would be
disruptive. The fewer means of communication they have to
control, the better. I have never even seen television. All I've
seen of the outside world have been airports and train stations.

"Television, and clubs! There's a gentleman named Max Gordon who runs a hot little place in New York called the Village
Vanguard. He wants you, Miriam!"

I can only think of the chains that bind me. "But my passport
won't permit me to travel outside Europe."

"*Details!*" Mr. Rogosin says. He brushes the air aside with his
hand as if he's clearing away the pesky little "details" that will
keep me from going to the U.S.

"Oh, it sounds wonderful, Mr. Rogosin. But, please, someone
stole all my shoes. Do you think I can go somewhere and buy
some more?"

"Shoes?" he almost shouts. "You want shoes? When we get to Venice, I'll buy you a dozen pair!"

At the car I meet a charming woman, Mrs. Rogosin, and the three of us drive south to Venice. At last I see the French countryside. I look, look at everything, and what I see makes my eyes grow wide. There are women—*white* women—who are cutting hay and carrying it on their backs, like the native women I have seen working in East Africa. And white men with handkerchiefs wrapped around their foreheads to keep the sweat from their eyes are digging ditches. At home you never see whites working like this. Such jobs are reserved for blacks. This is really something for me to see.

When we get to Venice, Mr. Rogosin buys me some shoes, and then we take the gondola to Lido Island. The city is very old and beautiful. The canals are like something from a storybook. We have rooms at the Excelsior Hotel, where all the producers and starlets are staying. Mr. Rogosin asks me if I would like to rest before going to the screening this evening. But I am too excited and restless. I decide to go out for a walk.

I do not get far before something strange happens. People begin to follow me. A few at first, but soon a whole crowd. I get scared. All these white people—why are they following me? Do they think I stole something? Do I need a pass to be in this part of town? It was foolish of me to leave the hotel without Mr. Rogosin. I do not know the laws of this country. I avoid the curious eyes of the Italians, and I go right back to the Excelsior. At the desk I get my key. A woman with three children comes up to me. She speaks to me in Italian. I don't know what to do.

The man at the desk tells me in English, "She is asking if you could please let her children touch your hair."

I am shocked. "Touch my hair? Why?"

The man speaks to the woman. She answers him, and he says to me, "Because she has never seen hair like yours."

"Oh!" I feel foolish, but I do not wish to offend these people. The woman looks sincere, and the three children are all excited. A boy rubs his hand against my arm. Then he holds his fingers close to his face to see if my color came off on him. I bend down for the children to touch my hair.

"Ahhhh!"

Then the mother herself strokes my hair. *"Bellissimo! Bellissimo!"*

"Very beautiful!" the desk clerk translates for me. The children saw my short, woolly hair, and they wondered why it does not hurt, like wire. But when they feel it they can see it is soft.

I learn that these people are fascinated by me because I am African. Yesterday, when a movie called *Orpheo Negro* was shown, the beautiful actress Marpessa Dawn caught everybody's attention. She is dark, but her hair is long and straight. Mine is woolly and very short. I stand out. When I go to the beach the photographers follow me. I do not wear a bathing suit because I am too shy. Also, I swim like a rock, so why do I need a bathing suit? I just put on a dress and some sandals. There are so many starlets around, and they are half-naked trying to get attention. They must be mad because the photographers are all following *me*, this little unknown.

For the big screening tonight, I wear a Western-style, strapless dress made out of a stretch material that is very tight. It is the fashion. Mr. and Mrs. Rogosin and I have to walk down this long passageway, inside and out, that takes us from the hotel to the cinema. It is lined with people, both sides. I cannot believe it, but they are waiting to see me! As we pass, they begin to shout: "Africa! Africa!"

Because it is a documentary, *Come Back, Africa* is not one of the major films entered in the competition, like *Orpheo Negro*. But it wins the Critics' Award.

Mr. Rogosin is very happy. He has big plans for the film, and he says it has already launched my "international career." We go back to London, where I am to wait for a visa that will permit me to enter a place I had once only dreamed about: America.

▼▼▼▼▼

Sonny meets me in London, where he has been pursuing his career as a ballad singer. I fall into his arms. It has been so long. As the French say, *il brille par son absence*—"He shines by his absence."

Being with Sonny again cures my homesickness right away, and I can begin to appreciate England. It looks as if I will be here for a long time. The South African authorities are in no hurry to process my visa application. They keep making excuses. I can only wait. Mr. Rogosin tells me that Steve Allen is working at his end, and also Max Gordon of the Village Vanguard in New York City, since he wants me to sing at his club. I am happy that so many people are impressed by the small part I played in the film.

One of these people is the wonderful jazz singer Cleo Laine. She sees *Come Back, Africa,* and when she hears that I am in London she throws a nice little party for me. I am delighted because, as the weeks pass, I do not have much to do. I see Sonny, I babysit for the Rogosins, and I walk around the neighborhood where I have a small apartment. There is a little kitchen in my room, which becomes very important. Sometimes I am *hungry,* but I am afraid to go into the restaurants. I look inside and there are all these white people. At home we are never supposed to eat with white people, and this way of living is hard to break all at once.

Policemen frighten me. If I see a police car while I'm walking along at night, I quickly look for the next corner to run and hide. You're not suppose to be walking the streets after eleven o'clock at home. But one time I get trapped. As I am walking I see two policemen ahead. The streets are long, and people have tall shrubs and locked gates in front of their homes. There is no place for me to go. I stand there, nervous, and the policemen can see that I am scared.

But when they speak, they are not rude or nasty. They are as proper as can be. "Is there something we could do for you?"

"Oh," I say meekly. "I think I'm lost."

They ask me where I want to go, and instead of telling me I am a stupid *kaffir* they are very polite and kind. "You're going in the right direction, all right. Just keep going down this way, miss, and you'll be right as rain."

"Oh, thank you!" I say, so relieved. For the first time in my life I feel safe and not threatened by policemen.

They can tell I would like to say something. "Is there anything else, miss?"

"I'm sorry, it's just that I was thinking—I guess I'm not in South Africa, anymore."

The "Bobbies" smile at me and touch their caps. "No, indeed, miss. G'night."

I finally get to see television. Mr. Rogosin has one in his flat. There is a program on the BBC called *In Town Tonight.* The producers learn that I am in town, and this night they ask me to come on the show. I have been in a recording studio many times, and I have appeared before the camera in *Come Back, Africa*. But this studio is something new. There is an audience, great big cameras that are pushed back and forth, and cables all over the floor that will trip you up if you are not careful. I am very nervous, but, luckily, all I have to do is sing "Back of the Moon," the song I did in *King Kong*. It is a bouncy number with a bongo rhythm.

Just yesterday, the Russians launched a spaceship that hit the other side of the moon, and the program tonight is all about this. Experts are talking about important scientific and political things. I cannot help them there. But I do sing my song, and everybody likes it.

> *Back of the moon, boys*
> *Back of the moon is where the folks unwind*

There is a gentleman from America who is in London to tape a Christmas show for the BBC. He is a singer we all know and admire in South Africa. As luck would have it, he sees me on the *In Town Tonight* program. The next day, at a screening of *Come Back, Africa*, he is there.

"Miss Makeba," he says after the film, "I am an admirer of yours."

I am almost in shock, but I remember to curtsy, because Mr. Harry Belafonte is a very great man. For years we have sung his songs, going back to the Cuban Brothers when they did "Day-O." We all saw him in *Carmen Jones*, and his hits have been translated into the tribal languages. I tell him all of this.

"That's good to hear, Miss Makeba," he says, "because I have a profound interest in your country. It is a very troubled place. But what a talent it has given us!"

This man is so handsome he could make a god jealous! When he compliments me I bow my head and mutter my thank you in a shy little voice. He must think this is cute, because he smiles at me. His smile could light up a village. He introduces me to his wife, Julie. She is a very beautiful woman. I tell them that I will be going to the U.S. to do this *Steve Allen Show* and the Village Vanguard engagement when I get my visa. Mr. Belafonte gives me all of his telephone numbers, and before he leaves he insists that I tell him if there is ever anything I need. We say good night, and I see him go to Mr. Rogosin. I believe they are talking about me and making plans.

A screening is a small thing, but this one becomes very important to me. A marriage is a big thing, but my marriage to Sonny is so sudden that we are almost surprised when we do it. When we saw each other again in London we knew the old fire was still hot between us. And I have been feeling so alone. I am not miserable when I am with Sonny. My visa situation is so strange that I do not know what the future would bring. So when Sonny proposes, I accept. This marriage is the most impulsive thing I have ever done in my life. After a few weeks, we wonder if it might be a mistake.

It does not surprise me to learn that Mr. Belafonte has all sorts of connections in the United States. I guess he really was impressed by my singing, because he wants to be one of my sponsors in America. Somehow, he has arranged for my visa. I am to place myself completely in his hands, and I am very glad to do so. The date for the *Steve Allen Show* and my appearances at the Village Vanguard are set, and I need someone like Mr. Belafonte who knows the American music business. There are so many arrangements to be made: what I will wear, what I must sing, where and how I will travel. But his organization is taking care of it all.

That leaves me to say good-bye to Lionel Rogosin and his lovely wife. He has brought me this far. I am so grateful to him.

Saying good-bye to Sonny is more difficult. We both realize we should have just stayed friends. Rushing into a marriage was unnecessary, and it just complicated everything. Now we have to bother with the divorce paperwork.

"My bride of three months," Sonny says to me. He really is good-looking when he smiles at me like a mischievous little boy. There is no ill will when we part. But we are sad. I missed Sonny before when we were separated, and I'll miss him again. I do love him. He says he loves me, too. But our lives must now go in different directions.

He sees me off at the airport. "Are you going to become a big star?"

"Oh, I should think so!" I joke.

But Sonny knows me very well. He can tell that I am scared. I do not know what the people in America expect from me. To them, South Africa must seem like that place in my song, like the back of the moon!

"Don't be afraid, Zenzi," Sonny tells me. "They will love you. Remember, you sing like a nightingale."

And if I flop, I also remember the source of my name: *uzenzile*, the expression that means "You have no one to blame but yourself."

▼▼▼▼▼

I first see America through the window of an airplane. I expect it to be big. It is. This is the next to last day of November 1959. The morning sun strikes the spires of these unbelievable skyscrapers below, and the windows light up like a million diamonds. What a rich country this is, to have buildings so high. I see the Statue of Liberty out in the harbor, and the blue United Nations headquarters. There is an independent black African nation there, now. The British let Ghana go her own way two years ago, and she is the hope and example of all Africa.

The plane lands at Idlewild. Mr. Belafonte has a car there to meet me. I am to go directly to his offices on West Fifty-sixth Street. From the ground, Manhattan is just as impressive. But there is no time for sightseeing. In two days I have to be in California to do the *Steve Allen Show*. And they tell me I am to open at the Village Vanguard here in New York in five days.

"Miriam!" After we hug, Mr. Belafonte says, "We haven't a minute to waste!" His entire organization is mobilized to help me. A musical arranger begins his work after I choose the songs I will sing. He must send music to California right away for the one song I will do on the *Steve Allen Show*. And then he must prepare the Village Vanguard songs. Meanwhile, Mr. Belafonte takes me to a designer named John Pratt. Mr. Pratt is very talented and fast. He begins working at once on two dresses. The design he creates is to become my trademark look for many years: a dress simple in style, strapless, with a cape over one shoulder. Mr. Pratt uses beautiful material for me, Indian silk. One dress is gold and rust, and the other is blue and green. The colors fade into each other. Mr. Belafonte, of course, has to see the completed outfits and approve them. Sometime during the busy two days, I start using my name for him, and it sticks: Big Brother.

A night flight takes me to California. The great American

continent is below somewhere in the dark, sleeping. I sleep, too. When I step off the plane, I receive a pleasant surprise: Los Angeles is sunny and warm! I am so happy to be in a place like this, after New York and London. I fall in love with California right away, because it is not too hot, not too cold. It's just right for me. Outside, where the studio car is waiting, there are palm trees, just like in Durban.

A young man in uniform who is the driver salutes me. I have never been saluted before. "Hello, Miss Makeba. I'm from NBC." I have a long car all to myself. The roads in Los Angeles are very wide, and they are filled with cars that are as long as two ox carts and have big tail fins like rocket ships. We go over some hills and come to a big green complex. Long, long corridors take us to the stage where the rehearsal is. I am introduced to a man wearing a tweed jacket and glasses; he is Mr. Steve Allen. He is a man who is intense and relaxed at the same time. And luckily for me, he is kind, because I am scared shaking. I rehearse and rehearse with the band. Mr. Allen can tell I am nervous. He takes me aside and says how much he enjoyed my singing in *Come Back, Africa*. I am singing "Intoyal," a song I did in the film, because he had liked this one.

I am dressed in the wonderful outfit Mr. Pratt made for me, and then I am made up. The show will be live. I think about making a mistake, and I can see all of America laughing. These thoughts do not help me any. I get more and more scared. I am here all by myself. There is no one I can speak Zulu to who can give me encouragement. I do not say much to anyone. But I don't have to, because the makeup lady just won't stop chattering away.

"Don't worry about a thing, honey," she tells me. "You'll be great. Don't even think about those sixty million people who will be watching."

"*How* many?"

She shrugs, as if it's nothing. "Sixty million."

The show begins. Mr. Allen does some funny sketches, but I am too nervous to laugh. When the time comes for me to go on, he comes to take me and says, "You're going to do just *fine*. Just sing the way I saw you singing." He grabs me and takes me to the stage, and he can feel I am shaking.

"The red light on top of the camera means we're on the air," he whispers. "Remember to smile."

Mr. Allen introduces me, and he is actually holding me up so I do not just collapse from fright. But then he must leave, and I am on my own. The lights are very bright, and I cannot see the audience. I imagine my mother sitting out there, and Bongi. The music begins to play. It is strange to hear the new, Western-style arrangement, so rich and full, made for my native song. "Intoyal" is a beautiful melody, and it touches a spot deep inside me. That spot grows, until it gobbles me up. I sway and smile, and move and sing. Somehow, I perform.

▼▼▼▼▼

I am back in the cold, in New York. I go out to look for shoes for the green and blue dress I will wear at the Vanguard. I think some of the nervousness from the television show is still with me, because I feel people are watching me. They look at me out of the corner of their eyes. I see them watching me from behind racks of clothes. I think, "What kind of trouble is this?"

A lady comes up to me. She looks at me kind of strange. "Aren't you the African girl who was on *Steve Allen?*"

I tell her that I am. Soon, another women comes up and asks me the same question. And then a real shock: a young man smiles and says, "Hey, man, give me your autograph!"

I apologize, and say that I have nothing to write with. They bring me paper and a pen, and I sign my first autograph. Now I am beginning to realize how important Mr. Allen's show was.

▼▼▼▼▼

The Village Vanguard is a little jazz club on Eighth Street. I do not know what I am doing here, because I am not a jazz singer, but Mr. Max Gordon, who did so much to bring me to the United States, seems very happy to have me. He has given me a contract for four weeks. I rehearse with the little band for my set of five songs. I will sing four songs and go off. The people will shout, "Hey! Hey!" and I will return for the fifth song. This is how we figure it. The set is short, only thirty to thirty-five minutes. But that's enough. A nightclub set is not supposed to be very long. Also, the musicians can only learn a few songs in such a short time.

The day of the opening, Mr. Belafonte's people take me to Harlem to get my hair made up for the show. I do not want this.

I like my hair the way it is: short and woolly. But the straight, long, elegant look like Diahann Carroll's is in. Seeing so many black people in Harlem reminds me of home, and I get a little sad. The woman who does my hair was once married to Joe Louis. She has a beauty salon, now, where she straightens my hair. I thank her, but I cannot look at myself in the mirror. I'm too afraid. When I get back to the hotel I see what has been done to me. I cry and cry. This is not *me*. I put my head in the hot water and I wash it and wash it. I am not a glamor girl. I'm just naturally myself. I still do not wear makeup. The big earrings that hang from each lobe and my large, colorful bead necklaces are all the decorations I need.

Still, when I get to the nightclub I hide in my dressing room. When Mr. Belafonte comes back and sees me, I tell him what I did. He says not to worry, and that he has a surprise for me.

He certainly does. When I peek outside I see that there is a long table in front. I cannot believe who Big Brother has sitting with him and his wife: Sidney Poitier, Duke Ellington, Diahann Carroll, Nina Simone, and Miles Davis. I have admired these people for years. They are great artists. And now they have come to see me. I wonder if they, or if anyone, will like my singing.

There is no time to worry. I am introduced. There is applause. The club seats about three hundred people, and it is jammed. I step onto the small stage and smile at the band. Big Brother has taught me a trick: In a nightclub, never start singing until everyone quiets down. I wait until there is a hush. Now it is my turn.

"Jikele Mayweni" is a sad song about an African warrior who has been defeated. It is a beautiful, lonely melody, and as I sing I can feel my emotion reaching out to these people. Very quietly they listen. The only movement is the slow swaying of my body and the thin clouds of cigarette smoke that swirl up into the white spotlights. When I finish, I bow. I swear, the applause is like the thunder that accompanied the lightning that once killed my girlfriend.

And the applause is like electricity to me. I next sing the bouncy tune, "Back of the Moon" from *Come Back, Africa*, and then the Xhosa song about a dreamy bride, which is called "Qonqgonthwane." In Xhosa, the tongue makes clicking sounds that one critic says are "like the popping of champagne corks." From this moment on I will be known as the "click-click girl."

The next song of my set is called "Seven Good Years." Sarah Silvia, the Jewish actress and the mother of Alfred Herbert, the producer of *African Jazz and Variety*, taught me this Yiddish song when I was in South Africa. I had to learn enough Yiddish to understand this song, because only by knowing what the words mean can I hope to convey their emotion.

When I leave the stage, the people call me back. I am happy to oblige, and I finish with another tribal song, a love ballad called "Nomeva." There is more applause, and then all sorts of people rush up to congratulate me. They say they've never heard anyone sing like me before.

"Oh, Mr. Belafonte," I say in the car, "I thought people in New York have seen everything?"

"But no one like you!" He is taking me to a party he is throwing for me at his and Julie's apartment. All the celebrities who were at the club are here. I am much too shy to speak to them. I can only smile and nod at their compliments. There are many white people at Mr. Belafonte's party, and I still do not know how to be comfortable with them. If they speak to me, I answer them. But as soon as I can I go sit in the corner and sip my Coca-Cola. I am having an interesting time just looking at the glamorous people.

Journalists come and ask me questions. I try to talk about my music, and they politely write down what I say. But they ask me questions about South Africa and apartheid. They want to know if I am associated with the African Nationalist Movement.

"Please," I say. "let's not talk about politics."

I must certainly avoid this. My mother, my daughter, my whole family is in South Africa, and they will have problems if I do something to displease the authorities. But I am getting bolder. What is happening in America is hard to believe, but it is true: I am becoming a success. *Look* magazine takes me to the top of the Empire State Building to photograph me against the city. The Vanguard shows are doing very well. I am becoming more confident.

At the end of one show, two men come to see me. I can tell right away by their Dutch looks, and by the way they look at me as if they *own* me, that they are Afrikaners.

The two men from South Africa do not seem happy. One of them says, "We came here because we thought we'd hear music from home. Why don't you sing any *lietjies*?"

A *lietjie* is a white folk tune in Afrikaans. I could say to these men that I do not know Afrikaans. That would not be unusual for a native. But, as I say, I am getting a little bit bolder.

"When you start singing in my language," I tell them, "I will start singing in yours."

7

I PICK UP *THE NEW YORK Times* and read about myself: "There are few cases in show business where a performer's life has changed more suddenly, more dramatically, and with so much promise."

This is certainly true. The little Xhosa girl from South Africa spends her first Christmas away from home at Sidney Poitier's house. For my first New Year's, a summertime holiday at home that is celebrated here in the middle of the winter, I am invited to Diahann Carroll's. I have signed on as a client of the great William Morris Agency. Negotiations are going on with RCA Records for my first album. And I have moved uptown, from the Vanguard in the Village to the Blue Angel Club on East Fifty-second Street. And now that I am singing for eight weeks in this East Side "saloon for sophisticates," where they are paying me $750 a week, the press really takes notice.

Newsweek says, "She sings with the smoky tones and delicate phrasing of Ella Fitzgerald, and when the occasion demands she summons up the brassy showmanship of Ethel Merman and the intimate warmth of Frank Sinatra." There is a quote from Mr. Belafonte in the story: " 'She is easily the most revolutionary new talent to appear in any medium in the last decade.' "

Time magazine writes, "She is probably too shy to realize it, but her return to Africa would leave a noticeable gap in the U.S. entertainment world, which she entered a mere six weeks ago."

Yes, it has been only six weeks. But like Dorothy says when she lands in Oz, "Things happen so quickly here!"

There was a bohemian feel at the Village Vanguard. Students would come on Sundays and sit on the floor when I sang. Black customers were much fewer than the white customers, who came out of curiosity or were students studying Africa.

In the Blue Angel, with its chic decor, low ceilings, and tiny tables, I look down and there is Lauren Bacall, really getting into my music. People wear jewels and furs and arrive in fancy cars. They come to hear the African girl. They are not disappointed, because they have not seen anything like me: I don't wear any makeup. My hair is very short and natural. Soon I see other black women imitate the style, which is no style at all, but just letting our hair be itself. They call the look the "Afro."

I am so excited I have to call home and tell my mother all that is happening to me. It is not easy to arrange, but my friends in South Africa finally bring my mother to the Black Artists' Union, where there is a phone.

It is so good to hear her voice. We cry more than we talk, but I manage to tell her all the news. Because of the Blue Angel dates, I have overstayed my visa, and I tell her I will not be coming home right away. Colleges are calling the William Morris Agency asking me to come and sing.

My mother's voice becomes grave. "Zenzi, you must bring Bongi to you."

For seven years my daughter has been raised by my mother. The separations have been painful, but necessary if I want to make any kind of life for Bongi. But now all of a sudden my mother wants to give her back to me. I ask if Bongi is ill. I ask if there are any problems at home, or if the authorities are cracking down on the natives and making life dangerous. But my mother will not discuss these things. "Take Bongi from here," she says. "She must be with you."

The next day I begin the arrangements to bring my daughter to the United States. My mother, the *isangoma*, is prophetic. I do not know what she thinks is going to happen in South Afrika, but I dare not go against her urgings.

I would like to have Bongi here with me. I am very lonely. *Time* might call me "the most exciting new singing talent to appear in many years," but I still go home at night to a miserable little hotel on Eighth Street. Lionel Rogosin found the place for me because it is close to the Village Vanguard. But I must move out soon because I cannot sleep. All night long I get strange calls from women. Their voices are low and intimate-sounding. They tell me that they like my short hair. They suggest things that frighten me.

"Please," I beg them, "it's the middle of the night. I'm just a girl from South Africa. I don't know about such things."

"Oh, baby, I can fix that . . ."

"Please, *please*, leave me alone."

But they don't. I sit at the edge of the bed and I stare out the window at the ugly brick building across the way. It is cold. I am so far away from the people I love. I pick up a book that was given to me by Langston Hughes, the great American Negro poet. He came to see me at the Village Vanguard, and I thought he was a very nice and kind old man. I read a poem of his called "Alone."

> We cry among the skyscrapers
> As our ancestors
> Cried among the palms in Africa
> Because we are alone,
> It is night
> And we're afraid.

▼▼▼▼▼

There is a kind family who takes me in until I find a place of my own. Mburumba Kerina is from Namibia, the country in southwest Africa. His wife, Jane, is from California. They have an infant daughter, Kakuna. Mburumba spends a lot of time at the United Nations. He is petitioning for the liberation of his country. Originally, the UN gave South Africa a mandate to govern Namibia temporarily. Now the UN wants its mandate back, but South Africa stays put. The Southwest African People's Organization, known as SWAPO, is being formed as an army of liberation. Africans are beginning to demand their rights. One part of this is the spread of the Nationalist Movement. When Jane and Mburumba take me to the United Nations, I meet the delegates of the newly independent black African countries. There are men and women from Ghana and Nigeria. This year, 1960, Senegal becomes free, then the Ivory Coast, and fifteen nations in all. The Belgian Congo changes its name to Zaire when it becomes independent. It is exciting to be with the delegates at this moment in history. There is so much hope and promise. It is the dawn of a new age.

I am getting used to New York. It is a very tiring place. Life is so fast! But I am still a little out of place. When I see a black man or a black woman on the street, I smile and say, "Sakubona!" I don't think twice about it. After all, they are my black brothers and sisters. So, I say, "Sakubona!", which means, "good morning." But, my, do they look at me strangely! And I then think, "Oh, yeah . . ."

After two months living with the Kerinas, I find a place for myself on East Eighty-second Street. On the day I decide to move, Mburumba is at the United Nations and Jane is at work. I am looking after little Kakuna. The Kerinas' apartment is on Seventy-ninth Street, not far from my place. I don't have many things: two suitcases, a little trunk, and Kakuna. I take a baby blanket and tie the child to my back, as I did with Bongi and other children at home. Then I take a suitcase in each hand, and the trunk I put on my head. I can carry a lot of weight on my head, which I learned to do when I was a little girl carrying the water up from the well to my grandmother's compound. The trunk does not weigh too much. With this load, I go out onto Seventy-ninth Street.

All at once I hear a squeal of auto brakes. One of these big American cars almost hits the back of a taxi. The drivers are looking at *me*. Everybody is looking at me as I walk along with the baby tied to my back, the suitcases in both hands, and the trunk on my head. I guess they are thinking, "Where did *this* one come from?"

After I am moved in, I get a call from Cicely Tyson. She is the young actress I met at Big Brother's. I like her a lot, and she admires me, too. She asks if she can come over.

"I'm supposed to play the role of a young African woman," she tells me when she comes. I boil some water on the stove and practice my hostess's skills on this pretty young actress. "How does a pregnant African woman behave?"

I am surprised, and I don't know what to say to her. "But a pregnant woman is a pregnant woman!"

Cicely laughs. "They are all the same!"

"Yes. Some crave for this, some crave for that."

We talk and have a nice time until I have to go to the night-club. This night a long limousine pulls up in front.

"Hey, Miriam!" a musician says. "Guess who's come? Bing Crosby!"

"What?" I say. "Bing Crosby coming to see me?" One of the things I wanted to do in America is meet all the people I have ever seen in the movies. And it is happening all the time!

After my set he comes to see me. I guess he wears a toupee in the movies, because he really doesn't have a lot of hair. But his smile is so familiar. "Nice show!" he says.

I think: Bing Crosby is thanking *me*? I am sorry, but things are turned around. I do what I always do: I ask for two autographs. One is for me, and one is for my friend in South Africa, Letta. I promised Letta I would do this. By now she has a nice collection.

Another big star from Hollywood whom I have admired for years is in town filming a movie called *Butterfield 8*. Elizabeth Taylor comes to hear me sing once, twice, three times. The third time she brings her co-star from the movie, Mr. Laurence Harvey. He was born in South Africa. They ask me out to dinner after the show. We go to a place on Third Avenue where they serve us Mexican beans.

Elizabeth Taylor is a nice lady. She is so beautiful I can't stop looking at her. And she is very interested in my life in Africa. I try to overcome my shyness to talk to her. But most of the talking is done by poor Mr. Harvey, who is very homesick. He does not meet many people from South Africa, and he is happy that I am here to know the places and things he talks about.

There are many singers I listened to in South Africa whom I am now meeting. When I find myself face to face with them, I say, "I can't believe this!" At the Basin Street East I go to hear Ella Fitzgerald. How I admire this lady! I've been singing her songs since I was a child. During her show, she tells everyone that I am in the audience. People applaud politely, but all I pay attention to is the great woman on stage.

Then I hear that one of my idols, Sarah Vaughan, is performing at the Waldorf in the Empire Room. You cannot get in unaccompanied, and I cannot find anyone to come with me. So I decide to be bold and go there myself. At the Waldorf I tell them that I am a young performer from South Africa. Would they please let me sit in back? I *must* see Miss Vaughan. Someone goes and tells her. The next thing I know, I am taken to a nice table right in front. Sarah Vaughan comes on, and I study her when she performs to see if I can pick up things. Afterward, she invites me to her dressing room. She says she saw me on the *Steve Allen Show*. Like all the American singers I have met, she is surprised to hear that her records are played and loved in South Africa. As usual, I ask for two autographed pictures: one for me and one for Letta.

On my way home, I pass the theater where Lionel Rogosin's film has opened. I cannot believe it when I see the marquee: "COME BACK AFRICA, STARRING MIRIAM MAKEBA." I am surprised, because I am only in the movie for three minutes. People say they go to see it expecting me, and they wait and wait. Finally, I come on, sing two songs, and I'm gone. But I am happy if my name will bring people into the theater, because the documentary is an important look at the terrible conditions we live in at home.

I learn that there are plans at home to speak out against these conditions. The people are going to stage a peaceful march to protest the carrying of passbooks. They say it will be historic. I should think so, because it is unheard of in South Africa to have any kind of organized march. The place they have chosen to do this is a black neighborhood outside the town of Vereeniging, a township called Sharpeville.

▼▼▼▼▼

My manager, Mr. Dave Baumgarten, whom I got through Mr. Belafonte, works through the William Morris Agency. He arranges my first college date. I go to the middle of America to sing at the Roland, Missouri, School of Mines. It is an engineering school. I find that Americans really do take their movies seriously. Their ideas about Africa are right out of a Tarzan movie. This makes me sad, since our land is so vast and complex. The people who think it is nothing but jungles and monkeys and half-naked villagers are really missing something. In private I try to tell the students and everyone else the way things really are—the good and the bad. But I do not make public speeches or give talks. They have not invited me to do this, and, anyway, I am too shy. What I do is sing. I was told that the people in Missouri are not as sophisticated as the people in New York. But they seem to like my native songs just as much as the chichi people who came to the posh Blue Angel Club.

I go to the big university at Madison, Wisconsin, next, and then it's back to New York. A lot of people have suggested that I take dance lessons. I don't know why I should, but I always like to learn things. I go to dance class once. The next day I hurt so much I can barely get out of bed. And I have to perform! My whole body is hurting. I say, "No more for me!" Besides, I have to get ready for Bongi.

The authorities have agreed to let my daughter out for a visit. I try not to get excited, because the South African officials might change their mind and cancel the trip at any time. They have done worse. But I cannot help but get excited, because I haven't seen Bongi in a year. Julie Belafonte brings over a big stuffed toy for my daughter, and we add this to all the other toys my friends have brought. I admire Julie because she is very intelligent. She is also a beautiful dresser. As an artist, a dancer, she understands other artists. She is a help to me.

I am so excited the night before Bongi's plane arrives that I cannot sleep. I stay up all night with a neighbor, a Jewish girl named Rene who has an apartment on the first floor of our building on Eighty-second Street. I have the basement apartment, which I took because it has a garden in back where Bongi can play. Rene and I talk and talk, and when it starts getting light we decide to take a taxi to Idlewild. We arrive hours before the plane is due to land.

I go upstairs and wait at the glassed-in balcony where visitors can look down at the passengers arriving from foreign lands. I keep my spot until Bongi's plane arrives. Rene is beside me. "Oh, is that her?" she keeps asking whenever a little girl appears. But Bongi does not show up. My heart is beating: boom-boom-boom! Then finally I see her, my little girl, hand in hand with a hostess. She is the very last one off the plane.

"There she is!" I jump up and down behind the glass and wave. She sees me and she jumps, too. Bongi has grown in the past year, and she is now such a slim and lovely little nine-year-old. When she is let through downstairs, she runs into my arms. My little girl is so excited she tries to tell me everything at once: how everybody is doing at home, how she has been following my adventures, and how my mother has taken sick. All this time she is looking around and asking a million questions. She laughs and points at everything while I try to find out the news, especially how my mother is.

When we get home, the apartment is filled with more toys and dolls and candy than Bongi has ever seen in her life. She just stands and looks at it all, as if she is in a dream. This poor girl from South Africa. In her I see myself as a little girl: How surprised I would be by all these many things, when to have any one of them would have seemed like Christmas. It makes me cry, because I know how hard life is at home, and I am so very grateful that I have managed to get Bongi out. This is especially true when I learn that my mother is not well enough to take care of her anymore.

Bongi begins her schooling right away. I enroll her in a private school because she does not speak any English. Bantu Education has seen to that.

▼▼▼▼▼

There are others from South Africa who also come back into my life, but only to haunt me.

William Morris has negotiated a contract for me with RCA Records. Plans are under way for my first album, which is to be called *Miriam Makeba*. Mr. Belafonte is involved. The four men who are his backup group, the Belafonte Folk Singers, will accompany me. Big Brother himself is writing the jacket notes.

But it seems that I already have a contract with Gallotone Records back in Johannesburg. It is a contract that never pays me royalties for my records, so I forgot about it after I received my last payment for a recording session a year and a half ago. But they now say they "own" me. This angers Big Brother, who does not like the idea of a black person being owned. To release me, Gallotone demands that RCA pay seventy-five thousand dollars. The sum makes my head spin. But Big Brother has lawyers, and they talk down the figure until it is forty-five thousand dollars. RCA pays. I will never see a cent from the *Miriam Makeba* album, even though it sells nicely. All the royalties will go back into paying Gallotone.

But at least the album is out, and people all over the country are buying it. The excitement of the Nationalist Movement in Africa has spread to the United States, and more and more there is an interest in things African. I find myself right in the center of this interest. Big Brother says I am a "diplomat."

There is much to be done and much to be said. The peaceful march in Sharpeville ends in horror and tragedy. The authorities at home are not willing to tolerate any kind of protest at all. The marchers are unarmed, of course, but they are met by soldiers. The army fires into the crowd. Many, many are killed in the massacre. Many others are wounded. I am on the other side of the world, trying to piece together the events from news stories. Then I get letters, and refugees begin arriving with word of my family. I learn the terrible news: two of my uncles have been killed. I weep and weep, and in my bitterness I can feel something hard, a resolve, form inside. My people all feel this in our grief.

But for now things quiet down in South Africa. People are too stunned. They have to think what they are going to do next. The ANC is banned by the authorities. Until the massacre of Sharpeville, the organization has been peaceful. But now it seems only a fight will save us from a quick genocide by massacre or from slow strangulation through the apartheid laws.

▼▼▼▼▼

I have not been able to call my mother. I cannot get through. Now I must leave New York. There is a club in Chicago that wants me for one week. Bongi is on vacation from school, so we go together. The day I am to open, I receive a phone call from Big Brother. It is the news I have been fearing: My mother is dead.

There is nothing that can be done for me. I am in such pain that I cannot concentrate on a thing I am doing. Somehow, I get to the club. I do not understand why the management insists that I perform. How can I, when I cannot stop crying? My mother had such a hard life, and I loved her so much that I feel brokenhearted that I could not have at least been with her at the end. I think of all the suffering she did, and all the things she taught me, and all the love she gave me. I think of these things when I am nearly shoved out on the stage. But it does them no good to insist. I stand in the spotlight with my head hung, and I cry.

The people in the audience are very concerned. "What's wrong? What's the matter?"

I explain what has happened. I hear some ugly sounds. The people are very angry with the management for making me go on.

Finally, I am permitted to go back to the hotel. But the next day I am told I must perform and fulfill the contract for all the shows of the week. It is very hard, but I do it. When I return to New York with Bongi, several days have passed and I must hurry to obtain my visa. I have certainly missed my mother's funeral—who knows how much time passed before Mr. Belafonte's office was contacted with the news?—but I can at least visit her grave and see my relatives.

I am nervous when I go into the South African consulate. Here I am once again nothing but a native black without rights. The darling of the American newsmagazines and music industry, the girl who charmed the New York sophisticates and started a fashion trend with her hair and clothes, here she is just a *kaffir* who doesn't know her place. The man at the desk takes my passport. He does not speak to me, but to himself when he says, "Miriam Makeba," as if he was expecting this moment.

He takes a rubber stamp and slams it down on my passport. Then he walks away. I pick up my passport. It is stamped "INVALID."

For an instant my breath catches in my throat as I realize what has happened. They have done it: They have exiled me. I am not permitted to go home, not now, and maybe not ever. My family. My home. Everything that has ever gone into the making of myself, gone!

I flee the building. I do not dare ask questions, because I know the answer: If I go back home now, jail awaits me. It is the same for anyone the authorities do not want. They are displeased with me. I have gone too far. I have become too big. Maybe they fear I will speak out against them. I have not said a word about politics in all the newspaper stories that have been printed about me. But I am still dangerous.

And now, with the single impression of a rubber stamp, I am in exile. I and my daughter, alone in a West that is bright and rich but is foreign to us. I hold Bongi tight and try to protect her from the terrible things I feel. But she feels them, too. I think of the poem Mr. Hughes gave me.

We cry among the skyscrapers . . .
Because we are alone
It is night
And we're afraid.

8

I AM IN ATLANTA, GEORGIA, in the American South, and my party is the first group of blacks permitted to stay in this hotel. Since Mr. Belafonte is such an important person and such a great talent, I guess this is as it should be. We are in this city to perform at a rally for the Reverend Martin Luther King, Jr. In South Africa, none of us had heard about Dr. King. But here in the U.S. I've heard nothing but all the great things he has done for black people and all of the difficult work that his organization is doing for civil rights. Dr. King is a very forceful man. When he speaks to a crowd, you have to sit up and listen. He has that power, that charisma. Sometimes people like that weigh heavily on you. When he comes to greet me after I sing, I am shy. His lovely wife sees this, and she is gracious to me. "How are you? Welcome to Atlanta."

But the welcome we get in Atlanta is good and bad. Yes, we are permitted to stay in this grand old hotel. But when Mr. Belafonte, Julie, I, and some other people go down to the restaurant for our dinner, we are not allowed to go in.

"Coloreds," we are told by the maitre d', "are not permitted."

"Oh, oh," I think, "here we go again." A new country, but the same old racism. In South Africa, they call it apartheid. Here in the South, it is called Jim Crow.

Mr. Belafonte is very composed. He tells the manager coolly, "I'll be back."

And he comes back. But this time he brings reporters from every paper and camera crews from every television station with him. He brings me along, too. I stand at his side at the entrance to the restaurant when he makes a statement. "What can we as Americans say to a guest like Miss Makeba? She comes from a land of oppression, only to find a situation like this."

I leave when the cameras leave. Big Brother goes away to plan a protest. The funny thing is, I did not want to go to the restaurant in the first place. Being shy, I would have liked to stay in a corner somewhere and eat by myself and be at ease. But being in a restaurant, with all the people looking at you because they know you from a concert or television, it's tiring. I call it "performing twenty-four hours a day." Who needs it?

But I understand why Big Brother made me go down to the restaurant the second time for the cameras. I admire the civil rights movement here in the U.S. All over the country, I see black people who are not just sitting down and letting everybody step on them. When you come to think of it, the treatment of black people in the U.S. is quite similar to the treatment of my people in South Africa. In the U.S., black people live in segregated areas that are not called townships but "ghettos." If you are black, you cannot live where you want, or go to whatever restaurant you like, or sit where you want on a bus. To me it's the same thing in both countries, except that the American government condemns racism in its constitution, and the South African constitution condones it.

At least they are making progress here. There is much to do. I find this on the road. William Morris has teamed me with a talented folk-singing group, the Chad Mitchell Trio, and we tour the country. Our shows are very popular at the colleges. But some of the campuses are in the South, or in rural areas. We arrive for a performance in Nashville, Tennessee. At the hotel, we are told that the Chad Mitchell Trio can stay, but my musicians and I must go. So, everybody comes over to the black area, and we find a hotel here. They give us rooms with jukebox speakers attached to the wall. I think of the Ready Fusion system that broadcasts propaganda to our homes in South Africa. In this place, the jukebox is located in the lobby. Every time somebody drops in a dime and plays a song, you hear it in every room. Chubby Checker's "The Twist." Over and over. So here we are, and the Chad Mitchell Trio is with us. At times like this, you can only kick off your shoes, laugh, sit back, and make the best of it.

In other cities, we cannot find hotels at all. Some of the college students give us their rooms, and we sleep in the dormitories. It is as if I am again in the production of *King Kong*.

The jazz opera has gone to London for the start of what will be a successful run. Auditions were held for the singer who must take my old part of Joyce. My friend Letta did a good job, but she is still too young to play the lead. The producer decided to use my cousin Peggy Phango. She is the one who taught me how to dress properly: how to match colors and select outfits. She had a strong idea about how I should look. She used to go with me to performances with the Cuban Brothers, and she would dress me for them. Since I didn't have much money, Peggy lent me her own clothes. Sometimes she gave them to me. To pay her back, I got her a part in *African Jazz and Variety*. And now she is in London with *King Kong*, along with my friend in the orchestra, Hugh Masekela. They are all being given a glimpse of life outside the cage of apartheid. There is always a danger that South Africa will consider these singers and musicians "corrupted" and not let them return. More and more, the authorities in Pretoria are becoming more hostile toward my people and more defensive toward the outside world. They become angry at some criticism by other members of the British Commonwealth, and they drop out of that body. Pretoria will just tell the rest of the world to go to hell if anyone tries to protest the treatment of my people. South Africa is a rich country, and as long as it has money, the government knows it can do what it wants.

It is this arrogance of the South African officials that makes so strange a meeting backstage at the Carter Barron Amphitheater in Washington, D.C.

I am spending the summers touring with Big Brother. The three-month circuit begins in Hartford, Connecticut. We go on to Massachusetts; Rochester, New York; Toronto; Vancouver; and then California. This year, 1961, is the first of many summers that I will spend this way. From time to time we also visit Boston, Philadelphia, and other cities. The billing is: "HARRY BELAFONTE, FEATURING MIRIAM MAKEBA." The tours help me a lot,

because everywhere we go I am seen by Big Brother's audiences.
Mr. Belafonte has his own band, and I bring my own musicians.
Mr. Belafonte uses my people in his set. Then Big Brother and I
do one or two songs with both bands playing and perhaps the
Belafonte Folk Singers backing us up.

Wherever we go, Big Brother holds press conferences before
our performances. We talk about the shows, of course, but also
about social affairs. Big Brother talks about the civil rights movement, and I talk about South Africa. Working with Mr. Belafonte
makes me learn a lot, and I grow up a lot in a way. All the
newspapermen and the radio and TV people give me a valuable
chance to speak up about the crimes that are being committed
against my people at home. I must no longer be shy. I ask
myself how many black South Africans enjoy the attention of the
press all the time, and I can only answer: one.

So, it is very strange when two Afrikaners come backstage
during intermission at the Carter Barron Amphitheater. I spot
them right away. Of course, their shocked expressions make
them very obvious. I have just changed into my outfit for the
second act. The other singers and dancers are rushing around.
Big Brother has assigned a wardrobe mistress to take care of my
clothes, my costumes, and everything. She is a nice lady named
Agnes, and she is a luxury that I am not used to.

The chargé d'affaires and the cultural attaché from the South
African Embassy here in Washington stop and stare at me and at
Agnes, this white woman who is down on her knees helping me
put on my shoes—me, this black girl that they would not allow
in their homes except as a servant to help them put on their own
shoes. When the gentlemen recover, they step forward.

"We are from the South African Embassy. We brought you a
gift from your tribe."

This makes me angry inside at once. Here they have exiled
me, and they do not speak of my home or my country, but my
tribe, as if it is a group of foreigners who are in their country. All
I can say is, "Which tribe is that?"

"Are you not from the Xhosa?"

They put a necklace of beautiful beads in my hand. Then the
cultural attaché says, "We would like to invite you and the
whole cast to the embassy for a reception."

This makes me feel even more angry. If I were to go to their reception the authorities would say to my people: "Look, she is with us." If I ever go to the embassy, I will be thanking Pretoria for putting me in exile and murdering members of my family.

I say to them, "Oh? Why didn't you invite me when I was at home?" And then I add, "Because, you know, I am no longer permitted to go home."

While we are talking, Julie Belafonte comes by. She listens for a minute, and then she goes to tell Big Brother. He comes at once. I can see he is not pleased.

"Who's on my backstage?"

I explain that the two gentlemen are from the South African Embassy. Big Brother is very short with them. "Listen, Miss Makeba is here on Belafonte time. If there's anything that anybody needs from her, they talk to me."

He asks them to leave. I put my hands behind my back. I'm not going to give back my Xhosa beads. Big Brother knows what the South African authorities have done to me, and he knows that I would want no part in any reception at the South African Embassy. He did not even want me to go home when my mother died. Because of Sharpesville, and the general oppression, he was against the idea.

Now Big Brother does not have to worry. I am his for the summers. And for special events. With Odetta, I join Big Brother for a concert at Carnegie Hall. RCA releases a record made of this memorable night.

Big Brother says that one day I will be a big star. If this happens, part of the reason will be Mr. Belafonte's help. Sometimes when people become big, they resent it that someone else helped them get to where they are. I hope I never forget Big Brother's role. He has taught me many things. The most important one is respect: respect for myself, for the stage, and for my audience. He teaches me how to conduct myself on stage: how to dress, and, especially, discipline. I do not think that anyone can become as good as Mr. Belafonte without a lot of discipline. I pay attention to him.

I also learn from other performers. I get to travel first class on planes, now, and on a flight from Los Angeles to New York I watch a good-looking young man walk by who I think I recognize. "Is that Johnny Mathis?" I think. "My goodness, he must be taking handsome lessons from Big Brother!"

Mr. Mathis sits behind me, and he asks if I am Miriam Makeba. Since I am, he is not disappointed, and we talk about a concert that he will give in New York. He promises me some tickets. I go, and admire the way he performs. He has a wonderful way with a microphone. There is never any popping to get in the way of his beautiful voice.

Carmen McRae is also a part of my education. At home I have most of her records. I love to watch her. She is also very skillful with the microphone. And her enunciation! This lady, you hear every word she sings. I say to myself that I must work on my diction until I can sound as clear as she.

In September, after my first summer tour with Big Brother, I make my first appearance at the Apollo Theatre in Harlem. I am told that for forty years this stage has hosted the great black entertainers of America. Ella Fitzgerald and Sarah Vaughan got their starts here as young girls when they both won amateur contests. Most of my idols have sung here, including Lena Horne, Eartha Kitt, Pearl Bailey, and Josephine Baker. And now the African girl comes.

Also, with the fall, it is time for the Chad Mitchell Trio and myself to tour the colleges. I am getting to know more and more about the United States. It is very pleasing to go to Tuskegee in Alabama, where they train black doctors. As a girl, I read about Booker T. Washington, who founded the school. The idea of a black scientist was as exotic to our way of thinking as a black king.

They tell me at last I am going to the American West. I am not disappointed by Laramie, Wyoming. Cowboys are everywhere, and they ride their horses just outside the town, whistling at the cows to go this way and that. There is only one hotel, which is old. I think, "Hey, Zenzi's in the West!"

But other parts of America are not so nice. I was not expecting to see poverty here. In South Africa, we really think that every American is rich. It's hard to disbelieve the pictures we see so many times in the movies. We all want to live like people do in the cinema, and so we think to do so we have to live in America. But here in the rural areas I see white families living in shacks. In the cities, poor people line up in front of the missions for handouts. Even black poverty is a shock. In South Africa, we get magazines like *Ebony* and *Jet.* You don't see poor people in *Ebony*. Everyone is gorgeous.

But I cannot complain about my own life in America. Bongi is doing well at school. The officials there tested her after her first months, and she was promoted up one grade. I feel that I now have enough money saved that I can make a more comfortable home for her. One bright day in 1962, we move from my basement apartment on Eighty-second Street to Park West Village on the West Side at Ninety-seventh and Central Park West. We have two bedrooms here: one for Bongi and one for me. We can see Central Park outside our windows. Our new home is very nice: a large kitchen, dining room, and living room. There are stores right downstairs, so I don't have to go out into the cold New York winters. There's a little market, and a bottle store, which is called a liquor store here in America. I do not drink, but I have guests who do.

A lot of artists live in this building. Ray Charles has an apartment upstairs on the twentieth floor that he uses when he is in town. Brock Peters, the actor, has a place here, and so does Abbey Lincoln, the jazz singer. Horace Silvel, the jazz pianist, has the apartment across from my own. He is not surprised when I tell him that we listen to all his records in South Africa. He gets fan mail from my people all the time. He brings one letter over. It is written in Zulu. I translate for him: A young couple is naming their new son Horace in his honor. He gets many letters like this one. There must be a lot of Horaces at home.

I see very little of the New York nightlife. I don't usually go out, especially when I am working. I'm too tired. I just want to stay home with Bongi. We have a television set, and she likes to watch *Bonanza*, which reminds me of Laramie, Wyoming. But I do go out to see my favorite musicians. I really like the pianist Randy Weston, who likes African music. I have to see Nina Simone whenever she is performing. And Carmen McRae and Sarah Vaughan. Every time.

Sometimes on weekends Bongi's friends come and spend the nights with her. I take her to the park across the street, and to the zoo. My friends take her out, too, especially to this place they have where you look at the stars: the Planetarium. Bongi loves the museums. You would never know it from her mother.

I have never been to any of the New York museums. They have so many things it makes me tired. My friend Carla takes Bongi out horseback riding in the park. But I prefer to sit and watch.

One day I come home and I get a shock. Who should be braiding Bongi's hair but Hugh Masekela! When *King Kong* finished its run in London, Hughie wrote to me that he would like to come to New York to study at the Manhattan School of Music. I wrote back that he should stay with me. And here he is, my old friend. I guess it is because I first got to know Hughie when he was fourteen years old, but to me he will always look like a little boy, with his cute fat cheeks and his big round eyes. But he is not a little boy. He is a young man of twenty-four, and he does not mind me telling him that he is good-looking.

Hughie stays with Bongi and me until I find him a place for himself on Eighty-seventh Street. I get him his own place because I think he should be alone. No one can say my faith in him is groundless; he starts to work hard at his music right away.

▼▼▼▼▼

It is strange how life works sometimes. Here I am reading about the big birthday party that is going to happen for President Kennedy at Madison Square Garden. Only the very top stars will be asked to perform. Marilyn Monroe will be singing "Happy Birthday." Marlon Brando will be there, and Diahann Carroll, Peter Lawford, and Mr. Belafonte.

And now Big Brother calls me up with the news that I will be performing, too.

I can't believe it. "Oh, no!"

"Oh, yes! You do two songs. Mark your calendar."

Little me, from Africa, singing for the President of the United States. But when the big night arrives, I am sick with the flu. I feel tired, and my head seems as big as a melon. I decide to sing my songs and then go home. At Madison Square Garden there are stars all over the place. Twenty thousand people are in the audience. The orchestra plays "Hail to the Chief." I look up and there are President and Mrs. Kennedy, waving from a box on high. The time comes for me to sing my songs. I have never performed before when I have not gotten stage fright. And I guess I won't be getting over it tonight. But I've never been shy on stage, either.

With my trio of male singers behind me, I stand back from the

mike and sing one of my most popular songs, "Wimoweh."
Some pop singers here in the U.S. have remade "Wimoweh,"
using new English lyrics instead of the original Xhosa. The song
is called, "The Lion Sleeps Tonight." It is a hit, even if the lyrics
don't make sense to me. I finish "Wimoweh," and another
African tune, "Nomeva," and the audience gives me a warm
ovation.

When I go offstage I see Marilyn Monroe standing in the
wings. I move up close to her. My eyes grow very big, and I
think, "Oh, wow! Look at her!" She is fussing with a tight
gown the color of champagne. They play a trick on the house:
Miss Monroe is announced twice, but she does not go on. A
spotlight shines on the empty stage. The third time she is called
she goes out. Mr. Lawford, the M.C., says, "Here she is, the *late*
Marilyn Monroe." Everybody laughs, and she sings "Happy
Birthday" to the President in a husky lover's voice.

Mr. Kennedy thanks all the performers in a speech. There is to
be a party for us. But I am feeling tired from the flu, so I go
home.

Bongi wants to hear all about how I sang to the President. I
tell her everything, and then put her to bed. But before I can get
to bed myself there is a knock at the door. A tall man in a dark
suit says he has come to pick me up.

"The President would like to see you. We have a car outside."

"Oh!" I am too flustered to make sense of myself in the
mirror. I hope I look all right.

The reception is at the home of Arthur and Matilda Primm. It
is a very large and lovely house, and I have been here before.
The Primms invite African diplomats to their home all the time,
and they ask me to come, too, because I am close to the African
delegates at the U.N.

I see Big Brother. Mr. Belafonte has been close to Mr. Kennedy since he campaigned for him in 1960. He tells me, "When
the President got here, he asked, 'Where's the African girl?' I
had them send a car to your place."

I am presented to Mr. Kennedy. He looks just like he does on
TV and in the papers. Very nice-looking, and a very nice smile. I
curtsy, which is my custom. I do not look him in the eyes. In my
country one is not forward like that toward people who are the
leaders of their nations.

Mr. Kennedy says to me, "I just wanted you to know, Miss Makeba, how very glad and how proud I am to have an African artist participate in my birthday celebration."

"Oh, thank you, Mr. President."

He introduces me to Mrs. Kennedy, and we shake hands. She is very nice. Her voice is very soft, like mine when I am not singing.

When I get home I am truly exhausted. But there is Bongi, again, wide awake. She won't go to bed until I tell her everything. This girl is proud of her mama.

▼▼▼▼▼

There are some black women in Washington, D.C., who invite African students into their homes so they won't feel lonely. The group is called African American Friends. They invite me to welcome Tom Mboya, who comes to raise funds for Kenyan students. Kenya is about to gain its independence, and Mr. Mboya will be one of the new nation's first ministers. The African American Friends ask me to sing wherever Mr. Mboya speaks. I do, and together we raise enough money to bring eighty Kenyan students here to study.

We are such a success that Mr. Mboya asks me to come back to Africa with him to raise money for the Mau Mau orphans. I want to help the poor children who are the victims of the terrible colonial war. But I have to admit that I am also very excited to be returning to Africa. Three long years have passed since I left.

Since my passport was revoked by South Africa, I am really a person without a country. I have no way to travel. But Mr. Mboya arranges some special entry papers, and we are on our way. Suddenly, I am in Africa, again, and so excited! At the airport in Kenya, we are met by a troop from the Starehe Boys Club, which is like the Boy Scouts in America. They travel with us across the wide country, with its famous game parks. Kenya is beautiful, but when Mr. Mboya tells me he is going to take me south to Tanzania, I am truly thrilled. Tanzania received her independence earlier this year of 1962. When we cross the border, I enter for the first time an independent black nation. I feel the same rush of pride as do all my brothers and sisters throughout the continent as we emerge from the long age of colonial domination.

President Julius K. Nyerere, one of the founding fathers of

African Nationalism, greets me. He knows that I am in exile. Within an hour he gives me a Tanzanian passport. I am so happy that I weep. From now on, whenever I go in and out of the United States, I will use this document. For the first time I feel that I am not only a South African native, but a native of all Africa.

▼▼▼▼▼

Baba Hemingway, as we would call him at home, once wrote: "*Kilimanjaro is a snow covered mountain 19,710 feet high, and is said to be the highest mountain in Africa. Close to the western summit there is the dried and frozen carcass of a leopard. No one has explained what the leopard was seeking at that altitude.*"

I stand at the base of Kilimanjaro, near the Kenyan border. I am far away from my homes—my old home in South Africa that is being denied me, and my new home in America. It seems to me that everyone is like the leopard in Mr. Hemingway's story: We all end up in places and we cannot say how we got there or why. All we know is we must keep on striving. I cannot hope to make sense of my own life. I can only hope to continue the struggle and keep on singing. I love to sing. I love my daughter. And I still have great hope for both of us. I stand at this beautiful place looking up at the western summit of Kilimanjaro, which is so blue until the ice and snow begin at the top above a crown of clouds, and I think that I have one thing in common with the emerging black nations of Africa: We both have voices, and we are discovering what we can do with them.

9

I SIT ALL BY MYSELF IN THE center of a long conference table, and I speak to the eleven members of the United Nations Special Committee on Apartheid. "Please," I say in my quiet voice, "I appeal to the UN to use its influence to open the doors of all prisons and concentration camps in South Africa, where thousands of our people—men, women, and children—are now in jail."

Since I first came to New York, I have been a guest of the African delegates to many functions at the UN. Last year, 1962, Miss Angie Brooks from Liberia asked me to sing for the delegates of the Trustees Committee of the General Assembly. I was happy to do a favor for the committee's chairwoman, who is really an intelligent and dedicated person.

But this day is my first invitation of real importance. This day I go before the Special Committee, and before the entire world, and say all that is in my heart about the war Pretoria is waging against my people. I am very nervous. But I have been preparing for this for years. Big Brother gave me this advice at the beginning of my U.S. career: "You must always be careful how you conduct yourself on stage and off, because some day you will have a chance to speak on behalf of your people." I do not believe I have done anything to disgrace my people. And the "some day" is this day. The committee members sit forward in their chairs and give me the respect of their full attention.

"My country has been turned by the Verwoerd Government

into a huge prison. I feel certain that the time has come for the whole of humanity to shout 'halt' and to act with firmness to stop these crazy rulers from dragging our country into a horrifying disaster."

I pause and take a deep breath. What I am about to do will be considered an act of treason by Pretoria. I think of my family who are back home, and how they may be harmed by this. Thoughts of them have been with me for days. But it is for them, and for all of us, that I must say these words.

"Most of the world's big powers have only paid lip service to the appeals of my people for help. Therefore, I must urge the United Nations to impose a complete boycott of South Africa. The first priority must be to stop the shipments of arms. I have not the slightest doubt that these arms will be used against African women and children."

I sit back in my chair, feeling drained but excited. At last I have spoken out!

The delegates praise me as I have never been praised for anything in my life. "Moving . . . stirring . . . eloquent . . . inspiring!" are the words I hear.

Kwami Ketosugbo, who is from Ghana, thanks me for "your great show of courage." Privado Jimenez of the Philippines says, "You are a true symbol of African womanhood."

I thank them for their kind words, and also Jose Aguirre of Costa Rica, who says, "All Spanish-speaking people pay homage to this woman."

Afterward, I tell the press, "I am not a politician or a diplomat." I am just a singer, I say. But in South Africa, when the authorities learn of my testimony, I become something else: a criminal.

At home, of course, all blacks are criminals. When something goes wrong, we are considered guilty until proven innocent. I am guilty of condemning the murder of my people. And my punishment is swift: From now on all of my records are banned in South Africa. It is illegal to sell my old records that I did for Gallotone and any of my new U.S. albums I do for RCA.

In reality, my records are still available to the people. They always will be. They are smuggled in from foreign lands. Secret shipments make their way into the stores of the townships, and my records are sold under the counter. From now on my importance with my people is greater, and with each song my commitment to them grows stronger.

Once again, a totalitarian state tries to drive a wedge between an oppressed people, and it only brings us closer together.

▼▼▼▼▼

And so I become a spokesperson for my people. My appearance before the UN Special Committee changes my life, or at least the way people think of me. The person Miriam Makeba is no longer just an African singer to them. I am a symbol of my repressed people. To be in such a position is to live with a great responsibility. It is as if I am more than myself. And it is scary, because I am afraid I will make a mistake and disappoint people. I am not a saint. I am just myself. But I do have three things that will help me when times get rough: a cause that is right, a belief that my family and friends who have been butchered must not have died in vain, and a certainty that the Superior Being wants a just and good world for us all.

People come into my life now because of this new role of mine. Bongi and I are staying in Los Angeles for a few weeks while I perform at a small coffeehouse called the Ashgrove. It is on Melrose Avenue in Hollywood. I was afraid that Los Angeles, which is warm in the winter, will be like an oven in the summertime. But it is very pleasant. The little coffeehouse, though, is hot and smoky. Mostly students come to the shows. It is for this reason that I do not believe the girl who comes back to my dressing room after my first set one night and says, "Marlon Brando wants to see you."

"Who?"

When she tells me again I just say, "Go on!" Honestly, I don't believe her. Why would Marlon Brando come to a place like this? The great movie star? All the boys in South Afrika used to impersonate him: *mumble, mumble, mumble!*

After I finish my second set, the girl comes back. "I'm not kidding. The man has been sitting out there through your first show and your second show."

"Well, I don't believe he's Marlon Brando." The girl disappears, and a moment later I look in the mirror of my tiny, two-by-four dressing room and there he is standing at the door. My mouth drops open and my eyes go pop!

"I'm Marlon Brando. I've been asking for you to join us at our table."

I go, but I don't know what to say. There is another gentleman, and two ladies. Soon it is time for my third set, and Mr. Brando stays for this one, too. After, he asks me, "Would you like to come and have some coffee with us?"

At first I am reluctant. I left Bongi at the hotel. We are staying at the Chateau Marmont, which looks like a castle on a hill above the Sunset Strip. I like the Chateau Marmont because it is quiet and nice. I stay there every time I am in Los Angeles. The hotel people know me, and the other guests do, too. Bongi likes the pool, and Pearl Bailey is giving her swimming lessons. This is good, because I cannot teach her. I swim like a rock. I just sit by the pool, listen to Bongi laugh, and hear that wonderful voice of her instructor: "Don't you go splashin' old Pearl, darlin'. Slow and easy with that kickin', now. I don't need no chlorine eyes if I'm going to sing tonight!"

I call up Bongi. She is going on thirteen years old, and she tells me that she will be all right. So I say to Mr. Brando, "Okay."

I think that we are going to a restaurant. But we get into his car and—vroom! vroom!—we are climbing up a Hollywood hill. We stop at his house. Through the trees the lights of Los Angeles are all spread out below. It is very beautiful. The ladies and men have coffee, but I never drink coffee, so I am given tea. Right away, Mr. Brando starts talking to me about South Africa. The next thing I know, we are *arguing*. He wants to know everything, and he has strong opinions. I must say, he is the first celebrity who has ever asked me about home. He wants to know when the Boers came. I tell him. He goes to the encyclopedia and says, "That's not true! That's not what it says here!"

I am mad. "Well, who wrote that?" I won't let Mr. Marlon Brando or anybody tell *me* about South Africa. I tell him this, too.

He laughs. "Miriam, you have a split personality."

"I do?"

"Yes," he says. "Because when you're singing you come alive. And then when you're off stage you're quiet. And now that I'm talking to you about South Africa, you become a lioness!"

I guess what he says is true. He pulls some steaks out of the refrigerator and asks if I'm hungry. Like a lioness, I am. "Yes!"

Before the steaks are cooked, the others leave. Mr. Brando and I eat alone.

"I think I'll get some sleep if you don't mind," he says. "I have a screen test at eight." He takes me up the hall and shows me his guest room. "You can lie down here. I'll have somebody wake you in the morning."

Before he says good night and leaves me, he takes my hand and looks into my eyes. He smiles in a quiet and almost sad way. "Miriam, you have something that most of us have lost. Something very special. And that's humility."

We say good night, and I go into my room thinking that this is a very nice man. In the morning I am awakened by a servant with breakfast. I never eat breakfast, so I just drink the tea.

"I'll drop you off at your hotel on my way to the studio," Mr. Brando says. But when we get to the Chateau Marmont, he wants to come up and see my little girl. When he looks at Bongi with her big eyes, he exclaims, "My goodness! She has such big beautiful eyes I can just scoop them out and eat them!"

After he leaves, Bongi asks me, "Who's that man who wants to eat my eyes?"

I tell her, and her eyes grow even larger. "Marlon Brando! I should have asked him for his autograph!"

"One day," I tell her, "if we see him again, we will ask for his autograph."

I am to see Mr. Brando again, many times. Before this busy year ends we are to become friends. In New York, I give my first solo concert at Carnegie Hall. Big Brother brings a large party to this event, my biggest concert. After, he and Julie throw a reception for me at their apartment. Mr. Brando is there. He says, "I'll walk you home."

This is okay with me, and we begin our stroll to Central Park West. He tells me, "We're about to premiere a new film of mine, *The Ugly American*."

"How can *you* star in a movie about an *ugly* American?"

"It's political, from the Graham Greene novel. The story is about how we Americans go to other countries and corrupt them. The premiere is in Washington. I'm inviting various diplomats. I was wondering if you'd come down with me and use your influence to get the people from the African embassies to come."

We are in front of my building, Park West Village. The two doormen step out when they see us. I agree to join him in Washington. He congratulates me again on the Carnegie Hall concert, and we say good night. When he leaves, one of the doormen says to me, "Excuse me, Miss Makeba, but was that Marlon Brando?"

When I say it was, the other doorman says to his partner happily, "Hey, man, give me my ten dollars!"

Mr. Brando sends a car to bring me to the airport, and his secretary is inside to tell me about the arrangements. When I arrive in Washington, I go to a press conference that is being held before the premiere. The reporters recognize me. "Oh, it's Miriam Makeba! South Africa!" I am nervous, but I speak about life at home. Mr. Brando is pleased that he can give me this platform.

There is much to say. In South Africa, Nelson Mandela is under arrest. From what I understand, he had returned from visiting some African heads of state when he was arrested in a white suburb. He was at a meeting with some people of the African National Congress when the house was raided. There is a trial. Mr. Mandela, who is a lawyer, defends himself. He is brilliant. But he is too great a leader, and the authorities have to get rid of him. They send him to prison for life. We are shocked, but we think that after a few years they will say he has been in prison long enough, and they will let him go. It always hurts when someone is taken from our community, especially when the person is very vocal and is trying to do something about our suffering. We love them. We want them to succeed.

▼▼▼▼▼

Singing at Carnegie Hall was very exciting. Performing at President Kennedy's birthday party was a highlight of my career. Touring with Mr. Belafonte, recording, doing TV shows— all of these have been very rewarding. But now I am to go back to Africa for a trip that makes me feel that my life is being fulfilled.

The continent is coming of age. My people are taking charge of their own fate. The independent nations are now meeting in Addis Ababa, Ethiopia, to form the Organization of African Unity. This will be like NATO without the military alliance.

There is great hope and excitement surrounding this meeting. All the heads of state will be there. But only one performer: me.

There is an Ethiopian student living with us in New York. I almost always have African students staying in the apartment. Bongi never forgets who she is and where she is from, because she is always surrounded by Africans. When they first arrive in the U.S., the young ladies stay with me for a while before they find places of their own. I ask this one girl from Ethiopia if she can teach me a song from her home that I can sing at the conference. There is not much time, only three days, but she teaches me one. I rehearse it with my musicians, and we are on our way.

The palace at Addis Ababa is beautiful and grand. I have never been in a palace before, and this one is too large for anyone to explore in less than a few days. I am brought to a reception room to await the emperor. Haile Selassie is the one black African leader we learned about in school. Soon I will meet this man of such great reputation. The palace room is lined with mirrors. I take a look at myself before he comes. I am still petite at thirty-one. I wear a size eight dress, the same size I wore when I came to the U.S. On my head is a silk hat that looks like a tall fez. I have a number of exotic hats in the African style. My wardrobe is a mix of Western and African clothes. My hair is still short. I haven't been able to find anyone in America who can braid it properly.

The announcement is made: "His Royal Highness, the Lion of Judah, the Emperor Haile Selassie!"

A very short, light-skinned man enters. But when he walks in we all feel that he is a big man. He has this great presence. A pair of tiny Chihuahua dogs are at his feet. They are always with him. I curtsy, and he welcomes me to Ethiopia. Rows and rows of colorful campaign ribbons are on the chest of his light-green, braided, military-style uniform. The emperor's hat is like a pith helmet, and the curly gray hairs of his beard start just below its rim. We get our pictures taken, and he invites me to dinner before the show I am to give tonight. Now it is time for me to leave. This must be done carefully. I have been told that I must never turn my back on the emperor. So, I bow and slowly walk backward until I get through the door.

"The Lion of Judah" they call him. And full-grown lions prowl the palace grounds. They are not caged. They go wherever they want. My musicians and I keep spotting them outside the windows during our dinner at the palace. My musicians are a lively bunch. They are from Africa and America, and they are experts at all kinds of folk instruments. They make jokes about the lions. Soon it is time for us to change for the concert.

Emperor Selassie is confused. He says, "But you are dressed."

"Oh, no, Your Excellency, I cannot wear on the stage what I now have on."

He tells an aide to take us to a room so we can change. We excuse ourselves. My musicians and I carefully back out of the room with our heads bowed. The boys do not snicker when they do this, which is a relief. They are very well behaved. But when we get to our "dressing room," and it turns out to be the emperor's office, we all feel like mischievous children in a grand house where the adults are away. There is a huge chair made entirely of gold in the center of the room.

"Now, if we can only take *that* home," I say.

My musicians try to lift the throne, but it is too heavy. There is no place to hang our wardrobe, so I drape my costume over the throne. "At least I can say I put my dress on the Emperor's golden chair!"

The jokes help to ease the tension, but right before I am to sing, I am struck with a terrible case of what the French call *le trac*: stage fright. People think of me as an important singer, but to myself I am still just an African girl. I think, "Look at me! My people are not even free, and here I am!"

Some of the most important leaders of our nations are waiting in the concert hall. This conference is a true moment in history. There is Gamal Nasser of Egypt, Habib Bourguiba of Tunisia, Sékou Touré of Guinea, Léopold Senghor of Senegal, Kwame Nkrumah of Ghana, Félix Houphouët-Boigny of the Ivory Coast, and other national leaders, all with their wives and diplomatic groups. And to think that they requested only one singer to entertain them!

I am thankful that I learned the Ethiopian song. When I sing it, the Ethiopians who make up the majority of the audience are very happy. They give me a big ovation, and this encourages me. But as I say, I am never shy on stage. Something takes over. Depending on the song, I am happy or sexy or angry or sad. But

I am in control, and the audience follows me. And so do the heads of state this night. They applaud for a long time.

I want to stay in Addis Ababa for the length of the conference. I would not think of leaving early. There is so much tension and excitement as the talks go on. At times major disagreements seem to bring an end to everyone's dream. Ghana's President Nkrumah wants an African High Command, a type of African Army. This causes a stalemate. There are other problems, and nobody knows if the charter will ever be signed. We get discouraged, but the talks do not end. They go on into the small hours of the morning. Finally, a pact is hammered out. Everyone cheers and embraces one another. It is a moment of great pride for all of Africa. The continent is growing up.

It is light outside when I return to my hotel room. The clock says seven-thirty in the morning. There is a knock at the door, and when I open it I am shocked. Two soldiers salute me. They speak French, which I don't. I think, "What do I do now?" But I hear the words "Sékou Touré," and I know they must be from the president of Guinea, which was a French colony. I curtsy and accept a book one of the soldiers gives me. They salute again and leave. I am very impressed. The book is written in French by President Touré. He has signed it for me. This is a wonderful souvenir, I think, for a great event. I am proud to be even a small, little part of it.

▼▼▼▼▼

The summer is coming to an end, and I am again in Los Angeles. Bongi is at the Chateau Marmont, and I am performing at a club called the Troubador on Santa Monica Boulevard at the border of Hollywood and Beverly Hills. For some reason, I am very tired. The days pass, and I complain to the Troubador's owner, Mr. Doug Weston, that I cannot get my energy back. I try getting more rest and taking vitamins, but nothing works. Finally, during a performance, something terrible happens: I collapse on stage.

"I'm sending you to my doctor," Mr. Weston says to me in my dressing room after I've recovered from my faint. I agree to go.

The next day a very concerned man name Dr. Lavet asks me, "When was the last time you had a smear test?"

I still do not know what a smear test is, even though I was given one four months ago. I tell the doctor this.

"Well, I'd like to take another." He does, and then we make an appointment for a few days from now when the test results will be back.

But I miss the appointment. Dr. Lavet calls, but I do not call him back. It's not that I am scared, it's that I am embarrassed that I missed the appointment. He calls and calls. Finally, when Bongi tells him that I am not in, he says, "It's very important that your mother phones me as soon as she gets back."

Because he insists, I do call back. I hear his very serious voice. "I'm coming right over to see you."

My drummer, Archie Lee, has come to my room at the Chateau Marmont to return my car. Whenever I am in Los Angeles, I rent a car for the week or the month. I do not drive, but one of my musicians takes me where I want to go. The rest of the time, when I'm not using it, I give the car to the boys to go around wherever they like.

Archie sits in the corner when the doctor comes. Dr. Lavet look very upset. "Miriam, I'm sorry to have to tell you this, but your test results came back positive."

"I don't know what that means," I say to him.

"It means, Miriam, that you have cancer."

Archie sits right up. I feel very faint. My voice is so small it is like a mouse taking a breath. "But no . . ."

He nods his head. "It's in the cervix."

The shock makes my voice stronger. "No! I just had a test four months ago."

"And in that short time you developed the cancer and it has spread."

"How far?"

"Very far."

He says he has made an appointment for me tomorrow with a gynecologist. There will be more tests. Dr. Lavet is very considerate and kind. He stays with me for a long time. When he leaves, I am weeping.

"Archie," I say to my drummer, who is very upset, "I've got to go tell Big Brother. Please take me."

Mr. Belafonte is performing in the amphitheater in the park, the Greek Theater. I am so upset that I do not even think, I just go right into his dressing room. He looks up from his chair and sees that I am crying.

"Miriam! What's the matter?"

For the first time I say the words: "I have cancer."

The news hits Big Brother so hard that he slips off his chair and falls to his knees. He covers his face with his hands. "Oh, God! But why?"

I stand and cry. When he gets himself together, Big Brother asks me, "Can I tell Julie?" I nod my head. He wants to know what Dr. Lavet told me, and he promises to pick me up tomorrow to take me to the gynecologist. Then I leave. In my fright, I did not even realize that I was seeing Big Brother not at the end of his show, but during the intermission. He has to go back on stage and do the second act, even though he is so upset. I feel very bad about this.

Back in the car, I say, "Oh, Archie, what am I going to do?"

He says, "Let's get drunk."

Archie must be very frightened, because he does not drink. I don't drink, either, but I say, "Yes."

We go to a liquor store on the Sunset Strip. Archie buys a big jug of this cheap wine, Gallo wine. We take it back to the Chateau Marmont and start drinking. But instead of getting drunk, I start vomiting all over the place. Archie just sits on the couch like a Buddha and stares off into space. If anyone ever cried over her own death, it is me this awful night.

Early the next morning, Big Brother comes to pick me up. I tell him I tried to get drunk, and he shakes his head. We go to see a second doctor. The results of the new test are the same as the original ones. Now it is up to both doctors to decide what to do with me. They agree to give me a biopsy. And then if, and only if, the biopsy says I have a chance, they will operate. The cancer has spread that far.

Dr. Lavet is not shy about telling me the truth. "Even if we operate, you will have only a fifty-fifty chance to live."

"Then why operate?" I ask timidly.

"Because if we don't, you'll have *no* chance. You'll be dead in six months."

The doctors decide to put me in the hospital to which they are affiliated: the Hollywood Community Hospital. But there are no beds available for three days. It is up to Big Brother and our friend Sidney Poitier to take my mind off my problem. Both men are both very nice. Mr. Poitier takes me to a preview of his new movie, *Lilies of the Field*. I forget. They take me to dinner. I forget. But at night, when I am alone, I think: I have cancer, and I am going to die.

I send Bongi to New York to stay with some friends. Papers are drawn up concerning her care if I should die. Big Brother tells me that he wants to be the guardian of my little girl. I cannot find words to thank him. I only weep.

But in New York, Bongi surprises everybody. She tells them, "I know my mother is very sick. I know she might die."

How does she know this? I have not told her anything. Everyone else has kept the news from her. For the first time I think that perhaps my daughter is displaying the kind of foresight that my mother and my sister Hilda had. My mother's ability was the first hint that we had that she was to be an *isangoma*. I wonder about Bongi. Is she also possessed by *amadlozi*? This could be a blessing, or it could be very bad for her. But it is too early to worry.

It feels like I am being sucked down, like something is draining everything out of me, all the hope and courage I ever had, and leaving only fear. I cannot think. I can't eat or sleep. I just lie in bed, and this terrible, terrible fear hurts like a pain. If it becomes more than I can stand, then I will carry out the resolution that I made before I came to the hospital: I will kill myself.

There are nineteen sleeping pills hidden under my mattress. I put them there when I came. No one knows about them. Each pill contains one thousand milligrams. Even in a hospital, if they find me in the morning after I have taken all the pills, there will be nothing they can do. The doctors tell me that if the biopsy shows that the cancer has spread too far, they will not operate. It will be a waste of time. I will get worse and worse, and there will be pain like I cannot even imagine, although it is all I can think about. I have seen other people die of cancer. It is horrible. "If they do not operate," I tell myself, "then I will take these pills." I lie in my bed and I think about them in their little bottle beneath me.

But the biopsy is hopeful, and my chances of survival increase by half: Now I have a fifty-fifty chance of living.

The operation comes. The place where life is created within me, and where my life might end, is cut open. My uterus is removed, and along with it they remove the piece of disease that would take my life.

Dr. Lavet is here when I open my eyes. "In six months we'll know if there's a recurrence. But for now, you must eat and gather your strength."

I feel relief. The waiting will be awful the next few months until we are sure that the cancer has gone away. With each pain I get and every headache that comes I will say: "My God, it's back!" But for now I can give thanks in my prayers that I am alive.

For fifteen days they keep me in the hospital. Mr. Brando is away making a movie, but each day he sends a vase of white lilies. Diahann Carroll and others come to visit, and I become very popular with the hospital staff because of all the special guests I bring in. Mr. Poitier is on location, too, but he telephones me twice from Athens.

When I talk to Bongi I can barely speak because of my crying. She tells me not to worry for her, because she is fine, and I tell her not to worry for me, because I am fine. When I hang up, it is with the thought that this little girl will be my only child. I do not grieve. I had Bongi way back. And since that time I have done nothing not to have another child. I never took birth control. But I never got pregnant again. Not by Gooli, or Sonny, or Hugh. Yes, little Hughie Masekela and I became lovers before he decided to go to London to work. He is a very sweet young man, and full of passion. But nobody has made me pregnant, and even before I got sick I was used to the idea that I may never have any more children.

But now I know for sure. I wish I was just as sure that the cancer was dead. The scare I have had has already taken so much out of me. I don't know how I am going to pick myself up and continue. I really do not know. I am so tired.

The room that I am in has all sorts of gadgets that I control from my bed. Lights and radio and TV. There is something I want to see on the news, so I tilt the bed up. Big Brother has gone to Washington to join Dr. King and thousands of others for a big civil rights march. I was invited to come along before I got sick. Big Brother sends a cable to the hospital: "*I know you will be with us in spirit.*"

I watch the whole march on television. I begin to feel bad that

I am not there with them. So many marchers, and each of them feeling so strongly about creating justice for the black people of America. And I realize: In my wish to be a part of this, and getting excited about it, I am feeling something again besides fear.

I see Big Brother at the front of the march. I think of another march back home, in Sharpesville. That one ended when the authorities fired into the crowd. But nothing like that happens here. The march finishes at the Lincoln Memorial. There are people as far as the eye can see. Dr. King speaks to them. He has the magic I remember from Atlanta. I think his power is even greater now. He says, "I have a dream," and he tells about his dream, about a world where children of different colors walk hand in hand and peace and goodwill exist for everyone. It is a lovely dream, and it is one that I believe everybody has in their heart.

And I think: "Yes, I have a dream, too." I would like to see my people free. I would like to see the black and white children of South Africa walk hand in hand. I would like to go home again.

This is something for me to dream about. And then I think, this is something for me to live for.

Here is a rare picture of my mother, the *isangoma,* taken in the late 1950s. She is seated second from the left. RIGHT: Once I started singing, I had to pose for "publicity photos." I am in my early twenties here.

The four Manhattan Brothers. They were truly my brothers, and my mentors. From the left: Rufus Khoza, Ronnie Majola, Joe Magotsi, and Nathan Mdlhedlhe.

Gallotone Records formed a singing group around me—The Skylarks. On my left are Mamie and Mary Rabotapi. My arm is around Abigail Kubeka. This is 1956.

In my costume for *African Jazz and Variety*. I sing
the closing number of the revue while the
chorus girls dance.

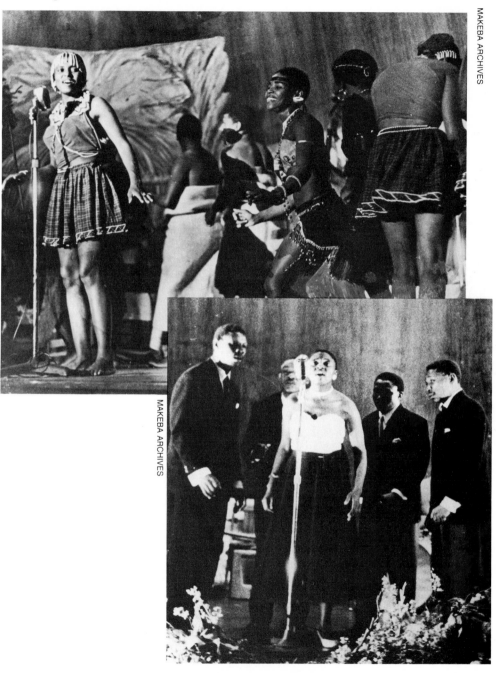

On stage with the Manhattan Brothers. Here I
am in 1953 with Nathan, Rufus, Ronnie, and Joe
in Alexander Township, South Africa.

Another publicity shot from South Africa. This shows me at home in Mofolo Village in the late fifties.

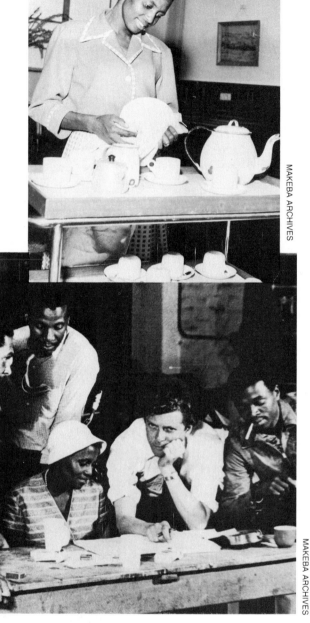

A planning meeting for the show *King Kong* in 1959. The show's star, Nathan Mdlhedlhe, stands above and behind me. To my left, leaning against the table, is our producer, Leon Gluckman. Joe Mogotsi, a Manhattan Brother like Nathan, is at the far left. And at the far right with the cigarette is Victor Ndlazdwane.

I am waiting at the Johannesburg airport for my husband, Sonny Pilay, and I must stand behind the bars of the segregated waiting area for blacks and Coloreds.

I was given this haunting picture by the photographer, and I carry it with me always: the burial of some victims of the Sharpeville Massacre, March 21, 1960. Two of my uncles were killed.

Backstage with Big Brother, Harry Belafonte. In 1966 we won "Grammy" awards for best folk record. LEFT: My first American publicity shot, 1960. They wanted to make me look glamorous.

I met U Thant, the Acting Secretary-General of the United
Nations, during a function in September 1962.

UNITED NATIONS

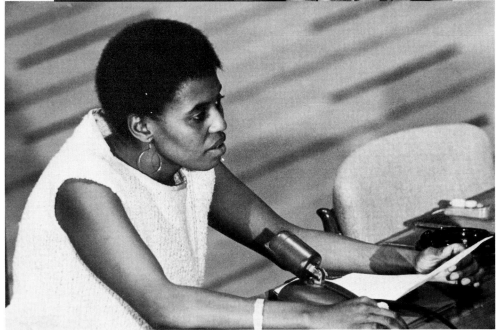

UNITED NATIONS

The first time I spoke out against the crimes of the South African
government was before the United Nations Special Committee on
Apartheid, July 16, 1963. In retaliation, South Africa banned my records.

My first trip back to Africa after I had been
exiled from my home brought me to Kenya in
1962. I was met at the airport by my friend
and idol, Dorothy Masuka. BOTTOM: A happy
celebration.

In Surinan in 1963, I performed with my Brazilian guitarist, Savuca, who is seated to my right. BOTTOM: Returning to Kenya in 1963, I was greeted by President Jomo Kenyatta backstage after my performance.

Hughie Masekela and I at our wedding reception in 1965.

MAKEBA ARCHIVES

Hugh and I do the gumboot dance of the South African miners with our friend Philemon Hou on the left.

I addressed the United Nations
General Assembly for the second time in 1976
during the International Year Against Apartheid.

Here is Jeanne Martin, one of the greatest women I have
ever known. I served under Jeanne in 1975 when she was
the Guinean Ambassador to the U.N.

My sponsor and the father of his country, Guinean President Sékou Touré.

In Guinea I revived the traditional hairstyle, the "Suki ya maboko."

My daughter Bongi.

My grandchildren,
Zenzi and Lumumba.

With my friend Samoa Machel, the President of
Mozambique, at his home in 1982.

MAKEBA ARCHIVES

MAKEBA ARCHIVES

A surprise meeting with Oliver Thambo, the President of the
African National Congress, 1982.

I sing at the Olympia Music Hall in Paris.

With Paul Simon on stage in Zimbabwe as part of 1987's "Graceland" tour.

10

THE GUINEAN DELEGATES
to the United Nations are getting to be like brothers and sisters
to me. So when they learn that I have been operated on for
cancer here in Los Angeles, the UN ambassador, Mr. Achkar
Marof, sends his wife Rosamond to look after me. She takes a
room at the Chateau Marmont.

But it seems that I have other guardian angels. Sometimes,
when you wake up after dreaming, part of that dream stays with
you for a little while. I am confused for a moment when I
awaken one day and see a man standing above my hospital bed
who looks familiar but whom I know I have never met before. I
know his face, but he has lost his hair.

He smiles at me and speaks with a beautiful deep voice.
"Hello, Miss Makeba. I'm Pernell Roberts."

"Oh," I say, "*Bonanza.*" On TV I guess they give him a
toupee to wear.

"I saw your show at the Troubador. I enjoyed it so much that I
brought some friends there last night. You were canceled, of
course."

Mr. Roberts learned where I was, and he is kind enough to
visit me during his lunch break from Warner Brothers studio. He
is a big fan of folk music. We talk, and he promises to come
back. He does, and each time he brings me steaks. The doctors
want me to eat and gain weight, but I don't like the hospital

food. I appreciate Mr. Roberts's visits. All my musicians are in New York, except for Archie Lee, who decided to stay with me.

After fifteen days in the hospital, I am permitted to leave. Dr. Lavet has been very kind. We talk and talk about all sorts of things. When I am released, he has to almost carry me out. He takes me to his house, where I spend a day with his nice wife and two sons. Pernell Roberts sends a limousine the next morning to bring me back to the Chateau Marmont. He comes and cooks for me. Rosamond Marof is also here, and my drummer Archie. He has a white girlfriend from Santa Monica and she comes, too. They cook and wash my clothes. I really am helpless.

Mr. Roberts takes me to his house. Some of his friends are folksingers, and they entertain us by the fireplace. He is living with a lady who is a classical singer. Everyone is very nice to me as I sit in my chair beneath a blanket, sipping tea and recovering my strength. When I am well enough, Mr. Roberts takes me to Warner Brothers for the day. This is the studio where they made so many of the films I adored as a young girl in South Africa. Right away I am introduced to Bette Davis. I am so excited and *very* happy. I have seen so many of her films. When we get our pictures taken together I tell her this, and she is kind enough to thank me for coming! Then I meet a nice television actor named Mike Connors and a very witty comedian, Mr. Alan King.

When I am better, it comes time to say good-bye to my friends in Los Angeles and return to New York, to my home and to Bongi. I find that I am also coming back to someone else. Hughie left London when he heard I had been operated on. When we meet again, we know how much we mean to each other. It is so good to see him, and he seems so happy and relieved to see me.

I gain back the weight I lost because of the operation, and then some. Before, I was size eight. Now my dress size is ten. This has got to stop! But at least I am well enough to do some singing dates I made before I got sick. There is a little club in Georgetown, in Washington, D.C. I sing until very late each night, and I sleep late at the hotel. One day I wake up and, as usual, order some tea. The waiter comes. He appears upset about something. He says, "Miss Makeba, the President has been assassinated."

There is so much political violence and so many coups in Africa that I ask, "Which President?"

The waiter is so surprised that he can only say, as if he did not hear correctly, "What?" He goes to the television set and turns it on. I see what is happening. I feel weak, and I have to sit down.

I remember the nice-looking man with the friendly smile. *"I just wanted you to know how very glad I am to have an African artist participate in my birthday celebration."*

I cannot believe it. I sit before the television, and I watch and watch. The club calls and says that I do not have to come in tonight to perform. I do not go out of the hotel much this weekend. Mr. Kennedy's body is brought back to Washington. From my room I can hear the guns that fire their salute at Arlington Cemetery. Some students from Guinea are with me. We have been watching the TV day and night, and talking about the President. It is truly terrible, because Mr. Kennedy was a very well-liked President in Africa. He did so much for civil rights. People in Africa are always interested in black people's fate in the U.S. In almost all African countries, stamps are put out in his image.

▼▼▼▼▼

We cannot forget our sadness, but we go on with our lives. This has been a very eventful year, and it is not over yet. I accept the invitation of President Kenyatta to participate in Kenya's independence celebration on December 12. This will be my third visit to that beautiful nation, where most of the movies about Africa are shot. I went to Kenya earlier this year after the OAU meeting. At that time Mr. Kenyatta was campaigning for office, and I made some appearances with him. To thank me, he invites me to the independence pageantry, and he asks me to bring along Mr. Belafonte. Big Brother is very pleased. This is his first trip to Africa.

I have never participated in an independence celebration before. It is truly beautiful. People are dancing in the streets. They clear the lanes only long enough for the many parades to pass through. My concert is one of several events.

The moment of independence comes during a ceremony that officially transfers the country's rule from the British authorities to the people. Thousands of Kenyans and foreign visitors fill a great outdoor stadium. The Queen's husband, Prince Philip, is here. All the tribesmen from the different parts of Kenya speak. The Masai, a very tall and beautiful people, come in their traditional dress of skins and long spears. They dance for us in front of the reviewing stand. The Belafontes and I sit right behind Prince Philip, and we are all impressed and moved. The big moment arrives: the drums roll and the flag of Great Britain is lowered. A moment later, the flag of the new nation of Kenya is raised. It is really wonderful to be here and to see this. I yell as loud as everybody else does.

Before I return to the U.S. I accept the invitation of President Houphouët-Boigny to visit the Ivory Coast. During my first trip to this country, I stay at the President's house. Mrs. Houphouët-Boigny, who is with the International Red Cross, is a kind hostess. We have breakfast and lunch together every day, and sometimes dinner. I brought with me a copy of *Come Back, Africa*, and the Houphouët-Boignys wish to see it several times. The Ensemble Traditionnel, the national dance troupe of Guinea, is in Abidjan this week. I see their show, which is very impressive. I remember that President Touré of Guinea gave me his book earlier this year in Ethiopia. To show my thanks, I now ask the dancers if they would give their leader my copy of *Come Back, Africa*. Now that I am coming back to Africa myself so often, it will not be long, I tell them, before I visit their country.

▼▼▼▼▼

But it is Big Brother who goes to Guinea before I do, in 1964. He is very well received by President Touré. I am busy in New York, where I go before the UN Special Committee on Apartheid for the second time. I plead for the release of all political prisoners in South Africa. The jails are more than full with my people.

I have been invited to sing at the Village Gate club, and because I am liked there, my string of appearances will last for four years. Nina Simone and I get just about the best salaries that anyone has been offered at the popular club.

Somehow, American show business has not changed very much this little South African girl. I am in my dressing room talking to a musician who has just arrived from home when a "hip cat" comes in. He smiles at me in a sly way and says, "Want some coke?"

"Oh, no, thank you," I say, "I don't care for anything cold to drink. It interferes with my singing."

He laughs at me. "Hey, bitch, who's talking about Coca-Cola?"

I do not have time to be startled that he is offering me cocaine, or to be embarrassed about my mistake, because the young man from South Africa jumps up. "How dare you call my sister a bitch!"

The two musicians start to yell, and there is a big commotion. People rush in before the fight becomes bad. I try to calm my guest by telling him that in American slang "bitch" isn't as bad as it sounds, although I don't think it sounds very nice, either. At least I have learned a new word: coke. Musicians also offer me marijuana to puff all the time. But I know that this is not what I want.

Many friends from South Africa come to America. A very talented singer-songwriter named Caiphus Semenya arrives in a musical from home called *Sponono*. Many people who think it shows an Uncle Tom stereotype of blacks boycott the show. It is a flop. But Caiphus and another man wish to stay in the U.S. I find an apartment for them and put them in a school for acting. They won't be allowed to stay in America unless they are students. Hugh, Caiphus, and I now fight to bring Letta M'Bulu here. After some months, we get her a visa. The day she arrives, I rent a car, and we bring Letta home past the World's Fair in a convertible Thunderbird. Little Letta comes to America in style! She is thrilled by New York.

Bongi now has another person from home to stay with us. My little girl is high school age, now. She is very good in math. Bongi also writes poems, and sings the songs she composes. There is a special place in New York called the High School of Music and Art. Only students who show they have some talent are accepted. Bongi hopes to enroll, and she goes in for auditions. She is so excited when she passes her tests, and I am very proud of her. A little singer is on her way.

Ever since South Africa, I have dated Hugh Masekela off and on. Sometimes we are like lovers, and sometimes we are like brother and sister. There have been times when I want to date another person, he would object, and we would fight. "Hey, you're too young for me," I'd say. "Get your own!" He might sulk, or he might go out and find a girlfriend. In America, like home, he comes and tells me his troubles with these girls. "She did this to me" or "she did that." I would listen, and then I'd say, "Well, you know, maybe you should handle it this way . . ." He would always listen, and then he would thank me.

But somehow, we always get together. It's that way with some people. They like each other. Time and places pull them apart. But after a while they always end up with each other again. This is the way it is with Hugh and me. One day, I realize that what I feel toward Hughie is something much more than "like." I ask myself all sorts of questions. There is a song I sing, called "Where Does It Lead." It is impossible to sing it now without thinking about my little boy trumpeter.

> *Where does it lead,*
> *this strange young love of mine?*
> *Only heaven and the lilies know.*

Hugh feels about me the way I do about him. In some ways, it seems like this had to happen. We have known and liked each other for so long. We decide that we must now do something about it. The song plays in my head.

> *Where does it lead,*
> *this strange young love of mine?*
> *Anywhere it takes me, I will go.*

And so, on the night that I introduce the new South African musician to my audience at the Village Gate, I do it by saying, "Ladies and gentlemen, I am very pleased to present to you my new husband, Hugh Masekela."

The wedding was a simple affair at a small church in Connecticut. We went there because Bob Bollard, the man who looks after me at RCA, wanted to give us a reception at his house. The only guests at the wedding were Mr. Bollord, his wife and children, Bongi, the African girls who are staying with me, and one of Mr. Belafonte's guitarists, who took some pictures. Bongi has always liked Hugh. The only worry she has is about her school. She likes the High School of Music and Art very much, and she does not want to give it up. She is doing very well. She writes a song that Hugh is going to record on his first album. The trouble is there is a lovely, three-bedroom house in Englewood, New Jersey, that I like and I am buying.

I tell Bongi that she can still go to her school. In the mornings, I put her in a taxi, which takes her to the bus, which takes her to Manhattan. This is a long trip for a girl. So I decide to keep my apartment at Park West Village and let Letta stay there with some other girls. Bongi can spend the week nights there, and I can have a place to stay in the city when I am performing.

The house in New Jersey is in a town where there are big lawns and plenty of trees. Our basement becomes a studio where Hugh can practice. Across the street live Dizzy Gillespie and his wife Loraine. Sister Loraine is very nice to me. She likes to pray, and she has a prayer room in their house. She takes Bongi in with her to pray. She is also very meticulous in her house. Everything is spotless. Sometimes Hugh and I eat there, and sometimes the Gillespies are our guests. Hugh is happy that he can learn his art from somebody like Dizzy.

Before long, we are a happy suburban family. Hugh and I paint the split-level house ourselves: off-white and green. Inside, I decorate the rooms with some masks and other gifts that are given to me when I travel to Africa. But I am not one for having wall-to-wall things. There is a leopard skin in the living room. The dining room has a table and wood chairs with turquoise seats. We bought the set very cheap at an antique store on Second Avenue in New York. But my favorite part of the house is the backyard, where I have my garden before the pine trees. And Hugh likes his studio in the basement, where the musical instruments lie about.

Hugh is a good cook. Sometimes when I come home he says, "You just rest. I'll cook."

"Oh, Hugh," I say at these times, "I do love you!"

We like to cook South African dishes. It is not difficult to find the ingredients in a place like New York, where they have everything. And we grew up on simple food. We love our cornmeal.

Every few weeks I have to say good-bye to Hugh and Bongi and go away for a show. When I perform at the Pan-African Festival in Algiers, the Algerian President gives me a diplomatic passport from his county. I now use this for overseas travel. I use it to go to the second meeting of the Organization of African Unity. The OAU is meeting in Ghana this year, 1965, and President Kwame Nkrumah invites me to sing.

When I arrive I have a surprise. The lady who meets me at the airport is from South Africa. Genevieve Marise is now the director of programming for Ghana TV. She asks me to stay at her villa. I accept, and as we are getting used to each other, she confesses, "You know, I was standing there waiting for you to arrive, and I was so nervous I was sweating."

I ask her why, and Genevieve tells me, "Earlier today, Josephine Baker arrived. And she came down the stairs from the plane in shorts! I was thinking, 'I hope that home girl of mine is not going to come here also wearing shorts!' "

"Oh, Genevieve, you know I wouldn't do that!" In fact, I came off the plane in a little dress I bought in New York that is a style they call the "woman's body-stocking." It is tight and pink, with a great big belt and a standing collar. This is the style, now, and it looks good on me because I have a small waist.

I am happy to know that Josephine Baker is also here. For a long time, I have admired this American singer who became a big star in Paris. We meet at the TV station, and then I go to visit her. They gave her a nice villa. She sits cross-legged on her bed and talks and talks. Josephine is very interested in social problems. Our situation in South Africa concerns her very much. If there is one person who wants all mankind to be united and at peace with one another, it is her. She tells me all about the children that she has adopted from all over the world. They live with her outside Paris in a chateau she calls Rainbow Village. But she is getting old, and it is hard for her to come up with the money to support her household, this marvelous family that symbolizes how people of different races and religions can live together in harmony. One of the things she wants to do here in Ghana is to solicit funds to keep her dream alive.

I enjoy watching Josephine on stage. Her costumes, the feathers and furs, are out of this world. And she is so lively! All the heads of state are in the audience. She just tells them, "Come along, everybody, clap your hands!" And they do! I say to myself, "My goodness, she sure is bold!" Emperor Haile Selassie is sitting there, just as regal as he can be. But I think that even he is smiling.

When I return home, there is Hughie, practicing his scales in the basement. Over and over. It makes me glad that I did not marry a drummer, because that practicing would really drive me crazy. But this is a very musical house. And it must be good music, because the neighbors never complain. One day a man walks in with a guitar and accordion. I look at Hugh. "Where is he going to play that?" An accordion? The man is named Savuca, and he is from Brazil. He is going to be my guitarist. He starts to play this accordion, and, my God, how he plays! He goes crazy. We all go crazy. It's fun.

Letta's music is coming along. Like Hugh, she is struggling. And also like Hugh, I give her a push by introducing her to my audience at the Village Gate. Big Brother is shocked. He asks me, "Why would you bring another singer from South Africa?"

But I say that the United States is a very big place, and it should be able to take in both of us. The night of Letta's show, I arrange a press conference for her. *The New York Times* prints a wonderful review of her singing. She is so thrilled, she shows the clipping to everyone.

Letta is a beautiful singer, and she can do things that I cannot do. I sing straight, but she can improvise. The way she embellishes songs is very exciting to hear. I admire her for this.

Letta and Caiphus decide to get married. The wedding is at my house. I make some pineapple brew just like we do back home from pineapple, yeast, sugar, and bread. There is another touch of home: One of the guests is Hugh's sister, who has come to live with us. For a wedding present, I find an apartment on 103rd Street for Caiphus and Letta. I fill it with furniture, and pay the rent for a year.

I enjoy helping my friends. They need encouragement, because the entertainment field can be so difficult. Hugh is not happy the way things are going for him. He does not come out and say that he is bothered that I am an "international star" and he is unknown, but I can tell by the way he acts sometimes. There is nothing I can do about what I am, but I let him know how much love and faith I have in him.

I hope that this will be enough. Sometimes when Hughie gets to feeling really down, he can be unpleasant.

▼▼▼▼▼

This year, 1965, is a difficult one for black people everywhere. In Africa apartheid is closing its grip on my people more and more. Rhodesia declares its independence from Great Britain and sets up a white minority government because it is afraid that Britain is about to grant independence to the country under a system of majority black rule. There are no signs of hope in South Africa, which is another British colony that broke away illegally.

Here in America, I am driving with Chad and the other members of the Chad Mitchell Trio to a date in the Pittsburgh area. There is a terrible winter storm. It is snowing, and very cold. We drive slowly, and still we get lost. I wrap myself up in my coat, and before long I am asleep. Chad wakes me up. His voice is concerned. "Miriam, listen to the news."

"What's happening?" I ask. The radio reports that Malcolm X has been shot. This is really shocking, as it always is when one minute a person is here and the next minute he is taken from us. Malcolm X was one of the first American black men who went to meet with the African heads of state seeking to bring together all the peoples of Africa—those who are on the continent and those whose ancestors had been taken away. He has been somebody we all listened to, and he had a lot to say. He was a powerful and charismatic man, and he was able to take young people off the streets and off drugs.

There is something else that Malcolm X said to black Americans: "The extent to which you reject and hate Africa is the extent to which you hate yourselves. You cannot hate the root of a tree without hating the tree itself."

For so long black Americans have been ashamed of their African roots. They do this because the whites, Hollywood, and everyone says that Africa is a primitive place, and it embarrasses those who come from there. I think that much insecurity and unhappiness must come from denying one's own ancestors. But this is changing. When I first came to America, the majority of my audiences were white. I was a curiosity to these people who came to the posh New York clubs. The only black friends I had were other musicians and artists. But more and more I am becoming known to black Americans. They are becoming more aware of themselves, and more vocal. Because of the ways they have been treated, some are becoming angry and militant. Our culture is asserting itself. Motown Records is having a great effect on pop music. Dress and fashions are changing also. The "Afro" hairstyle that I introduced to America in 1959 has gone beyond the women now. Men, too, are no longer conking and straightening their hair, but they are letting it grow natural.

With this interest in Africa, a concert is arranged for Letta, Caiphus, and myself in Los Angeles. Joining us will be a trombone player from home named Jonas Gwagwa. We decide that we will perform the gumboot dance in our show. This is the vigorous, leg-slapping dance the miners do wearing their rubber boots. Hugh and Jonas teach me some steps. After a while I decide, "Hey, I'm tired! You do all those complicated steps, and I'll do the simple ones." Some of the moves are very intricate. But the four of us pull it off on the stage of the huge Shrine Auditorium, where they have the ballets.

A few weeks later I come back to Los Angeles on my way to a show in San Francisco. Letta is performing here on her own at that same little coffeehouse on Melrose Avenue where I met Marlon Brando. Mr. Brando came to see me recently to ask if I could approach the African delegates at the UN for him. He needs a country to sponsor a resolution to allow an American Indian delegation to come to the UN and, as an occupied people, make a complaint against the U.S. But I had to tell him, "From what I can see, you're not going to get anyone to do it." None of the African delegates want to go up against the U.S. with something like this.

Dr. Lavet invites Letta and me to his house before her show. We hear the news about an uprising of black people in the Los Angeles ghetto, and we turn on the TV. What I see makes me think right away of South Africa. People are running, rioting. Buildings are on fire. There are police and troops everywhere. "Here we go again!" I think. Letta's show is canceled, so we go back to the Chateau Marmont. From the hill we can see the red sky to the south, and the dark fog that is made from the smoke rising above the Watts neighborhood. The rioting goes on for days. It does not seem to have a purpose, it is just pure anger. The whole country is shocked. But I am not really; I know that you can keep people down for only so long before they explode.

I think of my own people, who have been kept down for so long. They continue to struggle as best they can, and sometimes the things they have to do are very sad. Hugh's mother, who is Colored, divorces his father, who is black. For the sake of Hugh's two sisters in South Africa, Elaine and Sybil, Mrs. Masekela decides that they will "pass" as Coloreds, and live with the few pitiful advantages that are allowed to Coloreds and not to blacks. She changes their names from Masekela to Maskell, which sounds more "Colored." Hugh receives a letter from his mother that says he must always write to them this way, or else they may be "exposed." This upsets Hugh very much. He loves his father, and all of a sudden he cannot use the family name.

I try to talk to Hugh about this and about other things, but more and more he is becoming moody. His career is not going as well as he would like, and mine is like an express elevator, up and up. I cannot apologize for my success; I work very hard. At the end of the year I return to Africa, and I hope that, as they say, absence makes the heart grow fonder.

Christmas finds me back in Ghana, and I stay there through New Year's. I return to Tanzania, and then I go north to Sweden for my first concert in this country.

Back in the United States, my agents have been very busy. I have a new recording contract with Reprise Records. At the Apollo Theatre in Harlem, I have a big show with Billy Eckstine. We do a duet of a song called "Malaika." When I was at San Francisco State, some Kenyan students complained that I never do a song from their country. "Okay, teach me one," I said, and they taught me this beautiful song. "Malaika" is in Kiswaili, the East African speech of Kenya, Tanzania, Uganda, and Zaire. It is a love song. A man wants to take a wife, but he doesn't have the necessary wealth. He says, "I don't have anything, but I love you, Malaika." I love singing with Mr. Eckstine. I love his sound. He is a man who has a man's voice. But the Kiswaili language is difficult for him, and on the stage of the Apollo Theatre he forgets all the words. He just improvises by making vocals, and I cover for him with the lyrics. At the end, I bow to him, and it seems natural. We get a fine ovation.

The Village Gate shows bring in the people more and more. The management hires some bright young comedians to "warm up" my audiences. I have always had fine comedians who do their acts before I go on. When I was at the Blue Angel I had Carol Burnett. And now at the Village Gate as the weeks go by I have Bill Cosby and Dick Cavett. There is also a bold young man named Richard Pryor who uses language like I had never heard before on stage!

They can't seem to keep me away from the television, either. I do the *Ed Sullivan Show* twice, and the *Tonight Show* many times. I was told that Johnny Carson never sees his guests before a show. But I run into him in the halls of NBC at Rockefeller Center and he is very nice to me. He encourages me when I am nervous. He sticks his head in the dressing room and says with a smile, "Ready?"

I learn that when you do the *Today Show*, you do not sleep. I have to get up at four o'clock in the morning to be at NBC in time to prepare. But Barbara Walters is nice when she asks me questions. And so is Merv Griffin when I appear on his show in Los Angeles. Before long, I become comfortable doing all these programs.

When I travel to Philadelphia to do the *Mike Douglas Show*, I find that Mr. Douglas is also very nice. I bring along Hugh's nephew, Mabusha, who is two years old. I am taking care of the boy while I put Hugh's sister through Fordham University. When I carry him to the Village Gate, I let him sleep in the dressing room. Now, at the studio of the *Mike Douglas Show*, I place him in the Green Room. Mabusha is asleep when I go on the air and sing. But sometime while I am speaking to Mr. Douglas, he wakes up and wanders out into the studio. He peeks through the curtains, sees me, and comes right out. We cannot stop, because it is a live show. I don't know what to do. But Mr. Douglas is quick. He picks up Mabusha and puts him on his lap just as if it is part of the script. The audience always likes this kind of surprise, and Mabusha enjoys his applause.

Unfortunately, Mabusha's uncle is not getting all the applause he wants. I try to tell Hugh that it is a hard business, but this sounds funny coming from me because things are going so well in my own career. When Hugh is in a good mood, the smile between his chubby cheeks is like sunshine on a rainy day. But he can be sulky and immature, and then I do not care for the pout on his cute baby face. He has changed now that we are married. Of course, there are things that happen to us that would bother anyone. Sometimes, when we are out shopping, someone will say to me when they see Hugh, "Is this your son?" Or, "Is this your younger brother?"

I just laugh, because I am only thirty-four years old myself, and I don't think I look as if I can have a grown son. But Hugh gets very angry. And just let someone call him "Mr. Makeba." Oh!

The day comes when Hugh says he cannot stand his frustration any longer. He moves out of the house. I come home from a Village Gate show, and he is gone.

"Hugh," I ask him when he calls, "where are you?"

"I'm in Manhattan. I must be alone for a while to find myself."

"What do you mean, 'find yourself.' "

"You know, establish myself."

It is that old problem again of my name being bigger than his. I ask him what he wants, and he says he wants a separation.

"You know," I say, "you've become so Westernized! What kind of trouble is this? How can we work out our problems when one of us is on the other side of the bridge?"

I am not mad, I just know that this is not going to work out. I ask him to please come home so we can talk about it, but Hugh refuses. He tells me to come to Manhattan. We agree to meet for lunch.

It is a Japanese restaurant on Fifty-sixth Street. Hughie has definitely made up his mind. But I do not see the point in a separation. If a marriage is over, it's over. I finally say, "We don't need a separation. We need a lawyer."

Just around the corner, on Fifty-seventh Street, is my lawyer, Mr. Cohen. When he hears that we want to end our marriage, he tries to talk to us. Hugh starts crying. Then I start crying.

It is no good, and Mr. Cohen arranges a Mexican divorce. I cannot go to Mexico, because I am working. So Hugh makes the trip. He meets a white girl there who is also getting a divorce, and they start dating. But two months after our divorce, Hugh marries Cab Calloway's daughter, Chris. Their marriage lasts for two months.

I hope Hughie finds himself. He, Letta, and Caiphus want to be stars, so they all move to California. Motown has given them a record contract.

I think, "Ten years of friendship ended by less than two years of marriage." But this is not really so. I go to Los Angeles so much that I am always seeing Hugh, Letta, and Caiphus. Being a black exile from South Africa is like being a member of a family, and you can't divorce out of your family. I do not really want to.

It IS STRANGE, BUT THE SONG that boosts my career higher than it has ever been, and the tune that makes me known to people and countries that have never heard of me before, is also one of my most *insignificant* songs. I wrote "Pata Pata" in 1956, back in South Africa. It is a fun little song, with a nice rhythm. I just made it up one day, and I was thinking of a dance that we do at home. *Pata* means "touch" in Zulu and Xhosa. The original version was a hit in South Africa. Now, for my first album with Reprise Records, I make a new recording with English lyrics.

The album, which we call *Pata Pata*, enters the top five on the charts. It is my first truly big seller. All of a sudden, people who never knew I have been in America since 1959 are asking me to be on their television shows and play at their concert halls in 1967. In the discotheques, they have invented a new dance called the Pata Pata. Couples dance apart, and then they reach out and touch each other. I go to Argentina for a concert, and everywhere I travel in South America they are singing my song. Versions are recorded all over the world in several languages.

I will say one thing about success: It feels *good*.

Bongi and I travel to the Virgin Islands. She is seventeen now, and getting to be quite an attractive young lady: slender, with creamy-brown skin and big eyes. But she has one habit of a teenager: she is in love with an Otis Redding song, "Dock of the Bay," and she plays it over and over. Everywhere we go in the

Virgin Island I hear, *"So I'm sitting on the dock of the bay, watching the tide roll away . . ."*

"Bongi, please!" I finally say. "I love it, too, but enough is enough!"

The dock that Mr. Redding is singing about is in Sausalito, California, and the bay is the San Francisco Bay. There is a houseboat here in this little town north of the Golden Gate that I visit whenever I am in San Francisco. It is so beautiful to sit here with friends, put our feet up on the railing, and watch the moon on the water. Sevuca, my Brazilian guitarist, comes, and so does the American jazz singer Jon Hendricks. We jam all night in this little houseboat, until "the tide rolls away."

The "Pata Pata" girl gives a concert in London. When I lived here eight years ago, during my three-month marriage to Sonny, I was a timid and unknown singer. Now I am quite a sensation. In addition to writing about my clothes and hair and the usual celebrity things, the papers also permit me to tell of my hopes for a free South Africa.

I bring Bongi with me on this trip. She likes traveling with her mother, and I enjoy showing her some of the world. We have a suite at the Mayfair Hotel. Bongi comes running into the room. "Guess who I saw in the lobby! The Temptations!" I cannot say a thing, because she has grabbed a pen and paper for autographs and is out the door in a second. At times like these, Bongi is like any teenage girl; like when she is playing the Supremes records over and over. But there are times when she is alone and quiet when she seems to have a very deep sensitivity. This comes out in her poetry.

In New York, we live in a hotel on West Fifty-seventh Street. We do not have any use for the house in New Jersey anymore, so I sold it and said good-bye to Dizzy Gillespie, our neighbor. Sister Loraine says a prayer that we will be happy back in Manhattan. So far, we are, very.

On May 19 at the Apollo Theater I participate in another show, this time with Mongo Santamaria and my comedian from the Village Vanguard, Richard Pryor, who is getting more shocking and funny all the time. Then it is time to prepare for the annual summer tour with Big Brother. We will take the usual route: starting in New England and ending in California. Also as usual, Big Brother is the star, and no question about that. But because of the success of "Pata Pata," something new happens: More than just Belafonte fans come to the shows; some people come to hear me.

As we begin the tour, the news is filled with fighting in the Middle East. In one week, Israel defeats Egypt in what is called the Six Day War. Everyone is talking about it.

The tour is in Montreal when I get a call from some of the African delegates at the UN. "Egypt is an African nation," they tell me. "It is one of the founders of the OAU."

I know this, of course. The Arab countries to the north might sometimes not think of themselves as African, but they are. The delegates now ask me, "Would you please refrain from singing the Jewish song you have in your show?"

I am shocked by this request. Politics is strange business, anyway, and when it interferes with art the result is usually disaster. I tell the delegates, "But, sirs, these are love songs. They have nothing to do with war."

Since I told them that I did not appreciate their suggestion, I might leave the whole thing alone. But I am used to doing all that I can for my brothers at the UN. It bothers me that we disagree. I decide to go to Big Brother and talk to him about it.

Mr. Belafonte has a lot on his mind when we are on tour. Sometimes it is difficult to talk to him. He is there, but he is not there. It is one of these times when I see him in his dressing room before this night's show. We are alone in this room. Before too many days pass, I will wish that someone else was here with us, as a witness. Because the few words we exchange will become very twisted, and do terrible harm.

I tell Big Brother, "I received a call from the African delegates, and this is what they told me: They said that since I am from Africa, I should show solidarity with all my people. The Hebrew song that we do, and the one I sing by myself, they say are improper . . ."

Big Brother gets angry at once, even before I have finished. I am about to say that I told the delegates that I did not like their request. But Mr. Belafonte says the same thing I already told them, "But that's ridiculous! Miriam, the song we do is a love song. It's not political. Love is love anywhere."

"Okay," I say, "I just wanted to tell you that this is what they said. Whatever you say is okay with me."

I leave, because it is time for us to go on. I don't talk to him about this again. It does not seem important. But somehow, Big Brother has misunderstood our conversation. He thinks that the request from the African delegates is really a request from *me.*

The tour continues, and it ends at the Greek Theater in Los Angeles. When I check into my usual hotel, the Chateau Marmont, there is a stack of messages six inches high. I think: What kind of trouble is this? Something bad must have happened. There is a young man from Guinea who is studying cinema at the University of Southern California. He has left many messages, and I call him first.

"Miriam!" he says when he hears my voice. He is very excited and upset. "Did you see the paper? No, you couldn't, because you were gone. But Harry Belafonte gave an interview, and he said . . ."

I listen to the African student for a moment, and it is as if I forgot how to breathe when he quotes the article. I ask him to come over right away, and bring the Los Angeles newspaper with him. He does. Meanwhile, the phone is ringing off the hook. Other African students have seen the story, and they are also very concerned for me.

When the young man arrives, he gives me the paper. It is an interview Big Brother gave in Vancouver to a Los Angeles reporter for a story that is now released to publicize our show at the Greek. In the story he complains about "Africans dictating to me what I should do. Miriam Makeba is one of them. She does not want me to perform our Hebrew number, 'Erev Shel Shosha,' because Israel went to war with an African state."

"Oh, Miriam, this is terrible!" the student says. "The entertainment industry in the U.S. is owned by the Jews. Hollywood is a Jewish town!"

I try to calm him down. "This is a mistake. Don't worry. Julie Belafonte is Jewish, and she knows I am not anti-Semitic. She has had many fund-raisers for Jewish causes and I have sung for her. And then there are the fund-raisers for Israel that I do."

But I am very angry and upset myself. Big Brother and I have had disagreements before, like when I brought Letta to the U.S. and he did not care for her to compete with me, his protégée. It is not possible to work closely with someone for eight years and not have arguments. But this newspaper article is very serious and damaging. In it he tells the world the opposite of what I was doing. It is almost slander.

When I arrive at the Greek Theater, the rehearsal is in progress. Singers, dancers, musicians, and stage crew are all about. Mr. Belafonte is not in a good mood. He snaps at me, "You're late!"

But I am more angry than I can remember. I have the newspaper in my hand, and I just throw it at him. There is a gasp among the people. No one treats Mr. Belafonte like this. He is the boss. The cast will say one thing about him when he is not around, but they will never repeat it in his presence.

I point to the paper. "What is this?"

He does not answer. He just takes the newspaper and puts it aside. I turn around and leave. I do not even stay to rehearse. I am hurt; very hurt.

Big Brother will not talk to me at the show. But actions, as the saying goes, speak louder than words. When I look at the board that lists the evening's program, I see that he has canceled the Hebrew song, the duet that he and I usually do together. It is obvious to me what Big Brother is doing. People will think that because of what they read in the paper, I am the one who is refusing to sing the Hebrew song. Instead of admitting a mistake, he is trying to prove that he is right. I'm so mad that in my anger I say to someone that I'll never do another show with Mr. Belafonte.

He learns what I said and the next morning I get a phone call from Big Brother. He is furious. "You better show up at the Greek tonight, or I'll sue your ass!"

He hangs up. I am thinking: *Of course* I am going to show up for the concert. And Big Brother knows this, too, because he taught me so much about professionalism. He taught me how to be a pro the same way he taught me how to dress, and how to have discipline, and . . .

I start to cry. I cannot believe this is happening. He is slandering me in the press. He is threatening me with a lawsuit. Big Brother has always been my *big brother*! He is the man who gave me my start in the U.S. He is the man who said he would raise my daughter when I was sick with cancer and might have died. And now he will not talk to me. Off stage, he ignores me.

The whole cast meets at the airport. The show is going on to

Hawaii. But at the counter there are no tickets for me or my musicians. This is the last shock: We are being left behind. We are no longer part of the tour. I can only say good-bye to the other members of the cast. Nobody can believe it. The others get on the plane and go to Hawaii. We stay behind.

My musicians are panicky. "What are we going to do?"

"I'll tell you what we're going to do," I say. I have gone through a lot, from facing exile to facing cancer, and I have learned that it does no good to brood. I tell my musicians, "We're going home."

"Home? Where's home?"

"Africa!"

▼▼▼▼▼

President Sékou Touré of Guinea has invited me to his country to perform at a music festival. At first I had to turn down the invitation because of my concert schedule. But now the trip seems to be a gift from heaven. I need to get away, to see some of my people and forget about things. Arrangements are made for myself and my musicians, and we are on our way.

Big Brother tries to sue me because I am not in Hawaii. But the attorneys tell him that he can't. Because he did not leave tickets for us at the airport, he is in breach of contract. Years will pass before I see or hear Big Brother again.

Each time I go back to Africa, it is like being reborn. But it is bittersweet, because I cannot really go home—not to the place of my birth and family. People like President Touré know this, and they have this great desire to *adopt* me. For this reason, my collection of diplomatic passports grows and grows.

Because Bongi is on her summer vacation, I bring her with me to Africa. Guinea is a country rich with minerals, but it is poor. I do not speak French, and this place was a French colony until 1959. I am given an interpreter, a nice young woman named Jeanne Delavison. Before long, we are friends.

President Touré is one of the most impressive men I have ever met. I remember his handsome, strong face and beautiful smile from the OAU meetings. Even though he is a very busy man, he always has time to spend with his guests. President Touré has ruled Guinea since 1958, and he is very much respected throughout Africa. The nationalist movement has no greater supporter than this man, and he aids independence movements in all countries. When I am introduced to him he is dressed as usual in the traditional national dress of Guinea: the grand boubou. The fine white material of his robe was hand-woven in the country's interior by craftsmen. President Touré always wears a white hat and carries a white handkerchief that he waves at the children when he passes in his car.

The music festival is a beautiful event that is held every two years in Guinea. Local competitions are held all over the country for dancers, singers, and actors. Regional competitions follow, and now the national festival in the capital of Conakry. Every night we go to the People's Palace and watch the young people perform. By day we attend the sessions of the Eighth Congress, which is meeting at this time. I am very busy, and I am glad of this. I forget my troubles back in the States.

Or, as I discover, I trade one trouble for another. One day I come into the room I have with Bongi, and there she is, getting undressed. I can see that her figure has changed. She has put on weight. There is a bulge. Bongi sees that I am looking, and she hurries into the next room. But I follow. Even if I choose to disbelieve my eyes, I cannot ignore what my instincts tell me.

"Oh, Bongi," I say. "You didn't."

I must look sad and shocked, because my little girl starts to cry. Tears come running out of her big eyes.

All at once my world is shattered. I think of the things I wanted for my daughter, the same things that all mothers want for their daughters: an education, and a wedding where she wears a pretty white dress. I feel a little wronged, and I start to cry, too. My little girl! Only seventeen!

"Bongi, who is the father?"

"It's Nelson," she says. I have to think for a moment. I remember a tall, light-skinned African-American boy. He is nineteen, two years older than Bongi. I remember that at nights she would go out and meet him. One day I asked her where she was going, and she said, "Out to meet Nelson." I asked her to bring him to meet me. When he came, I said, "You should come here and take Bongi out and bring her back. You must not meet my daughter in the street." He said yes, but he never would do this. That was the only time I saw him.

I cry and cry, until I think that the reason is because I see myself in Bongi. I say to myself, "Well, *you* were pregnant when you were seventeen!" And I stop crying enough to talk some sense to my daughter. I am not going to make her have an abortion. And there is no point in telling her not to see Nelson when the baby is coming. She wants to go to him now. I have been invited to go up into the interior of the country with President Touré's party, and so I agree that this is the time for her to go home.

I say good-bye to Bongi at the airport at Conakry. It is the last time that I will see the little girl that I have known. From now on she will be different, changed. From now on the troubles between us will begin to chip away at my heart, and the bleeding will not end until there is madness and death.

▼▼▼▼▼

I could use someone's company once Bongi leaves, and I do not mind that a young man from America introduces himself at a reception. I have seen him at other embassy receptions, and passed him in the halls. I also recognize him from American TV.

"We've met before, Miss Makeba," Stokely Carmichael says to me. "At Harry Belafonte's."

"Oh? I'm sorry, but I don't remember."

"I was a student, and we came to get Belafonte's advice before we went down for the march on Selma. And later I saw you two give a concert at Forest Hills."

"Oh, yes, where they play tennis. Mr. Belafonte jumped around the stage like he was chasing a ball with a racquet!"

"I have always admired your singing very much."

I thank him, and he asks me to a party at the Gbessia Hotel. I go, and he tells me about his activities in America, fighting for civil rights and what he calls "black power." Stokely is considered very radical and something of a menace in the U.S. when he talks about black power, but I don't see anything wrong with it. Why shouldn't power be black? Here in Guinea, he tells me, he is representing black Americans as one of the international observers at the party congress. He then asks if he can come visit me at the place where I am staying.

I am very attracted to this tall, good-looking young man, but I have to say, "I don't know. I am a guest, here. And you are a guest, here. It will be difficult."

But I find a friend who manages to pick up Stokely at his hotel and he comes to my guest house. We talk and get to know each other. But from here we must go our different ways, hoping that we will meet again at some other place. My trip into the interior with Sékou Touré is about to begin.

▼▼▼▼▼

The journey up-country makes a great impression on me. Everywhere we go, the president presents me to his people as "our sister from South Africa." We stop in the tiny villages of this tropical land, where the mud huts with their thatched roofs are all together in a circle as if they are trying to protect one another from the thick, green jungle.

President Touré tells the people what South Africa is like, and what apartheid is doing to us. "Guineans should know there's still a part of Africa that is not free, where our brothers are still oppressed. We cannot be free until they are free." This is translated to me by Jeanne, and all the people look at me with such pity that I cry. I cry a lot during this trip. The journey really makes me think. Here I am: well-dressed, coming from abroad, a star in America. I'm being presented to all these bare-footed, simple people. And as the president talks, they look at me as if they are really sorry for me. It makes me feel how pitiful I am, because I know that you can have the best clothes, but if you are not free, you are a slave.

I find something very special in Guinea. I thank President Touré for being my host.

He does not want me to go. "Stay here. Live here."

"That would be wonderful," I say, "to live in Africa again. But I have to go home to America."

He shakes his head. "America can never be your home."

The president insists that I come back in a few months. I have always admired this man from afar. Now I am admiring him up close. I agree to be his guest later in the year.

▼▼▼▼▼

From Guinea I travel to another West African nation, Liberia. Next I go to Tanzania in East Africa. After my concert here there is a surprise: Stokely shows up.

"You didn't tell me you were coming here," I say.

"Well, you didn't tell me you were either!"

He is touring Africa, trying to hook up the struggle of American blacks and Africans. Stokely thinks that each can help the other. Since he will be busy in Africa for a few more weeks, he asks me to bring a letter with some money for his mother back to the U.S. I'm happy to do it.

When I return to New York, I cannot find Bongi. She has left without a word. I am very worried, and I search everywhere for someone who might know her boyfriend, Nelson Lee. I find them living together in a miserable little room in New York. I beg Bongi to come home so I can take care of her, for the sake of the baby. But she will not. She is acting very stubborn and strange, and she does not say why she disappeared. I talk to Nelson, and he agrees that I can rent an apartment for them. He has a job, but he does not make much. I find a nice place in Manhattan with a baby's room, a dining room, a living room, and a kitchen. I furnish it for them and get them started. Bongi agrees to see my gynecologist and do what he says. This gives me some peace of mind.

I go to find Stokely's mother. Mrs. Carmichael is from Trinidad. Stokely was also born in Trinidad, but he is now a naturalized American. I call up their house in the Bronx. One of Stokely's four sisters answers, and I say that Miriam Makeba is calling.

"Who?" She doesn't believe me. But I explain how I met her brother in Africa, and we make arrangements so I can come out to visit. The family is very nice. The mother likes me right away. And I like her. None of the children call her Mama, they call her "Mae Charles." Mae is her first name and Charles was her maiden name. Stokely's father died three years ago, and his mother will do anything for her only son.

When Stokely and I start to date when he returns to the U.S. I'll see him come into this house and yell, "Hey, Mae Charles! Got any food?" When he does this it is usually three in the morning, and Stokely has with him eight or ten of his friends from the Student Nonviolent Coordinating Committee. Sometimes I arrive in the morning and find them sleeping on the couch, in the halls, and on the stairs.

Stokely is always giving speeches at schools and appearing on TV. I am always giving concerts, sometimes at universities, and I sing on TV. But we get together from time to time, and when we do, we enjoy ourselves. Like Hugh, my last great love, Stokely is younger than I, by ten years. But this does not seem to bother either of us. It's as I have learned: If two people start to love each other, nothing is going to stop them.

▼▼▼▼▼

I have been thinking long and hard about President Touré's invitation to come and live in Guinea. The attraction of living again in Africa is very strong. But right now I cannot take it very seriously. There are so many things keeping me in America, things that I do not want to give up: the music industry; the television shows; the concerts at the major halls in all the cities and universities; my manager Bob Schwaid, who keeps bringing in the business; and the good life as an American celebrity. None of these things exists in Guinea. But what is there are my roots, and I have found that these roots cannot be transplanted.

In December I return to West Africa. Janet Carmichael is my traveling companion. Stokely's sister always dreamed of going to Africa. More and more I am finding that this is the hope of many black Americans. So I make the arrangements, and Janet gets her wish. She is very excited, but also a little scared. She has heard that there are many coups in Africa. Because she knows nothing about Guinea, or the popularity of Sékou Touré, she is afraid that she might be caught in some fighting here.

When we arrive in Conakry, we are asked to join the presidential party for a tour of the country by plane. This sounds like fun, because I am enjoying myself with Janet and my translator, Jeanne Delavison, another American woman, Catherine Black, and my old friend from Ghana TV, Genevieve Marais.

On Christmas morning we get up late and we have to rush to the airport. I am wearing my hair long, which is unusual for me. I don't care for it this way, because I have to comb it, and this morning there is no time. I just put a hat on over it.

We arrive late, but there is a delay. The airport is foggy. President Touré is anxious to go, so we board.

The weather clears up a little, and the plane takes off. My friends and I sit in back, make jokes and have a good time. Genevieve tells us about the terrible coup she lived through in Ghana. Such talk makes Janet nervous. She seems to think there is a coup in Africa every minute. But she takes something, and after awhile she falls asleep.

President Touré is seated at a table in front. I see that a stewardess with a worried expression keeps coming back from the cockpit to talk to him. The president shakes his head and sends her back each time. But she returns. I wonder what is going on. Jeanne hears bits of their talk, and she translates for us. "The stewardess reports that the pilot feels we should not land at our destination. There is zero visibility. We should go to another city."

But President Touré insists. "No, we better land right now, right here."

We are told to fasten our seat belts. Janet Carmichael is asleep, so we fasten hers for her. I like to sit by the window on planes. But when I look out I can see nothing but gray. The plane goes down. Whoosh! It comes back up. We circle and go down again. This happens three or four times. Down and up. The fifth time we go down, I hear a grinding sound and a bump from below. I have been flying long enough to know that the landing gear has been brought up. But why, when we are about to land? An announcement is made in French. Jeanne tells me, "They want us to take off our shoes."

"What? Why should we take off our shoes?" I leave mine on. I look out the window. Suddenly, I see trees below. They are at a crazy angle. It does not look as if we are going down, it looks as if the trees are coming up! I crouch down and cover my face with my hands, and I wait for the boom.

The plane hits the earth on its belly. We skid for a long time. The noise and shaking are terrible. Genevieve panics. She stands and is thrown down to the aisle. The motion tosses her between the seats like a rag doll. Things are falling all around. People scream. The motion finally stops, but now there is fire from the back.

All I can see are people running. Women are screaming. This is a Russian-built plane, and the doors are jammed. The President's soldiers start to smash out the windows with the butts of their rifles. At this moment, Janet wakes up and looks around to see smoke, the passengers running, and the soldiers with their rifles.

"I told you people!" she shouts. "I told you we shouldn't come here! You see? Now there's a coup!"

I never knew that a person can go through one of those little windows. But people do. A door in front is opened. President Touré stands beside it, shouting to everyone to get out. But I am on my hands and knees. I am looking for my hat! I know that I did not comb my hair, so I cannot get off without my hat! Jeanne is also down on her hands and knees. Through the smoke we look at each other in surprise. "My cigarettes!" she cries. "Where are my cigarettes!"

I am in such a dizzy state that when I find my hat, I put it on, even though it is wet and ruined. Juice, milk, and coffee have spilled all over it. The milk and juice drip down over my face and dress. *Now* I can leave the burning plane!

President Touré is shouting, "Where is Miriam Makeba? Where are the others?"

"Here I am!"

"Get out!"

I jump and start to run. There are people all around. We are at an airport, but the plane is far from the runway. I look back at the plane and it is completely wrecked. It is on fire in the back. The grass is burning where the plane first struck. Guinean women are beating the flames with their robes. The women here wear two robes, and they are using their outer garments to extinguish the fire. A big crowd has been waiting for the President. They were screaming and screaming, thinking we are all dead. When we start to come out they rush forward to help.

The ground feels uneven beneath me and I cannot see straight. Things shake like an earthquake. It is because I have one shoe on and one shoe off. I don't even have the sense to take off this other shoe, which has a high heel. I walk along, limping. Finally a Guinean woman rushes up and takes off my shoe for me.

President Touré is the last one out of the plane, and it is hot in there! His feet never touch the ground. The people lift him up and carry him to the terminal. They are cheering.

My friends and I are in complete shock. But no one is hurt, not even a two-month-old baby who was aboard. Genevieve is all black and blue because she panicked and was thrown around the cabin. Jeanne is angry. "This is Sékou Touré's fault. He insisted that we land."

Someone remarks that it is like the kings in the olden days who would die and have their servants killed with them. In the afterlife, the servants lie down and use their bodies for the king's mat. I think, "What kind of trouble is this? I was about to die so I can become a mat for the king!"

The next day, President Touré tells us we must get into a new plane to continue our journey. We all cry and beg not to go. But he insists. We get on board, and we are scared to death. The night before, every time I tried to get to sleep, even though they gave us tranquilizers, I kept seeing trees coming up at me. Now I look out the window and I see more trees. We're going to land in the forest! The plane goes down, and the pilot lands on a narrow dirt road. Everybody claps. I'm so relieved, I do, too.

Later, the president asks me, "Do you know why I did that—made you all go on the plane right after the crash? It was so you would get over that fear, because I knew you had to take planes to get back to your countries."

This man has common sense, I think. And he is right. On the overnight Pan Am flight back to New York, the air is bumpy and I am wide awake. Every time there is a bump I think, "Okay, this is it!" But thanks to President Touré's psychology, at least I have the courage to fly at all.

When I arrive in America, it is 1968. This year, too, will be a bumpy ride. I will soon be thirty-four, and I am beginning to think that just about everything that can happen to a person has happened to me. But, really, things have only just started for me.

12

*T*IME CALLS STOKELY A "Black Powermonger." White America seems to panic when he goes on TV or gives a speech with his statement: "I say to black people, you gotta get your guns!"

Some of my friends say to me, "I can't believe you're seeing Stokely Carmichael!"

"We love each other," I tell them. And this is true. For a long time we have been going together, and no one has spoken about love. Then, one day, Stokely says, "Miriam, I love you."

I'm pleased. "Oh, yeah? I love you, too."

I tell my friends, "It has nothing to do with politics."

But, really, everything in my life seems to involve politics. Anyone else can go home and see their family, but for me to do so would require changing the political system of South Africa. Any other singer can sing a love song and the audience will think about lovers lost or found, and feelings sad or beautiful. But when I sing a love song it is, like one critic writes, "a metaphor for the yearning of a subjugated people to be free." Ed Sullivan introduces me on his show, and sometimes he even pronounces my name right, and half the audience sees me as a symbol of African nationalism, protest against apartheid, and black pride. Not that I mind; it is an honor to be associated with these things. But when Miriam Makeba falls in love with a black militant like Stokely Carmichael, people are going to say more than, "Oh, isn't that nice!"

And there is gossip about our ages, because Stokely is younger than me. He was dating a girl from Washington before we met. She calls me up and curses me out.

"You're old enough to be my mother!"

I let her have it. *Pow!* "You should be ashamed that your mother could take your boyfriend away from you. It means you ain't good for nothing!"

I go with Stokely to the colleges where he speaks. This is one way for us to spend time together, since he is so busy as the president of the Student Nonviolent Coordinating Committee—SNCC. I sit in the audience like anybody else, and listen to the questions and answers. He introduces me, and I curtsy to the people. After, if he goes to a planning meeting, I just go back to the hotel. The man's activities do not interest me, only the man himself.

Stokely is very articulate and intelligent. But he is full of passion, and his passion makes him angry, and his anger makes him say things that sound very threatening to some people.

My style is so completely different from his. I could also make inflammatory statements about my country if I liked. I sincerely believe that blacks in South Africa are in worse shape than our brothers in America. But I don't do this because such things only make people excited and defensive. They don't listen to you, they just close their doors against you because they think you will do them harm.

I never tell Stokely what to do. I never involve myself in his politics, so I don't really know what he's up to. But as a performer, I can make suggestions about his style.

"You have to be careful, and think about the effect of the things you're saying," I tell him. "You have to build, and be constructive, and bring people together, not pull them apart."

Stokely listens, but he does not agree.

There is another part of his "act" that I do change. When I was growing up, we were poor. But we were clean, and we took great pride in the way we dressed and looked. Stokely and his American friends, who are not poor, dress like vagabonds. Stokely wears dirty jeans and torn jackets. He and his friends say that being dirty and wearing tattered clothes means that a person identifies with the masses.

This makes me mad, because it is just wrong and it sounds

patronizing. "Hey, man, I grew up with the 'masses.' We were not proud of our poverty, we were proud when we could be clean and presentable and show that we were above our poverty."

"I dress this way to show that I'm a revolutionary."

"What you're doing is not revolutionary. You don't fight a revolution to stay in the mud. You fight to get out of the mud. If you want to stay in the mud like a pig, then you don't have to do nothing."

Stokely does not like to be called a pig. That's the name they use for police.

"No, man," I say, "you've got to dress fine." I take him shopping and buy him some shirts and suits. Mae Charles, Stokely's mother, is very happy that he is dressing nicely for a change. But his fellows at SNCC are not pleased when they read in the paper that I am buying him things. They say he has gone "counterrevolutionary."

And they are serious! Everyone is very serious in America, now. And with the Vietnam War, the student protests, and the riots in the ghettos, everyone is scared. Everyone is afraid that there will be a great black uprising. The government is afraid that Stokely will be a leader in this revolt. The FBI never leaves him alone. And because he is a native of Trinidad, which was a British colony, he is banned in all the countries of the British Commonwealth. This is thirty countries. There is concern that he might stir up the local people to riot.

Well, I think, he's got his problems, and I've got mine. But we are two sturdy people, and we are in love. When Stokely does not propose that we get married right away, I put the suggestion in his head. And then I use the arts that a woman knows to make him like the idea, and think that it is *his* idea. If a woman wants a man, he's done for.

In February, we make the announcement to our friends that we will be married the following month. Many people see it as a union of two black worlds: the old and the new.

This comes at a time when I am busy and excited about my first business. I am about to open a dress boutique in the Bahamas. The shop idea of mine came from the country's efforts to attract black businesses to the islands. I got to know the Bahamas last year when I was invited by Prime Minister Pindling to sing at his inauguration. Big Brother came also, and so did

Sidney Poitier and Bill Cosby, the clever young comedian who worked with me at the Village Gate in New York.

The officials are pleased that I am opening a business, and they were very helpful when I came back to look for a location for the shop. I chose to open a dress boutique because there is a very talented lady from Trinidad who designs beautiful clothes in the local style. She sends her designs to me in New York for approval. There is much work to be done, but I do it. There is much money to be spent, but I spend it.

To kick off my business, I arrange a fashion show to raise money for a charity for the blind. Janet Carmichael, who suffered with me through the plane crash in Guinea last Christmas, comes along. Janet is a model, and she shows off many of the boutique's original designs in my show.

The very day of the fashion show, when the public gets to see my boutique, the papers carry the story about my engagement to Stokely. I think this is a happy coincidence: the public learning the same day about two things of joy for me. A government official shows up and tells me that Prime Minister Pindling wants to see me tomorrow.

I go to the office expecting congratulations, and maybe a thank you for investing in their country.

But the prime minister acts differently from the man I have met before. He is cold and short with me. He does not even ask me to sit down. I have to find a chair myself, which I do because the things he says make me feel weak.

"You are thinking of opening a boutique here in the Bahamas?" he asks, like a police inspector.

I am shy at once. "Why, yes, Your Excellency. Excuse me, but I think you know this."

"But I did not know you are engaged to the American revolutionary, Stokely Carmichael."

I feel tense inside. I know what is coming, but I cannot believe it.

"You must get out of the Bahamas," he says.

I think of my dream of owning a business, something that no black person can do at home. "But why? *Why?*"

"Because Stokely Carmichael is an undesirable here."

The prime minister says that his nation is part of the British Commonwealth, where Stokely is banned. I ask what my husband-to-be has to do with my business. But it is no use. Mr. Pindling must be one of those who thinks that a woman exists only as a part of her husband, so my affairs are really Stokely's.

I cry; I cannot stop myself. I think of all the work and money that has gone into my shop. And this is the very day it is to open.

"What am I going to do?" I ask the prime minister.

"You just can't have it."

He dismisses me. I go to my lawyer, who has helped me with all the legal arrangements.

"My hands are tied," he tells me. "There is nothing I can do. There is nothing you can do."

His hands are tied, all right. This is because my lawyer is employed in the law firm that is run by Prime Minister Pindling himself.

But there is one thing I can do: I can leave this horrible place right away. I pack my bags—the entire inventory of the shop. It is a big job, and I am crying while I do it. I am hurt; really, really hurt. I cannot believe that a black-ruled country would do this to me. They used me. They used my name, and they had me sing at the inauguration. I get on the plane to New York, and I say that I will never go back to the Bahamas ever again.

"Okay," I think when I stop crying, "this is another one of those things you will just have to put in the back of your head and say *c'est la vie.*"

But the loss of my business is not to be just one disappointment. Disappointments—and worse—are just beginning.

The wedding is in New York. Stokely works in Washington at the SNCC headquarters. I have been commuting by jet to see him. Now it is time, I decide, to move out of the hotel in New York and rent a place here. Stokely likes the idea, but I am a little mad at him. Even though the wedding is a civil ceremony and only the two of us are there, he shows up in jeans and a tattered jacket with patches on the sleeves. But he promises to look good at our wedding reception in a few weeks. President Touré of Guinea is so pleased by our marriage that he has ordered his ambassador at the UN to throw a party for us.

All of my friends and associates can see how happy I am, and they are pleased for me. So is Bob Schwaid, the tall, dark-haired white man with glasses who is my manager. But when he phones he sounds very disturbed.

"Miriam, they're backing out."

"Backing out? Who?"

"*Everybody*. They're canceling your bookings right and left."

"But why?"

"I think you know why."

I feel that tenseness inside. So, I think, it is starting, again. I ask Mr. Schwaid, "Don't we have contracts?"

"Sure we do. But this is show business. Their attitude is, 'Go ahead and sue.' "

Not everybody cancels my shows. Some realize that I am Miriam Makeba first and Mrs. Stokely Carmichael second. I am a singer, not a revolutionary. I keep reminding the press of this. But interviewers won't leave me alone about my husband's politics. I tell them, "Look, Stokely speaks for the family. I sing for the family."

I am happy that my biggest show of the spring goes on as scheduled. At the famous Coconut Grove in Hollywood I am booked for one week. This is one of the most important places for entertainers to perform. Marlon Brando telephones and says he would like to introduce me at the opening.

My first night is very special. Even though I have had a falling-out with Mr. Belafonte, many friends and celebrities show up: Eartha Kitt, Pearl Bailey, Nina Simone, and Mr. Brando, who gives a little speech about me before I go on. When I do my act the house really comes alive. So do I. The reviews come out in the Los Angeles papers and in the motion picture trade journals, and they are fantastic.

The crowds come and pack the house for three nights. And then we get the news that shocks everyone until we are either mute or crying. Martin Luther King has been shot. His death is a blow to all of us. I think of the time in Atlanta when he came to my defense when I was banned from the restaurant there. He liked my singing, and I was so moved by his power and eloquence. I remember seeing him on TV during the march on Washington, and listening to his words that helped build my spirit when I was recovering from the cancer operation.

But there is more in store for me. I get back to the hotel room, and there is a telephone call from New York. It is Bongi. She has given birth. I now have a grandson. My daughter is well and happy. I put down the phone and collapse on the bed. And I cry. I cry out of sadness and gratitude. I fear for what is happening to our beloved leaders. I am happy that Bongi is well. A great man is dead. A child is born. My head feels so full, I just lie down and let all the confusing feelings roll over me.

▼▼▼▼▼

Now that Dr. King is dead, everything shuts down. The wedding reception that the Guineans were going to give us is postponed. I tell the management of the Coconut Grove that I cannot continue, and they kindly release me from the rest of the week's contract. Stokely and I must attend Dr. King's funeral in Atlanta. I go from Los Angeles to Washington to pick up my new husband.

With the death of Dr. King, who preached nonviolence, it is as if the anger of black Americans cannot be expressed nonviolently anymore. All over the country, riots set the cities on fire. In Washington, a curfew is in effect when I arrive. The taxi takes me through streets that are deserted and empty. From the townhouse that I am renting on Sixteenth Street I can hear the sirens and see the light from the fires that are consuming blocks and blocks. The news says that fifteen thousand troops are being sent here to restore order.

On the television there is nothing but pictures of burnings and people running. All over the country. I think, "Goodness me, what's going on?" And I am getting scared, because there is no Stokely. I get a call that he is coming. I wait and wait, but nothing. Outside the window, the fire engines and police cars race by, and then there is an awful silence. Way off there is gunfire. Somebody runs by fast, because nobody is supposed to be on the streets. But it is not Stokely. I am scared to death. What if the rioting and fire comes this way?

Finally, Stokely knocks on the back door. I run to let him in, I am so happy.

"How did you get through the curfew?"

Stokely only laughs. What is a curfew to him?

We go to Atlanta for Dr. King's funeral. The place is packed with people, press, and dignitaries from all over. I see Big Brother. This is the first time I have laid eyes on him since the breakup. But he is with Mrs. King, and they are busy with all the people so I cannot get close to him. I escape the crush as soon as I can, and take a plane to New York. When I get there I go right to the hospital. Bongi looks like such a little girl that I cannot believe she has had a baby. And then they bring in the child. He is one of the sweetest-looking things I have ever seen, and I have to weep. Bongi cries, too. We are both very happy. The baby is light-skinned, like his mother. She is calling him Lumumba. Lumumba Lee, even though she and Nelson are not married.

"I love you so much, Bongi," I say.

"I love you, Mama. You're the best mama in the whole world."

I leave the hospital a grandmother. It is strange, because I have only just turned thirty-six years old.

▼▼▼▼▼

A weekend in mid-May is set for our postponed wedding reception. This is being hosted by my friends Achkar and Rosamond Marof, the UN Ambassador from Guinea and his wife, at the request of President Touré. Rosamond came to Los Angeles to take care of me when I was recovering from cancer, and they are happy that the President wants to throw this party for me. But Rosamond's mother dies, and they can no longer be hosts. Friends from Tanzania step in. The UN Ambassador, Akill Daniel, and his wife offer to have the reception at their home in Mount Vernon, New York. One hundred and fifty guests are invited. Over five hundred show up.

Stokely dresses nicely for the party, in a grand boubou. I am in a grand boubou that Madame Touré gave me when I last visited her country. Journalists, entertainers, diplomats, black activists, and all sorts of people crowd the rooms and cover the lawns. Stokely's mother says she has never seen anything like it. She and I are very good friends. But I cannot bring myself to call her Mae Charles. To me, it sounds disrespectful. It's the way I was brought up. I call her "Mamo." Mrs. Carmichael is very happy that her son is married to me. I know that she must be disappointed that he can never have any children by me, but she never says a word about it.

▼▼▼▼▼

Stokely's term as president of SNCC comes to an end. He is replaced by H. Rapp Brown. For a while, Stokely works as a field secretary for SNCC. Then, like some other SNCC members, he is attracted to a new organization, one that has its headquarters in Oakland, California. It is called the Black Panther Party for Self-Defense. This is a very, very controversial group, and although Stokely does not become a member, the fact that he is working with them really puts the pressure on us.

The FBI, which has been following Stokely everywhere he goes for a long time, now begins to follow me, too. Every day there is a car in front of the house. The car is always behind, even when I am alone. I have a feeling they must hear what we say inside the house, because when I get to where I am going, there are FBI men there, too. How do they know where I am going if they do not listen to our conversations? It can be Stokely's mother's house in the Bronx, or it can be the airport. They are there. These faceless white or black men in their suits sitting in their cars and looking at me. When I arrive in a city, they come to meet me. They are easy to spot because they are conspicuous. I know the difference between strangers who look at me because they saw me on TV or like my music and these men who look at me because they are studying me. After I rent a car, I see them at the desk getting the address of the place I am staying, and when I get to the hotel, they are there. When I leave my key at the desk, they ask what room I am in. I guess it is so they can bug it. We call them our "babysitters," but I am really scared. It is nerve-wracking, and it is something I never would have expected in America. This is really nasty treatment from a country that is supposed to be free.

I tell Stokely that I feel as if I am in prison. We even have the impression that someone is listening when we are making love. He says, "Never talk to them. Don't look at them."

I try to do as he says. Stokely is used to all sorts of intimidation. The U.S. government took away his passport because he went to North Vietnam, China, Cuba, and other countries where they say he is not supposed to go. He goes anyway to these places. But he does not use his passport, even though it was returned to him. Instead of traveling as a U.S. citizen, he goes as an individual.

I have my own travel problems. When I arrive on the island of Jamaica for a concert, at first I am glad to find an airport where there are no FBI agents to trail me. The concert goes very well. In the audience is Dudley Thompson, a cabinet minister in the government of Prime Minister Manley. He knew me from a time when we were in Kenya together.

But when my musicians and I go to the airport to return to the U.S., I am not permitted to board.

I am shocked. "Why? What has happened?"

The agent is very cool. "You do not have a visa."

For many years I have traveled on a Tanzanian passport, and because I am not a citizen of the United States, I obtained the necessary visas to go into and out of the country. But things have changed, and I tell them, "But I am married to a U.S. citizen."

This does no good. I send my musicians on their way, and I go to Dudley Thompson's house. He agrees to put me up, and after I drop off my bags I go to see the American Ambassador. I sit and sit, but the ambassador will not see me.

When I do not go away, he comes out of his office at last. But he will not talk to me. He will not even look at me. Instead, he says to his secretary in a very nasty voice, "Tell her I'm not giving her a visa."

The ambassador goes back into his office and slams the door. I go to Mr. Thompson's house and call Stokely. He is furious. He says he is coming down right away.

The first thing Stokely does is contact the people he knows in the Congressional Black Caucus in Washington. They are also made angry by my treatment. He checks to see if Prime Minister Manley has lifted the ban that kept him from entering Jamaica, which is a British Commonwealth country. This has been done, so Stokely takes the plane down and meets me.

By this time the American newspapers have gotten wind of my problem. The stories say: "MIRIAM MAKEBA BLOCKED IN JAMAICA." The press stories are making an embarrassment, and the Congressional Black Caucus is putting on pressure. But the American ambassador tells Stokely, "I'm still not giving her a visa."

My husband just smiles. He is so cool. "Fine. I'm going to spend the *whole* weekend here, in Jamaica."

We leave. Stokely being on the island makes the ambassador nervous. Many officials in America are very paranoid about him. In Maryland, where Stokely was speaking just before Dr. King was shot, the governor there, a man named Spiro Agnew, is blaming Stokely for inciting the black people to riot in the city of Baltimore. It is as if the assassination of Dr. King had nothing to do with what the people did.

We get a call at Mr. Thompson's house. The American Embassy is closed, but the ambassador wants us to come over right away. He looks uncomfortable when he speaks to Stokely. "Well, you know, your wife can have her visa, and you can leave anytime you want."

Stokely just sits back and laughs. "I'm glad to hear that my wife can go back. But, you see, I've decided I want to stay. I have a lot of meetings here with the people, and a lot of folks I want to see."

The ambassador looks wretched when we leave, because Stokely won't go, and I get to enjoy the island for a few days until my husband is ready to go home.

But home is becoming more and more hostile. My manager, Bob Schwaid, gives me the terrible news: My concerts are being canceled left and right. I learn that people are afraid that my shows will finance radical activities. I can only shake my head. What does Stokely have to do with my singing? People say, "You married a radical." But I never saw Stokely kill anybody. The police during the demonstrations and riots, *they* are killing people.

It is frightening. There is an expression about seeing the handwriting on the wall. I think of what they did to Paul Robeson, here. He was not given work because of his political beliefs. But what have I done? I have never expressed any views about American politics. This goes back to the days when Big Brother told me, "When we give a press conference, you speak about your people in South Africa. But when we march and demonstrate, you go home."

And I never said anything to offend people in the U.S. I am a guest here. The only thing I ever protested was apartheid. I did nothing to be treated the way I was in Jamaica by the U.S. government. And the people in the entertainment industry, are they passing the same judgments about me? I can see the proof with each concert that is canceled. I wonder if they will strangle me. It is an awful feeling to think that this might happen, that it is already happening.

If my marriage to Stokely is giving me problems, his marriage to me is causing him trouble, too. This may not be the time to look for another house to rent in Washington, but I do. There is a very nice place on Bladgen Avenue N.W. near the Carter Barron Amphitheater, where I have performed. I make some inquiries. The next day there is a story in *The Washington Post* and another in *The New York Times*: "CARMICHAEL IS RE-PORTED BUYING $70,000 HOME."

Stokely is not going to buy a house. I am the one who is looking. And I'm not buying, either. I want to rent. But the damage is done. There is much rivalry among the black militants, and some of Stokely's enemies jump on this. They treat it the way they did when I bought him some suits: "Look, he's no revolutionary. He's bourgeois! He's buying himself a rich man's house!"

We deny the story, but it is no good. For years Stokely will be called a hypocrite because of his imaginary purchase of a house.

▼▼▼▼▼

America seems to be going crazy. Half the people seem to be out in the streets protesting or rioting, and the other half are at home behind closed doors, scared. The "establishment" is cracking down on the people who want to topple it, the people in the streets. And it is cracking down on those who are associated with the people in the streets.

The end comes for me when my recordings stop. My contract with Reprise calls for three albums a year. We have been putting them out very profitably like clockwork. I always get a call from my Artist and Repertoire man when it is time to start work on the next album. But as the summer of 1968 grows older, no phone call comes. I would have to be more than illiterate, now, if I could not read the handwriting on the wall. I would have to be blind.

But I am not blind, not deaf, not dumb. I think very clearly about what is happening. I have been put down and threatened all my life. It has never been easy, but I have never given up. By now I can say I know how to survive.

"No," I say, "they are not going to strangle me." When I was not wanted in the Bahamas, I packed my bags that very day. I am not going to stick around in the U.S. the way things are. I could sue Reprise for breach of contract, but what would be the use? That would just drag me down and tie me to the past. Because it is over, now. This wonderful dream come true—the little African girl who becomes a big star in America—it's all over.

I refuse to let myself cry. This part of my career is finished, but I am not finished.

▼▼▼▼▼

I pack up everything that is in the townhouse. I have done this hard work before, so many times. I am hurt; very hurt. I do not know why this has to happen to me. But I always think this when the terrible things strike: Why me?

Bongi has her life here with Nelson. My grandchild is an American. They will stay.

I am going to Europe for a three-month concert tour. France, Switzerland, Scandinavia, and other countries. Stokely is coming with me. And after?

I have been considering President Touré's offer. When he asked me to live in Guinea during my trips to his country last year, I liked the idea very much. I could not do it, then. My obligations in America were so many. Now, I have only one obligation to America: to get out.

But they want me at home, in Africa. Not just Guinea, but other countries have asked me to come and stay. The diplomatic passports they have given me are their way of saying, Come, be with us.

After the nightmare that has happened to me in America, it is nice to go off and work for three months, and then be welcomed by a head of state to live in his country. I think this to lift my spirits when I get on the plane at Dulles. But I must think about it very hard, because leaving is difficult.

Things happen so fast in America. They always have. Look how quickly I became a star here. I wonder how soon it will be before they will forget me. Probably no time at all. Then there will be all sorts of changes, because America is always changing. Maybe one of these changes will bring me back. In the meantime, I must live my life elsewhere. There are people who know me all over the world. I will go and see them. Maybe somewhere I will find some peace at last.

13

"THAT IS VILLA ANDRÉE," President Touré says to me. "It is named after my wife."

He points ahead to a group of round white houses. They are together in a compound that was built for guests of the government. Stokely and I are in the back seat of the President's white convertible Cadillac, which was a gift from the U.S. government when Guinea became independent in 1960. President Touré is at the wheel. He always drives himself around the streets of the tiny capital city, Conakry. With one hand he steers, going very slow. With the other hand he waves to the people with his white handkerchief. I have never seen a leader act like this. Anyone could take a shot at him. But the only ones who rush the car are children. They adore their president. The people on the street cheer him. The women chant in Sousou, the native language, "*Sékou, we want you to stop and say hello!*" He does. After the greetings—because the women of Guinea are the darlings of this man—we continue on our way.

Stokely and I are given a house in the Villa Andrée compound. We both adjust very well to life in Africa. Stokely likes it so much that for a year he does not return to the U.S. He begins studying African politics with the former ruler of Ghana. Kwame Nkrumah has been living in Guinea since he was overthrown in a coup in 1966. I travel to Europe, where I have concert appearances to do. With my career in the U.S. over, William Morris no longer represents me. If concert promoters wish to reach me for a show, they contact me through Guinean diplomatic channels.

Guinea is very poor, like all of Africa. Its land is about two-thirds the size of California, and it is on the Atlantic coast in the tropical portion of the continent. Mangos and coconuts grow wild during the two seasons: the summer rainy season when the thick mud is bright orange and the wild trees are so green they glow in the sun, and the winter dry season, when the earth, rich with bauxite that is exported to make aluminum, becomes dust and covers everything indoors and out with a red film.

Conakry is an oversized village made up of fading French colonial buildings and tumbledown shacks where the poor try to live. The beaches have no sand, because the people took it all away to build with. But this type of sand makes poor concrete, and all over town walls and posts are crumbling down.

It is hard for Conakry to repair itself because the engineers have no city plans or blueprints to work with. When the French left in 1960, Charles de Gaulle came to ask Guinea to join the commonwealth of former French colonies. But President Touré said no, and he said no to the general in public, at a big stadium rally. I am shown films of that day: of President de Gaulle leaving the stadium angry and in a hurry to get out of the country. De Gaulle is a proud man. But so is President Touré. In his memoirs, de Gaulle says that Sékou Touré is a nationalist like him, and that if Sékou Touré was a Frenchman, de Gaulle would have made him a cabinet minister. But because Sékou Touré is not a Frenchman, de Gaulle made his life miserable. He ordered all the French colonial engineers to leave, and when they went they took the blueprints to all the electrical wiring, telephone lines, and sewage systems. President Touré turned to the U.S. for aid, but de Gaulle asked President Kennedy to refuse. Kennedy honored the request of his NATO ally.

The countryside of Guinea is also poor. But it is very beautiful; especially around Dalaba, a mountain region five hours from the coast. When Sékou Touré asks me where I would like to live, I tell him I want to build my house at this place. Plans are drawn up, and I commute to the site in a government limousine that the president gives me to use. In no time, a round house, whitewashed and with a thatched roof, is finished. The house is in the local style, and it blends into the grass and forests that surround it as if it just grew there naturally. Anyone could find peace in a lovely setting like this, and I do. Goats and chickens wander around the little dirt yard, and there is a water pump out back by the commode. The neighbors come by and say hello. They call me "stranger," but they are friendly. Some get to know me when my songs are played on the radio. And sooner or later everyone gets to see Guinean TV, and sooner or later I show up singing in a film clip.

When I go to Sweden, I visit the Volvo factory and buy a car. It is shipped to Conakry, and Stokely uses it to drive me to the big, open-air market or to visit friends. My car is the first Volvo in Conakry. A couple is here whom I have known since 1964, when they lived in California. Gilbert Minot was a film student in Los Angeles, and Audrey grew up in Oakland. They got married and came back to Gilbert's home. He makes documentary films, and Audrey runs a school. The Minots, Stokely, and I take the boats out to the coastal islands during the dry season when the ocean is not rough. We lie on the sand in the shade of the palm trees, drink wine, and talk.

Before Stokely left America, he formed a group in Washington called the African People's Revolutionary Party. He corresponds with the home office while he is in Guinea, and after a year he goes back to America. I return to the country myself, but it is only to see Bongi, my grandson, and Stokely's mother. One time I come from the airport to my daughter's apartment, and I find she is about to go out. When she tells me that she must visit the hospital, and that Nelson's father is very ill, I put down my bags and leave with her at once.

Mr. Lee is dying of cancer. He is very pale and weak, but his eyes light up when he sees me.

"Miriam Makeba . . ."

He holds out his hand, and I take it. I am very moved, because it is difficult for him to speak. But he struggles.

"I . . . have always wanted . . . to go to Africa."

I am weeping when I leave. I have never met any of Nelson's family before. And I won't again after this. Bongi is changing now that she is with Nelson. I can feel her withdrawing from me, and becoming more distant. She is still so young, only eighteen, and I think this may be a phase she is going through. Just because she has a baby does not mean that she is an adult. I tell myself that living in Africa, I don't have to worry about getting in her way. But I miss the Bongi who was an innocent and carefree little girl.

My visits to the U.S. are very brief, and nobody knows about them. But when Stokely goes back, there is all sorts of noise. He gets into an argument with Eldridge Cleaver, who is the minister of information for the Black Panther party. The argument ends badly, and Eldridge Cleaver says he will kill Stokely. I am glad when my husband is out of America and back with me.

We go to Switzerland together for a concert. My reputation in Europe is very solid, now, and I am invited to festivals in many countries. After the show, we return to Guinea by way of the African country of Sudan. But first we must change planes in France. While we wait to board at the airport in Switzerland, two French military men come up to us. They ask Stokely if he is going to France.

"I'm going to Sudan," he answers in a voice that says he has nothing more to say to them. He tells me that he has been banned in France. Last year he was invited to Paris by some students to speak about college kids in the States becoming radicals. When he left, Paris was on fire. It was May 1968. Stokely had nothing to do with the student riots, but he was banned anyway. Now, a year later, he is still considered dangerous.

I learn how afraid the authorities are of my husband when the plane lands in France. The steps are brought up to the door, and a military man comes inside. He tells Stokely and me to remain seated. All the other passengers leave. When we finally get to go out, there are five soldiers at the bottom of the stairs waiting for us. Each one has a machine gun.

Stokely says, "What's going on?"

An official tells him, "You have to be under guard until you leave France."

We are escorted to a little room. I ask if I can go to the duty-free shop. They tell me no.

Now I get a little angry. "But what did I do? I just want to buy some perfume."

They let me go to the duty-free shop, but I am taken there by a soldier with a machine gun. People look at me, and they don't know what to think. Am I a public enemy? I get so mad I forget about the perfume, go back, and wait to leave.

But even when I travel on my own, and no mention of Stokely is made, politics still gets in the way. A few months after the incident in France, I go to Dakar, the capital of Senegal, for a show. Senegal is on the northern border of Guinea, and the two countries have been at odds for years over foreign policy. When Senegal gained its independence from France, it joined the commonwealth of former French colonies, and Dakar always follows the French lead. President Touré wants independence in everything.

About the time that I go to my concert, things are getting bad. Insults are being traded every day. None of this seems to affect my show: The people are very enthusiastic and they receive me well. I am to perform four times. After my first show, representatives from the government come to my hotel room. But they have not come to give me flowers.

"You sang a Guinean song last night. You are a guest in our nation, and we do not wish that you sing it again."

"Which one was it?" I ask. They tell me, and I promise not to sing it again. The men leave. The night of my second show, I keep my promise. I do not sing the song the officials dislike. Instead, I substitute another Guinean song. I know many, and I can sing a new one each night.

But I am not going to get a chance. The day of my third show, Friday, I am visited by the same government officials. They are not happy.

"You must leave Senegal!"

"Oh, but that's impossible," I say. "My shows . . ."

"Canceled!"

"But how am I to leave? The next plane out is not until Monday."

"Just stay in your room," they tell me. "Don't even go to the market. Because if you do, the Senegalese people will *kill* you!"

All I can say to this threat is, "Oh, yeah?"

On Saturday, I go out to the market to buy some flat shoes. On Sunday I walk around the streets of Dakar, and go to the bazaar. The Senegalese recognize me, all right. They come up and speak to me, and they are worried.

"Why didn't you sing last night at the stadium?"

"Ask your authorities."

On Monday, the plane comes and I return to Guinea. A year passes, and I am invited back by a group of artists. My musicians and I leave Conakry at nine in the morning. We arrive in Dakar at eleven. As soon as I step off the plane, I am handed a letter signed by the man who has just been elected prime minister, Abdou Diouf. The letter says that I am declared persona non grata in Senegal. I am not permitted to leave the airport. Air Guinea brought us here, and so I say, "Air Guinea, bring us back."

By two o'clock, I am again in Conakry. I go directly to President Touré's office. I show him the letter. He takes it from me, and soon the two nations are engaged in their "dialogue." It all seems strange to me, since I am not a Guinean citizen. But I just cannot seem to get away from political conflicts, wherever I am. The worst thing is that my singing is hurt. Concerts keep getting canceled, in America, and now in Africa. I am an artist, and I am losing my audience. This hurts.

It seems that I have little time to stay in Guinea and enjoy the government's guest house in the city, or my country home in the mountains. There are many invitations from other heads of state to visit them.

It is north to Algeria for me, Stokely and little Lumumba. Bongi has given me my fourteen-month-old grandson for a few weeks, and I am enjoying every minute. But the trip loses its happy feeling very quickly. Eldridge Cleaver is also in Algeria, at a conference. When he and Stokely had their fight in California, Cleaver threatened to kill him. Now he repeats his death threat. I am very nervous. Stokely tells me not to worry. But I can tell that he is bothered himself.

I have my work to do. I go to rehearsal. When I return to the hotel to rest before the concert, Stokely is not in our room. And Lumumba is gone. There is a note: "GONE TO MEET CLEAVER. LUMUMBA WITH ME. S."

I am scared at once. Part of me says that the men have decided to meet to work out their differences. But another part of me fears a trap, an ambush. I am terrified. And Stokely took my grandson with him! I call everywhere I can think of, but nobody knows anything. The hours go by without a phone call or message. I am so panicky I cannot think of anything but the terrible picture of my husband and grandchild dead.

The time comes to do the show, and still no word. I have to perform. Once I go on stage I have to forget about everything, and I do. The audience cannot see the terror inside me, because the part of me that I show them is the joy I feel being able to sing to them, and the excitement that makes me shake and move when I am on stage.

As soon as I finish singing, I ask for messages. There are none. I rush back to the hotel. Stokely is sitting in a chair, as calm as can be. Lumumba is playing on the floor. I drop to my knees and embrace my grandchild, kissing him. I glare at Stokely. I have never been more angry with him.

"How *could* you?"

At first, he pretends. "I had to bring him. Who was I going to leave him with?"

I am so mad I cannot speak. He sees this, and he admits the truth. "All right, I knew that if I took Lumumba with me there would be some second thoughts about killing me."

"What if there hadn't been any second thoughts?"

Now Stokely gets defensive. He points to the floor. "Well, there's your grandson. As you can see, he's all right."

My husband forgets that he brought a baby along as a bullet-proof vest, and he grows sulky that I am not more concerned about him. I have to swallow my anger, put down Lumumba, and go take care of my other baby.

Stokely gets to know Africa. It is more than just adjusting to the climate and the food. The spirit of the place must get inside you. There are things that cannot be put into words that rule life in Africa. We respect these things, even if we cannot explain them. We know what our ancestors can do if their will is ignored. So we pay them homage with sacrifice. We know that the spirits of the dead inhabit the *isangoma* in order to help the living. So we seek out the tribal doctors to cure us. We know that certain animals and places are more than they seem. So we respect them.

One day, Stokely is driving me in the Volvo from my house in Dalaba to Conakry. He sees a snake in the road ahead, and slows down.

"I'm going to run it over."

I am afraid, and I cry out, "Oh, don't!"

"Why not?"

"Because at home, they say that if a snake isn't bothering you, you leave it alone. Or something bad will happen."

"Oh, that's junk."

Stokely aims the car and runs over the snake. He looks back, and he is happy. I just sit and sigh. We drive on. The roads in rural Guinea are full of potholes. It seems that we are driving from side to side in order to avoid the potholes as much as we are driving forward. A car approaching us swerves toward us to avoid a hole, and Stokely almost hits it. We wind up in a ditch. Neither of us speaks the native language, and we are faced with four angry people who want to beat us.

"You see," I say. "You should have never run over that snake."

Stokely is angry. "I still say that's junk."

He has much to learn. And things will get worse for him until he does.

In 1969, a malaria epidemic sweeps Guinea, and Stokely gets it bad. I nurse him night and day, and he regains his health. A few months later, a cholera epidemic hits the country. It is very serious. Everyone gets vaccinations. President Touré sends some of his cabinet ministers to Europe to be treated when they get sick.

Stokely refuses a vaccination. "I'm not a baby. I'm not going to take that."

"I'm not a baby, either," I tell him. "But I'm getting a shot."

He refuses, and he is hit by cholera. We are in Dalaba when he is struck, and he gets it bad! A sister of mine—a woman from South Africa—is living in the village, working at the clinic as a nurse. She arranges for an ambulance for me to take Stokely to the capital. After we put Stokely in, she comes with us on the long trip. Normally, the drive is five hours. But with the bad weather, it takes us seven hours to get to Conakry. Stokely is so sick that I am terrified. He never stops groaning and vomiting.

When we finally arrive in town, President Touré puts many doctors at our disposal. I am so frightened about Stokely's condition that I cable his mother. In three days time she arrives from New York. I feel so much better, because I do not want anything to happen to Stokely when I am all alone here. He is close to death. Mae Charles and I never leave him. President Touré makes his daily rounds of the cholera patients, including the prime minister and the minister of state, and he drops by to see Stokely and chat with me.

Days pass before we know: he will pull through. It takes him a long time to recover, and he will never regain the weight that he has lost. Stokely was a big man when I married him, but not any longer.

Now that I am certain that my husband will survive, my body tells itself that it's okay for me to get sick. I do. It is not malaria or cholera. I am simply exhausted. I check myself into a hospital in London. For years I have been meaning to go to this place that has been recommended to me for allergies. I know I have allergies, and now is the time to find out what they are.

Mae Charles comes up from Guinea on her way back to New York. She is good company. I also send for Bongi. My daughter arrives and is very shy. Something is on her mind.

I look at her very closely, and when I do she drops her head. My look goes down from her pretty face to her belly.

"Oh Bongi," I say. "Are you pregnant again?"

For the second time I see it before she tells me. And for the second time she does not answer. She just cries. She is worried that I will not like her because she and Nelson are having a second child and they are still not married. I am very weak, but I lift up my arms to her. She comes over, and I embrace her as she lies beside me on the bed.

"Oh, Bongi, I love you. Don't be scared. There's nothing to be scared about, and nothing to be ashamed of."

It is so good to feel my daughter again.

▼▼▼▼▼

At the hospital, they start to make a list of all my allergies. They give me tests and vaccinations. Some of my allergies are terrible: My eyes water, my face swells, and my voice gives out. This is bad for a singer. Two tests come back positive: cat fur and house dust. I have always been afraid of cats, ever since I saw that nasty one kill the woman relative at home when I was a small child. And now I know that their hair makes me ill. As for house dust: I am a very thorough house cleaner, but the dust of the winter's dry season in Guinea is very difficult to escape.

I have a food allergy, too. Almonds. Every time I eat almonds

I vomit. From now on I don't eat cake, because I never know if it has almond extract in it. And, of course, people are always offering me cake. "No, thank you," I say. But they insist. I still refuse, even if they feel hurt, because if I ate it I would vomit and they would get disgusted. They might even vomit what they ate! Then things would get really bad, because I cannot watch anyone who is getting sick without getting sick myself. I vomit in sympathy. This happens a lot. With Bongi and Lumumba, and Stokely in the ambulance, every time they start vomiting, I do, too. It makes me glad that I decided to become a singer and not a nurse.

▼▼▼▼▼

Stokely and I are both at home, recuperating at Villa Andrée by the sea. The sun is setting behind the palms, and I am in the kitchen making dinner. The beef you buy at the market is freshly slaughtered, and since it has not been drained well, it is tough. I pound and pound the meat to make it tender. These hands are not the hands of a singing star who spends two hours doing her nails. They are hands that have always worked.

It is late November, and the skies above the pale blue sea are growing dark earlier each day. Stokely and I sit on the porch with some wine and we watch the lights of the cargo ships that sail into the harbor. Then we eat, and watch a little of the Guinean television station, trying to improve our French. He takes me in his arms, and we go to bed.

There are many noises that can wake me up at night. A cat will howl. Or a dog will bark. A coconut will fall off the tree and hit the roof. But this night I am awakened by a different noise. A popping.

Stokely wakes up, too. He listens. "Gunfire."

The shooting grows louder, and closer. All of a sudden it is like we are in the middle of a battlefield. Men are outside, running up from the beach. They have machine guns and they are firing away at everything.

"Get down!" Stokely says. I lie on the floor for hours. Every few minutes I try to get up to get the matches by my sewing machine and to try to reach my pants. "They're not going to find me naked!" I tell my husband. The voices outside are foreign. We do not understand the language, which is not French.

At dawn other voices come. I get up and see Guinean soldiers everywhere. Stokely goes outside to take a look. The windshield of my Volvo has been blown out. I call up President Touré's house. My French is bad, but I can understand a little of what they tell me. Guinea is being invaded.

I find Stokely. He has been talking to the soldiers. They have a radio, and we listen to President Touré as he addresses the people: Mercenaries have been hired by Portugal, and they have come from the neighboring country of Guinea-Bissau, which is still a Portuguese colony. I know the Portuguese: They are always collaborating with South Africa. President Touré always helps independence movements, and he has permitted Amilcar Cabral and the other leaders of the Guinea-Bissau Liberation Movement to work out of Conakry. The invasion is meant to flush out these men, and to get back at Sékou Touré.

We look out to sea, and there is the giant troop transport ship that brought the mercenaries. Along the beach are the small boats that brought them to shore. The invaders came right past Villa Andrée.

President Touré asks the citizens to take up arms to defend themselves. We are told the mercenaries are dressed just like Guinean soldiers, only they have light green bands around their arms so they can identify themselves to each other.

Soldiers go from house to house and hand out firearms. I have faced many times of crisis, but this one gives me something new. In my hands I now hold a Soviet-made machine gun.

I know how to use it. In Guinea, everyone learns how. Here they have a people's militia. Students go when they finish school, and other young men when they get to a certain age. And everybody else receives training with weapons. Every man and woman. When I first came to Guinea, I told them that I would like to learn, too, like everyone else. And like the neighbors, I go to the district meeting every Friday night when the mayor tells the news to the townspeople, who are called militants. The militants use these meetings to make complaints. We are told what head of state is visiting Conakry so everyone can mobilize: dress in white, line the streets, go to the stadium. Of course, if a citizen does not attend the weekly meetings, the penalty is a loss of rations. Ration cards are needed for everything—rice, oil, sugar, tomato paste—since almost all foods are imported.

I spent some time at the rifle range, learning how to fire this big gun. I do not have to use it, now, thank God. I would do so if I had to defend my home, but it never comes to that. Troops are brought to Conakry from the interior, and the citizens of the town prove that they really are a people's militia. The mercenaries are pushed back. One day the big transport ship that brought them is gone. Many foreign soldiers are stranded. For a while there is sniper fire, and then, one by one, the mercenaries are found. The kids of Conakry are very active and they flush them out of many places. The women in the marketplace are very effective. The mercenaries get hungry and they try to buy some food. As soon as they pull out their foreign currency, the women shout: "Portuguese! Mercenary!" Between the kids and the market women, the invaders don't have a chance. They are captured.

▼▼▼▼▼

Stokely and I are back at the house, talking about the events. Now that we are safe, my main problem is getting a new windshield for the Volvo. I will have to send away to Sweden for one.

We sit and look out to sea, but there is a tension now in the view that was not there before. This tension will become less with time, but it will never go away, because Stokely has learned, and I have been reminded, that Africa is an unpredictable and violent place.

Guinea will not be invaded every day, but this scare has shown me that it is an illusion to think that I can find true peace here. This is because Guinea is friendly to me, but it is not my home. And true peace can only be found at home.

My home is South Africa. And so I have to ask myself a terrible question: Will I ever find peace in my lifetime? Will I ever go home?

14

MY GRANDDAUGHTER IS born at Mount Sinai hospital in New York on the eleventh of March, 1971. My gynecologist, Dr. Truppin, delivered the girl, as he delivered Lumumba before. I am traveling, but I come as soon as I can.

Bongi is so proud as she holds her tiny baby. She smiles at me. "I am naming her after you, Mama. I'm calling her Zenzi."

I am very happy. My name comes from *uzenzile*, the expression that means "you have no one but yourself to blame." When something goes wrong, I am always saying this to myself—*uzenzile!* —usually after the damage is done. But even if it is a bit strange, it is my name, and I am very pleased that Bongi should remember me like this.

But it hurts that such happy moments are fewer between us. When I arrive in New York, Bongi tells me that she and Nelson have gotten married. I am shocked to hear that they would do this and not tell me. I love my daughter, and I would have liked to have been a part of the wedding. In a quiet way I tell her this. But Bongi just laughs, a nasty laugh that mocks me.

"Oh, we just pulled a bum off the street to be the witness."

I am hurt, but I do not know what to do. Bongi not only makes me no part of her wedding ceremony, she also keeps me out of her married life. I can sense that she and Nelson are having problems. My daughter never went back to school after she had her first child at age seventeen. She took a course and became a court reporter. Nelson has a job with a collection agency. At least they have money to live on. But my daughter is confused and dissatisfied. I do not know the details about her life with Nelson, but I know it is not a happy life.

There is another reason for her unhappiness, I know. My daughter is feeling the effects of being taken from her home. Bongi is a South African girl. Our people and our ways cannot be found in America. The loss is terrible for me, and I know it must be terrible for her.

▼▼▼▼▼

Back when I was living in the U.S., I was asked to do benefits for civil rights groups. I sang for Dr. King's Southern Christian Leadership Conference, and for the NAACP. Now I am asked by another black leader, the Reverend Jesse Jackson, to come to New York for the founding of his new organization, People United to Save Humanity—PUSH. The American singer Aretha Franklin, whom I admire, is coordinating the guest list. After the Operation PUSH ceremony, she invites us to a birthday party she is throwing for herself at the Americana Hotel.

I wish her a happy birthday, and she says, "Miriam, I need your advice. I've been asked to go to South Africa."

In an instant my mask of sociability drops. When it comes to this subject, I am always very honest. The authorities back home love to gain status and boost their image by bringing international stars to perform in the clubs—clubs that are for whites only. The UN has finally applied limited sanctions against South Africa, and one of these forbids artists from performing there. But the Americans I speak to don't seem to know anything the UN does. I hope that Aretha does not want me to give her my blessing for her trip. But I don't have to worry; she seems to be sincerely concerned if it is right.

I tell her, "Aretha, you are the Queen—the Queen of Soul. You have a big name, and you are loved everywhere. I don't think you need a concert in South Africa. Whether you know it or not, you'd be helping the people who oppress our brothers and sisters. No artist can go to South Africa without getting dirty herself. It's true what they say, you can't roll around with pigs and not end up covered with mud."

Aretha understands. She tells her managers to turn down the offer. I have conversations like this with other artists.

But I am not long in the U.S. In London I give my first concert in England, at the Royal Albert Hall. It is *some* place, and, if I do say so, *some* concert. The reviewers are so enthusiastic that I have to be impressed with myself!

In Guinea I also perform. Visiting heads of state, because they know I now live in this country, ask Sékou Touré if I will sing for them. All these evenings are the same: a cocktail reception, dinner, and then everyone goes to the People's Palace. There are two dance troupes, the Ballet Africaine and the Djoliba Ballet, and together they make up the Guinea Ballet. These excellent and exciting dancers travel throughout Africa and the world. Before they perform at the People's Palace, a local group dances, and then I sing. My musicians are Guineans, now. I take them with me wherever I give a concert. All the artists in Guinea are civil servants. They are paid by the government to rehearse and to perfect their craft. They are paid whether they are working or not. President Touré's political party, the *Parti Democratique de Guinea*, feels strongly that it is necessary to revitalize African culture.

My musicians never studied music, just like me. But they are excellent, and with the permission of the Ministry of Youth, I borrow four of them—Kemo, Famoro, Amadou, and Abdu—from the national orchestras. My fifth musician, Sékou, is also from Guinea, though he has been living in the country of Liberia.

President Touré also invites me to march in the annual Independence Parade. This year, 1971, I have invited Letta M'Bulu to come from America and visit Guinea. She marches right beside me, and she is impressed by all the spectacle. The people love this holiday. They line the streets, everyone wearing white, and wave flags. Letta and I wear white dresses when we join the parade inside the stadium. The cheering, music, and spectacle are something for us to remember. The Guinean tribesmen from the countryside dance in their feathered costumes made from beautiful skins.

We have to dance, too, just looking at them. I look down at my moving feet. Usually, I wear high heels because I am short. I prefer flat shoes. I really prefer going barefoot. These shoes are flat, but they are white. I hate white shoes; they make my feet look big. I've got a nasty-looking foot. It's short, wide, with no arch. My mother used to tell me, "Oh, you poor child, you have ugly feet like your father." And it is the truth: If there is one thing that's ugly about me, it's my feet. My mother had pretty hands, pretty feet. *I'm* the performer; *I* should have such pretty hands and feet!

I guess I think of these things because in 1972 I turn forty. But the photographers are still all around me, taking pictures that will appear in the European magazines and on the covers of my albums, which are now recorded in France. I still like to experiment with my clothes and hairstyle. In Guinea there is a traditional way of wearing ladies' hair that has almost disappeared. It is called the Sahi ya maboho. The women today think it is old-fashioned. But I find it fascinating: The hair is braided over a wooden plate that is placed on its side on top the of the head, in the center. A friend jokes that a person looks like she is wearing the rudder of a boat. There is an old woman near my country house in Dalaba who knows how to do hair this way. I go to her, and when I return to Conakry, people are impressed. President Touré is very pleased that I have brought this traditional style back. He takes all the pictures I have just had made of myself—leaving me only one—and he places them in the guest houses where the heads of state stay.

At a dinner, President Touré gives me a compliment about the trends I start in his country, but only after he says his piece about women. "Women! You need ten pairs of shoes, but you can only wear one at a time. You need a big house, but you can only live in one room at a time."

He looks at me and says, "Anyway, you did help us here. Before you came, our women needed twelve yards of cloth to make a grand boubou that would drag in the back it was so long. When you came you had your simpler dress. You used three or four yards. And our women started copying you. It is good for us—we, the men, can pay less now for the material." And he laughs and laughs!

"You are going where, next, my sister?" he asks me.

"Cuba," I answer. "It will be my first time."

"Cuba! Say hello to our friend, Fidel!"

I promise, because it is Fidel Castro's officials who invite me to sing. The government arranges all the entertainments on the island. Stokely does not come with me on this trip, but I have my grandchildren. Lumumba is four years old now. He has a curiosity much larger than his size. And Baby Zenzi is one year old.

In Cuba, I see people working very hard to build up their country. They are isolated, here, and they have little. But with what little they have they are doing many beautiful things for themselves. The emphasis is on education for the kids. The children have everything they need. No matter how poor a child is, he can learn.

I once heard someone say about Cuba that there are only old buses driving around. I remember this when I hear Mr. Castro say in a speech, "We prefer to take lights to the villages and the schools than to have neon signs of publicity shining all over our streets. We prefer to have buses that can transport everybody than to have millions of cars in which we will not have anywhere to drive as time goes on—because we are a small country, an island!"

Mr. Castro attends some of my performances. After my last concert, I receive word that he would like to see me and the children. I do a TV show, and then I go from the studio to Mr. Castro's office with Lumumba and Zenzi. Mr. Castro always wears the same olive-green uniform. He does not have his famous cigar when he greets us.

Mr. Castro understands English, and he can speak it, too. But he won't. He prefers Spanish, and this is what he uses when he speaks to us through the interpreter.

First, Mr. Castro's minister of foreign affairs presents me with an honorary Cuban passport. I am always flattered when a country gives me a passport, but I know it is because they want to show solidarity with my people. It's symbolic. I made the decision to always talk about the problems of my homeland, so those governments that feel compassion toward my people and want freedom for my people take me as a representative of my brothers and sisters. Every time I receive an honorary passport from a country, I accept it in the name of my people. I do this now.

Mr. Castro gives Baby Zenzi a doll. The doll is bigger than she is! He shakes Lumumba's hand and gives him a little Cuban military uniform. It is a miniature of the type Mr. Castro wears himself. He also gives my grandson a toy machine gun.

But Lumumba is very bold. Something is bothering him. He looks up at the president with a frown.

"Are you a revolutionary?" he asks. Lumumba is only four, but he hears the word "revolution" all the time when he comes to Guinea—from Stokely, from President Sékou Touré. He knows what a revolutionary is.

"Yes," Mr. Castro says. "I am."

"I saw you on TV talking for your people?"

Mr. Castro nods his bearded head. "Yes, that was me."

"You fight for your people?"

"Yes."

Lumumba raises his voice. "You *kill* for your people?"

Mr. Castro looks at me, and then down at my grandson. "Yes."

I am embarrassed, and surprised. But I think they are good questions.

Lumumba is very confused. He twists his face and blurts, "Are you *white*?"

Poor Lumumba thinks that only a black man like Stokely or Sékou Touré can be a revolutionary. Mr. Castro sits down and puts Lumumba on his knee. My grandson's lower lip sticks out like a challenge. The president strokes Lumumba's head.

"Well, you see, young man, in Cuba, there are people from Africa. There are people from Spain. We are black and we are white. But we are all Cubans. And we are all revolutionaries."

Lumumba will have to think this over. We thank the president and go off to catch our plane to Berlin. I have an engagement to sing at the First World Youth Festival. My grandson wears his uniform on the plane. He holds tight his little machine gun. Before we arrive in Germany I want to take him to the back and dress him in his suit. But he will not take off the uniform. He howls until I leave him alone. He is a revolutionary!

East Berlin hosts the World Youth Festival, which is held in a different country every four years. I am to perform outdoors, at the Alexanderplatz. When the day arrives it is pouring rain. I leave Lumumba and Zenzi at the hotel, and I go alone, expecting the show to be canceled. But it is not. When I arrive, the place is *packed*. The rain pours down on the audience, but nobody moves. I wish they would leave, but they don't, so I go on. In a few minutes I am sopping wet. The beads that click at the ends of my hair braids drip water. I'm scared to death of the microphone. I'm afraid I'll get shocked. But I always do my best when I sing, and today is no exception. My set lasts an hour. Before I finish they bring a canopy, too late to do much good. When I leave the stage, the audience cheers. The festival officials are so grateful that I was not intimidated by the weather that they say they hope I will be part of the World Youth Festivals from now on. Drying myself, I say that I will try.

But there are other places this year where my reception is much less kind. In Denmark, I finally get to perform in Copenhagen. I remember the last time I was booked in this city, I got terribly sick and Bob Schwaid, my manager then, had to cancel the show. My appearance now is received with much enthusiasm by the Danish audiences. It is wonderful how my African music is accepted in such different countries: in Cuba, Germany, and now Denmark.

My musicians and I prepare to leave the theater after the show. But when I step out of my dressing room there are three men waiting for me.

"We have come to take the money that you earned tonight."

This is so crazy that I don't know what to think. Are these men bandits? I ask, "Who are you?"

One man says, "I am the promoter of the show that you failed to appear in. You took my deposit, and never sent it back. Now, give me the money."

I have an envelope of bills given to me by the concert promoter, and these men, one of whom is a policeman, look as if they are going to jump me. Fortunately, my musicians gather around. I say, "Please, I did not take your money."

Since I do not book myself, I explain, only my old manager could straighten this out. I start to leave, but the men try to block me. My musicians form a wedge around me, and we break through. The hotel is across the street from the theater. There is a girl there who is looking after Lumumba and Baby Zenzi. I tell her to take good care of my grandchildren, because something awful is happening. There is a commotion outside. The police have been called, and the photographers. I give the concert money to a friend who lives in Denmark, and ask him to take it to his house for safekeeping. This is done just in time, because there is a knock on the door.

The Danish police do not play. They *drag* me to a police car. My Guinean musicians are angry; they shout and curse. When a photographer runs alongside to take a picture of me, one of the musicians knocks him down. The girl who is minding my grandchildren picks up the camera and she is going to throw it on the ground.

"No, no, no, don't do that!" I say. I am afraid that they will be arrested, too. "You all just go back in the hotel."

Once again, little Miriam is the public enemy. I am driven to a woman's prison with two policemen on either side of me. They walk me up to the fourth floor, where I am locked up in a tiny cell. I look around in the gloomy light. There is just a basin to wash your face, and a little bed. When I try to sit on it, the bed goes down like a hammock. I say to myself, "What should I do? Sleep? Cry? Sit? Well, the night is long."

I sit on a chair and stare at nothing. "My God, even in Denmark, Miriam has to go to jail! And for what?"

Every hour a woman guard comes by. "Why don't you sleep?" Finally, I say to her, "I can't sleep on this thing. So, just leave me alone because I'm not going to run out of here and jump from the fourth floor!"

At dawn somebody comes by and drops in a tray. Coffee and brown bread. I don't even look at it: I don't care for coffee or breakfast, anyway. I check my little watch. It is seven in the morning. At quarter to nine, I am taken away to what is said to be a court of law.

When I enter the room, I see the same three men who confronted me last night—only one of the men, the one who I thought was a police officer, turns out to be the judge. I look at him, and I say, "Oh, wow! Even in South Africa it is not like this. I've never seen the policeman who comes to arrest you be your judge the next day."

"Quiet, prisoner!" They tell me that if I don't give them their money, I will be sent back to jail.

"I don't care. I will go there. I never took anybody's money."

"Well, your managers did."

"Why don't you go after them? After all these years! I'm not going to give you money I did not take."

They ask me what happened last night. "I'm not going to answer that because the man who knows what happened yesterday is the very man sitting there who is supposed to be my judge!"

There is a recess, but they do not permit me to see any of my people. I would love to have one of my musicians outside get me something to eat. And I would like some word of my grand-children. This is the one thing that bothers me the most, this separation from Lumumba and Zenzi.

I am told that the ambassador from Guinea has arrived. They will not let me see him. Ambassador Seydou Kerta works out of Rome, and he represents Guinea to many European nations. When I was arrested, the news got on the radio. President Touré always works late at night, and the radio was on in his office. He heard the story, and he telephoned Ambassador Kerta to tell him to go to Copenhagen right away. When I see him, it is in the court, after the recess.

"How much is this money?" the ambassador asks the court. He is not happy, and he gets angrier when the promoters go from one figure to another: It is six thousand; no, four thousand; no, five thousand.

"Goddammit, how much is it!" Ambassador Kerta finally yells. "I am ready to pay whatever it is. This woman is worth every-thing to us. She is very dear to the African people, especially in Guinea. She does not have to be treated like this."

He points out that because I am traveling on a Guinean diplo-matic passport, my arrest was illegal in the first place. But I am just glad when the amount they ask is settled at four thousand, and this is paid by the ambassador. I rush out to see my grandchildren.

I am to go to Algeria, and Mr. Kerta will not let me leave him until he takes me all the way there and gives me to another Guinean ambassador. Then he returns to Rome to file his report. I finish my tour, and then reimburse the Guinean government for the money they put up to keep me out of prison. It is a strange experience; one that showed me that no place is free from danger. Who can blame me for being nervous, when I suddenly find myself being whisked away to jail in Copenha-gen, of all places, and for somebody else's mistake?

Of course, Guinea is never entirely free from danger. Stokely and I are passengers in President Touré's motorcade, which is greeting a visiting head of state, the President of Zambia. The drive is slow when we move from the airport. Along the road, people dressed in white are cheering. As usual, President Touré drives himself in the convertible car in front. In the passenger's seat, where he can be seen by the people, is Zambia's president. I can see President Touré ahead, waving his handkerchief to the crowd. Suddenly, a man runs out and jumps into the car. There is a quick glimmer as sunlight flashes on a raised knife. I shout. Sékou Touré is not a tall man, but he is big, and broad in the shoulders. He also knows judo. He throws out his attacker. The man lands on the pavement, where a policeman shoots him. This all happens so fast I cannot believe it. By night, some people are arrested, but nothing in the schedule of events changes. I still sing for the President of Zambia; the Guinean Ballet performs; and at the reception, all is normal.

▼▼▼▼▼

Sékou Touré is not a capitalist, and for this reason he does not congratulate me or say anything when I do finally get to open my own business. He knows about it, of course. He knows everything that happens in his country. Zambezi is the name of my boutique. I named it after the river in Rhodesia that has the Victoria Falls. Ladies come expecting to find outfits like the ones Miriam Makeba wears, but they will not.

I sell baby clothes. There is a real need, because such things are very hard to get here. My suppliers are from Spain and East Germany, and my prices are very low. I feel so sorry for the poor women who come in and just stare at the merchandise that I lower the prices even more. I am not a good businesswoman. People know this, and they come in, buy things, and take their purchases to other stores that resell them for higher prices. I put a stop to women who buy in bulk, but whoever is controlling them just sends in different women each time to buy and buy. I see my things down the street at a markup. But my store is doing all right, and the poor ladies have somewhere to shop.

▼▼▼▼▼

Ever since they were born, I have taken my grandchildren for weeks and months at a time. I love to travel with them, and Bongi does not mind. She loves Lumumba and Baby Zenzi, as anyone can see, but motherhood is hard for her. Her marriage is hard, too, although she loves Nelson very much. There is something very troubling about their relationship, and I am frustrated, because she keeps things from me. But a long series of problems finally catches up with her, and one winter day early in 1974, she wakes the children up early in the morning, dresses them, and takes them out into the cold to find a taxi. When they locate one, it drives her away from her married life.

I am in London, on tour. Bongi comes to me and tells me about her separation. I support her as best I can, and agree to take the children. Bongi is very upset. Nelson was the first man she knew. Somehow, she must try to sort things out with him.

In Liberia I have found a very dear friend, Gertrude Brewer. I call her Sister Gertie, and she really is my sister. She is also a botanist. We walk through her garden in Liberia, and she tells me the names of all the plants and trees. I cannot remember them, and I admire her for her knowledge. There is a private school where she lives that teaches in English. Sister Gertie agrees to take Lumumba, who is now eight, and Zenzi, who is five, while they go to school here. I am very grateful.

When we are alone, I have a serious talk with my daughter. It is clear that no matter what she says about Nelson, she is deeply in love with him. I hope that now that she is back in Africa with her own people, she will begin to rediscover herself and become less confused. Bongi tells me that she really wants to pursue a musical career. She has never stopped writing poems and songs. She says she wants to study. Bongi is only twenty-four, and she is so slim and lovely she could be a model. Her voice is lovely, too. I encourage her to give it a try.

I think that maybe, since she has the soul of an artist, Bongi might have felt stifled by her married life in New York. But at least she was stable during those years. That is about to change; and it is about to change disastrously.

15

In FEBRUARY OF 1975 I RE-
turn to New York for a Saint Valentine's Day concert at Lincoln
Center. It has been seven years since I left the United States. In
that time, young people have grown up who have never heard
of me. There has not been a month when I have not been
performing somewhere. But not here, and this place, the second
country from which I have been put into exile, is special. The
U.S. is the capital of the entertainment world. You can make it
anywhere, but if you do not make it here, you are not truly an
international star. For ten years I was so big in America that they
knew me everywhere I went. Now I visit New York, and I am a
stranger. It is sad, but do I not dwell on it.

Some performers are "on" twenty-four hours a day. But for
me, for the two hours only that I am doing a show, I am a star.
As soon as I get off, I leave that coat on stage. I put on my
ordinary coat. I have known entertainers who have really flipped:
One day people are asking for your autograph, and the next
time they just look at you as if they do not know you. A person
who has known what it's like to be a star has got to be very
strong to take that kind of thing and not crack up. Some artists
who have been up there turn to drugs and alcohol when the
time comes for them to hit the earth again.

But for me, I have always known what goes up must come
down. And vice versa. For instance, my people cannot be kept
down forever. And sooner or later, I will return to the U.S.,

when they forgive me for marrying the man I love. I do not have a great big ego, although I do have some pride and some good feelings about myself. These I must have, if I want to survive.

The concert at Lincoln Center is like a glimpse of what once was and what may be again. Tickets are sold out weeks in advance, not long after the announcement is made that I will be appearing. When I arrive at the dressing room, I can barely see the mirror because of all the flowers of well-wishers. Friends and musicians I know show up by the dozen, and the reception afterward is a real reunion. I tell them that I miss New York, which is true, and they tell me that they miss me, which I think is also true.

I am to live in the city for three months this year, but not as a singer. President Touré asks me to be one of the Guinean delegates to the United Nations. One by one, as the African nations have become free, I have gotten to know their delegates, some as friends. I am very honored to join them. But I do not kid myself: I am not a diplomat and I do not know the first thing about this important work.

There is no need to worry. The Guinean ambassador to the UN is one of the most impressive women I have ever met. My boss, Jeanne Martin, who is in her fifties, is also one of the most respected of African women. Dark-skinned and in her colorful dresses, the swirling fabrics of the grand boubou, she passes through the corridors of the UN headquarters with great dignity and assurance. With one look, people know that this is *somebody*. Her intelligence is second to none. Guinea, and the African people in general, are well-served by her.

Every morning, I leave my apartment, which is owned by Guinea, and I go to Jeanne Martin's office at the UN. She assigns each delegate to a committee. I always go where I am told, although when I get there I am as lost as a sheep in the subway. I sigh when Jeanne says, "Today, Miriam, we need you at Maritime Regulations," or "Global Ecology," or "the Special Hearing on Monetary Reform." My head spins, and it goes around faster when I attend the meetings and try to take notes. I sit for hours hearing about the reunification of Korea, and getting a headache, and asking myself, "Why am I here?"

The next morning, I am to say what went on at the meeting I

attended. At the end of three months, a big report about the session is prepared for President Touré.

"I'm sorry," I have to apologize to my fellow delegates, "but I honestly didn't understand a word that was said."

Jeanne laughs. "Nothing at all?"

"I'm afraid not."

The other delegates crack up, but they are kind to me.

I begin to worry that I am only window dressing here. I see Pearl Bailey in the halls, and we chat. She is another celebrity delegate, with the United States. But she is always active and doing things. I admire her. Sékou Touré told me that he wants me, as an artist, to learn the political side of things, since this is a way for me to also help my people. But I would like to make a contribution.

And then, my reason for being here is given to me. Ambassador Martin tells me that President Touré wants me to deliver the annual Guinean speech to the General Assembly, a speech that is usually given by a nation's foreign minister.

"When you speak," Jeanne says, "you will, just by your presence, bring the problems of South Africa to the forefront."

The words are the government's, not mine, but there is a condemnation of apartheid in the speech. The day I face the General Assembly I have to wonder if I have ever been so scared in my life. The room is huge. I look out and see all of these people from every nation in the world; not to mention the press and the small army of interpreters behind the long windows on the sloping walls above. Kurt Waldheim, the secretary general, introduces me, and the applause gives me a little boost. But I am very nervous. When I give a concert, I suffer stage fright every time. The musicians behind me are a comfort, and I already know the songs. This is something else.

The microphones pick up my quiet voice, and my words are translated into other languages. The delegates hear me talk about the problems of Africa, the accomplishments of the nationalist movement, and the need for the superpowers to aid us and, at the same time, leave us alone. When I begin to speak about apartheid, more emotion must creep into my voice, because the delegates interrupt with applause. When it is all over, they give me an ovation. I bow to these men and women who have the difficult job of keeping the world at peace.

As a diplomat, I am beginning to lose my amateur ranking. I now travel with the diplomatic passports from eight countries. Shortly after Angola receives its independence, I am invited to this new nation by President Neto. It has sort of become a little tradition in Africa: Become free, and have Miriam come and sing.

For a month and a half I travel all over the country, along with the Guinean Ballet. There is no admission charge for the people. The government is paying for everything. This is a troubled country that I am visiting. The civil war is very violent. I am awakened one night by gunfire. Outside our house, some rebels and soldiers are shooting at each other. Whistling bullets hit the outside walls. *Ping!* The original owners of this villa fled during some earlier fighting, and the governor of the district put us up here. My musicians and some members of a Guinean film crew that is with us come in. "Don't nobody go to sleep and leave me!" I cry. I am scared. We stay up all night playing cards.

We perform at places where no one has ever seen a show before. In one country hall, there is a riot that ends in tragedy. The place is packed, and the people outside begin to push to get in. The dancers and I are not yet in costume when we hear noise and shouting. We come outside into a nightmare. People are running, falling. Children are being trampled. When it is over, thirty people are dead. Nobody thinks about performing, we just rush to help the injured. The dancers and I work to separate the bodies and free the people who are trapped. Children's shoes and books are all over, and some girls, crying, pick these up. Doctors come to treat the injured. I hear a woman's voice. "Which one is Miriam Makeba?"

"I am Miriam Makeba," I say. The woman is dying. Blood flows from her mouth and from wounds that I can see through her torn skirt. "How can I help you?"

But she only wants to look at me. I fear it is the last sight that she will see. Nothing like this has ever happened anyplace where I have sung. The concert is not canceled; that would cause another disturbance. But it is very, very hard for me to go on. It's about the hardest thing I have ever done. I keep seeing the bodies on the ground, and that poor, torn, dying woman.

▼▼▼▼▼

Usually when I meet a nation's leader, I am shy. I answer yes or no, and then I am on my way. But President Samora Machel of Mozambique and his wife Graça are different. I am invited to the independence celebration of their country. I am part of the Guinean delegation; in another trip I will come back to sing. The Machels put me in their guest villa, and I am more free with them than with any head of state, except President Touré. Graça Machel is a lively little woman. She brings her children over, and they are so well-behaved that they listen while the mother and I have our chat. Her husband speaks Zulu, so at dinner we talk merrily away in my native tongue.

Getting to the independence ceremony is difficult. The new nation, which has been devastated by its war of independence, does not have the skills to coordinate all the elements of a pageant. There is no transport, and we have to walk through the mud to get to the stadium. I am thinking, "What kind of trouble is this? Walking through the mud?"

But when we arrive, everything is wonderful. Graça Machel may be a small woman, but she charges up the people when she speaks. Fifty thousand of her countrymen stand up and cheer. She encourages women to work, and she says that independence does not mean we can sit down. Now is the time for the people to really be working to build a nation.

This country is on the northeast border of South Africa. Being here brings me closer to my home than I have been in sixteen years. But when I return to my hotel, I find that I am closer than I think. I get a call from the police.

"There is a man here who is under arrest for entering the country illegally. He has come from South Africa without a passport. He says he is your brother."

I just about drop the phone. "My brother!"

A voice comes on that I do not remember. It has been a long time, and I am suspicious of tricks. I am suspicious of anything that comes from South Africa, and I think I have good reason.

I say, "What is your name?"

"It's Joseph, Miriam."

I do not feel anything.

"Your African name?"

"Mefika."

Oh! "Brother, what did you call me when I was small?"

"Kiri!"

Yes! The *knobkierrie*; the skinny little body with the great big head. I scream. I cry. I beg him to come to the hotel right away.

The police oblige, and soon my brother and I are together. I do not eat or sleep this night. I can barely talk because I am crying so much, seeing a member of my family after so, so long. I touch his face and hands and hair. I kiss him and hold him. He is older, and a little gray. But he is still good-looking, still tall, and he is still my Joseph. Joseph Mefika Mahlangu. His name Mefika means "one who just arrived." And this arrival of his is the happiest I have ever known. I am so surprised that I even forget to ask how our mother died.

Joseph says, "I heard on the radio that you would be here. And I came."

Our life together comes back to me. I remember when he was gone from the family for a long time. I was a girl, fourteen years old. My mother's oldest sister, who lived in the black township of Orlando East, told us that Joseph was living in Orlando West. He was there to get a job. I went to Johannesburg, all alone, to find him. My brother came back and I was sitting on his porch. I was scared, and I was crying. "Please, please come home. Everybody wants you to come home." Joseph was very touched, and he came home with me.

Now, it hurts that he is the one who has come to find me, and I cannot come home with *him*. I even have to leave before he does, because I am part of the Guinean delegation. It hurts me so to go away. I beg all the officials to see that my brother gets home all right. It was very brave of him to come. I cry and cry when we say good-bye. Will it be another sixteen years before I can see him again? Everything I have I give him to take back to his family. My jewelry, my clothes, even my suitcases I give him to bring to his wife and children. When I get back to Guinea, I have nothing. I have nothing but a memory of my surprise reunion with my brother Joseph. It is like something from a dream, or a moment of warmth in the chill of an exile's nightmare.

▼▼▼▼▼

Bongi goes to visit Sister Gertie in Monrovia so she can get a divorce and put an end to her marriage with Nelson. Their differences cannot be mended, although it is clear that she still loves him, because she seems to look for Nelson in each new man she sees. In Liberia, a person can obtain a one-party divorce. A notice is put in the newspaper for three weeks. If the other party wants to contest the divorce, he or she has this time to do it. Nelson is not going to read a Liberian paper. But even if he did, he would not respond.

Bongi's behavior is growing more and more disturbing. Her mood swings are like a little child's. One moment she is happy and singing, and the next moment she is throwing a terrible tantrum. When she comes to Guinea, she is upset by the sight of so many poor people. But the sight makes her generous. She goes to the hospital and brings food to the sick. She gives away clothes to strangers on the street. I am happy to see her open her heart this way, even if the clothes she hands out she gets by raiding my closet and taking anything she wants. What truly bothers me, and makes me suffer, is when she comes flying through the house, nervous and high-strung, and shouting, "I hate this place! I've got to get out! I'm suffocating!"

Bongi abuses everyone when she is in one of her moods. Her bad behavior is so sudden and ugly that we are shocked. What makes her act this way? I thank God that the children are away at school, because when they have seen their mother like this they became confused and upset. I decide I must try to get my daughter some help.

But she is like a hummingbird that will not stay put. She is always here and there. She shows up at a rehearsal with my musicians, and I see that she is close to my percussionist, Papa. He is a fantastic conga drummer.

I tell her, "Look, you must not meet with the musicians, because it is not good for our working relationship."

Bongi laughs. I am too late. She is already pregnant. This time, she does not act guilty or cry when she tells me.

My family has no secrets from President Touré. He considers us part of his own family. He has known that Bongi is disturbed, and he offers to help. There is an excellent psychiatric hospital in Algeria. He arranges for my daughter to go there. The president really does his best for her. When Bongi makes the trip, she stays as a guest in the Guinean Embassy. But pregnancy just makes her torments worse. She throws such a fit that everyone is afraid she will hurt the baby. And after one of her tantrums, she just leaves.

When Bongi returns to Guinea, she acts perfectly normal. She goes to see Andrée Touré, the president's wife, and she apologizes for causing embarrassment for the Guineans in Algeria. Andrée and Bongi are friends, and it pleases me that my daughter has this lady to talk to.

A boy child is born, and Bongi names him Themba, which means "hope." In Guinea, even if a man is not married to a woman, he at least makes what is called a *baptême*, which is a baptism. The man says, "I acknowledge the child, and give him my name." But Papa does not do this. He refuses to recognize the child.

I worry how Bongi will take care of the baby, because her behavior has been so unpredictable. And then I come home to find that my daughter has disappeared, and so has my grandson. I search everywhere. But I cannot find her in Conakry, or anywhere in Guinea. Finally, Sister Gertie in Liberia says that Bongi is in the capital, Monrovia. Since she left me without a word, I do not know what to expect, but I take Papa with me so we can both talk to her.

Bongi has rented a room in somebody's house. When we get there, she is not at home. But there is Themba, alone, lying in a basket. There is a woman somewhere else in the house whom Bongi asked to look after the baby. I am shocked by this negligence, and I take Themba with me. Papa leaves word with the woman to tell Bongi that we are baby-sitting.

When Bongi comes to us, she is *mad*. "How dare you steal my child!"

Papa and I have been talking, and he is firm but understanding when he speaks to her. "You know, you should let your mother take the child with her. We found him lying in a little basket and you were not there. So, if the baby is with your mother, it's better for you and better for the baby."

After we discuss this for a while, Bongi agrees. I take my grandson home to Guinea, and there he stays for a few weeks. One day, Bongi comes back and takes the baby. She again leaves the country with him. I am sick with worry, because she does not tell me anything. Then the company I record with in Paris, Disques Espérance, gets a call from her: She is in Sierra Leone and she needs two tickets to Paris. The company sends them to her, and they phone me to be reimbursed. This is how I discover where she is. But who is the second ticket for? A friend in Paris tells me that Bongi is living with a man from Guinea.

My record company calls again: Bongi says the baby needs winter clothes. She asks for funds that could outfit a dozen babies. Because I know that my daughter is disturbed, I approve the funds. She still won't talk to me. Bongi's requests to my record company for money become more and more frequent. Finally, they call and say the Guinean man is always phoning and demanding money. I tell the company: no more. I am really suffering now. It sickens me to think that my daughter is using my grandchild to extort money for her friend. I know that if I go to her she will get mad, but I feel I must.

But Bongi does not throw a fit. She is glad to see me. The man is not around, so I don't have to worry about hitting him with a skillet and maybe hurting my wrist.

"Let's go home, Bongi."

She says quietly, "All right, Mama."

It is not long before the cycle begins all over again: the storms, the calm; the days of happiness and generosity and the days of tantrums and abuse. I love my daughter, and I am afraid for her.

Lumumba is eight, now, and Baby Zenzi is five. They come to Guinea on their school vacations. A friend of the family, Philemon Hou, who is a musician from South Africa, teaches them a little poem of his. Stokely likes it, and whenever we sit down to dinner, he recites it with the children like a grace, and they clap their hands to the rhythm.

> *We are an African People*
> *An African People!*
> *An African People!*
> *We are an African People*
> *And don't you forget it!*

When I take the children back to school in Monrovia, I thank Sister Gertie. "They have such wonderful manners. And they owe it to you."

To show my thanks, I take Sister Gertie with me to Cuba, where I am asked to sing at the second World Youth Festival. Nations from all over march in the opening ceremony, and we see displays of the things that young people do: dance, acrobatics, music and art. My friend is thrilled by the trip. "I am the first Liberian ever to go to Cuba!" she says.

There is another return trip for me this year; one that is not so happy. The United Nations has declared 1976 the "International Year Against Apartheid." President Touré feels that it is appropriate for me to again give the Guinean address to the General Assembly. Once more I face the delegates, the press, the visitors. But there is added interest this year. There is an urgency and emotion in my voice and in the reception I receive that was not there last year. This is because my people have suffered the worst massacre that anyone has known in my lifetime. A new word enters the consciousness of the West, and from now on it will be associated with oppression, outrage, and blood. It is Soweto.

All of the black townships that are together in the southwest section of Johannesburg—Orlando East, Mofolo, White City, and the rest—are called Soweto. That is what Soweto stands for: South Western Townships. The word did not exist when I was growing up, but all of the inhuman treatments that make up our way of life were well known. Sixteen years ago, in Sharpeville, a march was held to protest the Passbook Law. This ended in slaughter, and the people were so intimidated that for years there was silence.

This ends with a great uprising that is started by the students. These are the young people who represent the first generation to suffer under Bantu Education. They see the hopelessness of their lives and the oppression all around them. In many families, the children take the lead in the fight for liberation.

A son will say, "Father, I beg you, please do not go to work today. Join the strike. Otherwise, my friends will burn our house down. And I won't be here. I'll be out burning down the house of another who won't observe the strike."

I am in Mozambique when I hear the news over the radio. The uprising spreads throughout the townships, and violence by the government does not stop it. Each day I expect it to be over, and I am awed when it goes on and on. President Machel and his wife have me as their guest while I perform. At dinner we sing revolutionary songs and have fun. But our good times are cut short by the news at home. I go from Mozambique to Europe for a concert, and there I see the first pictures of the revolt. The tear gas, the shootings and burnings: It is shocking. I am scared because I do not know if any of my family is involved. Two of my uncles died at Sharpeville. I wonder how many are suffering, now. Not knowing makes it worse.

The students who started the uprising must flee South Africa. They are many, and they are scattered all over the world. It breaks my heart when I see the unhappiness of their lives, the sadness of their exile. Many of these young men and women find their way to me. I see them in airports, at concerts, on the streets. I listen to their stories and try to help them any way I can. As the years go by, many of them will come and stay with me.

The Soweto uprising never really stops. The authorities declare that "peace is restored," but from now on movement against the Pretoria regime grows. It is not as it was after Sharpeville. Now, the people do not rest. They get shot at, but they still go out. This is new and surprising for the authorities, and from this moment they will have to sleep with one eye open.

$\blacktriangledown\blacktriangledown\blacktriangledown\blacktriangledown\blacktriangledown$

16

$\blacktriangle\blacktriangle\blacktriangle\blacktriangle\blacktriangle$

IT IS 1977, AND I AM IN NI-
geria for Festac, a festival of arts for black people from all over
the world. Since I am African, they ask me to be a hostess.
Stevie Wonder arrives from America, and I am asked to take care
of him. Stevie remembers me from the Copacabana show of his
when I gave him an African statue because I admired him. I
admire him still, and he is quite a success. Stevie is looking like
an African, now, his hair all braided with beads. For the month
that we are together, I am his guide. I will see that he has all he
needs during his stay.

"Miriam," he says, "I love you!"

"*What?* Stevie, I am old enough to be your mother."

"Miriam, age ain't nothin' but a number."

We all laugh, and I go home, thinking, "*Age ain't nothin' but a
number.*" But age is other things, too. It is wisdom, if one has
lived one's life properly. It is experience and knowledge. And it
is getting to know all the ways the world turns, so that if you
cannot turn the world the way you want, you can at least get out
of the way so you won't get run over.

But what have I to tell Stevie about the ways of the world? He
is on top of it. His album, *Songs in the Key of Life*, has been
nominated for seven Grammy awards. But he does not want to
leave Festac to attend the Grammy show in Los Angeles. I am in
my hotel room when we come up with an idea. Suppose I find a

way to get a TV hookup here in Nigeria so he can give his acceptance speech in Africa and be seen in America live?

Much work must be done to accomplish this. I go to the nation's Ministry of Information, and ask to arrange a satellite connection. "Festac is a festival of all black people around the world," I tell the officials. "But it's ignored by the world press. To get them to take notice, we need a personality like Stevie Wonder, who is loved everywhere."

It is agreed, and a hookup is made at the National Theater. Other artists are performing right up to the time of the awards show, which we watch on monitors. Stevie wins his Grammies, and the people in the U.S. are impressed to see him saying his thank yous from the other side of the world. The setup is considered very innovative and daring. Stevie thanks me. I was glad to help, because he is one artist who always gives of himself for not only black causes but causes for all people.

Festac is a lot of work, and I am tired when I return to Guinea. There is a ballet performance at the People's Palace, and I have been invited. But I do not attend because I am sick. It is one time that I am thankful to be ill. When President Touré enters the theater, an assassin throws two hand grenades at him. One goes off to his right and explodes, killing a man and wounding a woman. The second lands at the President's feet, but it does not explode. Several people are injured in the panic that follows. But Sékou Touré is all right. His luck is amazing.

▼▼▼▼▼

I introduced Hugh Masekela and Letta M'Bulu to my audiences, and they were well received. Now I introduce another young talent to my audiences, and she, too, is well received. I was happy for Hugh and Letta, but for my own daughter, Bongi, I am both happy and relieved. She is serious about her music, and I encourage her when I see this is giving her life a direction. I do not know if singing is the cure to what is ailing Bongi, but I hope it will help her.

The work that Bongi has put into her singing is paying off. She is a natural performer. Her voice can be sweet or jazzy. She has her own sound, which is not a copy of mine. Her stage movements are also her own. When I start giving her a song to do in my concerts, she pulls it off with confidence. The ovations she receives are encouraging. She really does have talent.

So, I think, "Good for her! Maybe she will take off this way."
In Paris, the reviews are wonderful, and she shows them around.
Everyone is happy for her. My record company wants Bongi to
consider a deal with them.

I guess I am a little nervous when Bongi tells me she wants to
come out from under my wing and go out on her own. She must
do this sooner or later, and I say that I will always be here if she
needs me.

Meanwhile, I have her one-year-old son Themba to take care
of. And I have adopted a South African girl. I met Muntu
Mvuyana in Lagos, Nigeria. She was an orphan there with no
papers, and I brought her back to Guinea. She is a lovely girl in
her twenties who likes it here. Muntu gives me a nickname:
Mazi. "Ma," from mama, and "zi" from my name Zenzi. The
nickname catches on quickly. Soon the students who stay with
me, the help around the house, everyone calls me Mazi.

There is a Guinean boy named Ousmane who comes to us and
soon becomes one of the family. He runs errands, fixes things,
and does all sorts of chores to help out. Ousmane is one of those
big, lovable boys who is always smiling, and who makes you
want to smile, too. But usually it is hard for me to have servants,
because I have spent so much time cleaning house myself that I
can't stand just sitting around while they work. I have to work,
too, and I get so involved I end up working more than the
people I am paying.

▼▼▼▼▼

My grandchildren Lumumba and Zenzi have gone to school in
Zaria, Nigeria, for a year. I visit them on my way to a concert in
Angola that I must do with the Guinean female orchestra, the
Amazons de Guinea, and the Ballet Africaine. The Ballet Africaine,
which does the traditional dances in traditional costumes, is not
only the best in Africa, it is versatile. When we tour Angola as a
present from Sékou Touré to mark the conclusion of that poor
country's civil war, the dancers have to build our stage at a
former drive-in movie theater. I help. Why not, when I can drive
a nail as well as the next person?

President Neto, his wife, and their children have me as a guest
in their house during the Angolan trip. The Netos are very polite
people. They invite me to breakfast, and they will not eat until I

eat. Breakfast is one meal that I never eat, and I have to force myself the first day. The second day I am more miserable; my stomach just won't take the food. On the third day I beg them to excuse me, that I don't eat breakfast but, please, please, eat without me. I am grateful for their hospitality, and it is very sad when, a few weeks after I leave the country, the President dies.

In Cannes, I have been invited to sing at a banquet of the MIP TV, an organization of all the color television stations that use the French system. I take Bongi with me, and she sings, too. It is at Cannes that I meet the great American writer James Baldwin. He is the type of person I meet again and again during my travels, and we are always happy to see each other. His sister I know, too. She is married to a man in Sierra Leone, in West Africa south of Guinea. In New York, she and her husband have a house next to the Guinean residence where the ambassador lives.

This is the year, 1978, when Stokely and I celebrate our tenth wedding anniversary. This will also be our last anniversary. If I were to say it has not been an exciting and sometimes painful ten years, I would be lying. But none of the pain has been Stokely's doing. Considering all the traveling that we both do, and the time that we are away from each other, and the fact that he *is* a good-looking man, people are amazed that he does not chase after the women here in Guinea. If he did, I would not fall to pieces, because men are known to be naughty. But usually when Stokely comes home from his travels he is so tired he sits down and reads his books. He does not have the time to go around and do those mischievous things that most men do.

So, for ten years, I do not worry. And then the ten years end. There comes another woman, a Guinean woman. Stokely does not just have an affair with her. Affairs come and go. I would have been hurt if he had done this, but it would not be the end. What happens is more serious. My husband falls in love with the woman. This love of his is so great that he takes chances for it, and he does things that would seem foolish for a man who has far less intelligence than Stokely has.

It is one thing for a man to go to his mistress's place, and another thing for him to bring her to his wife's house. For me, this makes all the difference in the seriousness of the affair and it also shows how much the man respects his wife. Stokely begins to take advantage of my trips out of the country. One time he takes his woman up to my home in the mountains for an entire week. He brings our young friend Ousmane to cook for them. Guinea is a Muslim country where polygamy is common, so Ousmane does not see anything wrong with a man having more than one woman.

When Stokely starts to bring her to our house, he is so out of his mind that he does not see that she is planting things. I come home and I see the traces: a shoe I don't know who it belongs to. A comb. I think, "This chick, here, she does this on purpose." She is sending a message.

I do not have to ask Stokely anything. I am not a stupid woman, and I can see why he has become more distant. My first reaction is to be very charitable: I think, these two people love each other very much. I do not want to stand in anybody's way.

And then the bad part hits: I realize I have lost my husband. When you love a person and you are together so long, you grow to depend on that person. I depend on Stokely. How could he do this to me? I have sacrificed so much for our love.

The hurt is very bad for me. I have lost my man to a younger woman. I am forty-six. I have lost him to a woman who can give him children. I am barren. To stop the tears, I tell myself, "Goddammit, it's happening. You'll hurt for a little while, but time heals all wounds." I can bully myself by talking this way all night long, but I cannot stop the hurt.

When Stokely comes, I tell him, "Get out." He packs his things and leaves. To be suddenly separated from someone you have been close to for so long is difficult. I have to force myself to be strong. "I'll start my life again," I say. "It'll be all right."

President Touré does not want to give us a divorce. It was to him I went to receive a blessing when I first married Stokely, and he acts like a father toward us. Stokely's mother, Mae Charles, also will not give us her blessing for a divorce. She and I are very close. She does not blame me for not fighting to get my husband back, but she always asks me why I allowed it to happen. I can only say that I am used to being where I am wanted, and I never force myself on anyone.

President Touré drags his feet for so long that I finally have to go to his office and be bold. "Please, I *want* my divorce."

He agrees without pleasure. "All right. Go see the prime minister. He'll arrange it."

I never have to go to court. It is all handled for me. Stokely speaks to someone in the government, and they give him a house in Villa Andreé, where we both first lived. I stay in our new place at Villa Camayene.

I find things to do. My boutique for baby clothes only lasted two years before the government banned private enterprises of this sort. I have been thinking of opening an entertainment club, but thoughts are all that this has been up to now. And there is my singing, always my singing. My concerts do not stop, not for divorce or for anything. The people want to see me, and I want to give the people my message.

▼▼▼▼▼

"I was sorry to hear about you and Stokely."

"Thank you, Big Brother."

Mr. Belafonte and I had our "divorce" twelve years ago. We are together again as guests of the Cuban Youth Festival. We are formal toward each other, but it cannot be said that we are enemies. It is strange what time can do: As the years grow old, big things seem small and horrible things seems less evil. Big Brother has put on a little weight, and a little gray, but so have I.

"You are an African, again," he says.

"I have always been an African."

And this I have been, for better or worse. It is never easy living in Africa. The politics, the poverty, the terrible diseases are all hard on the soul. It takes courage, hope, and real love for the land and the people to live here. But since I have these things, I continue to make this place my home.

Lumumba and Zenzi come to live with me in Guinea for good, now. Bongi lives here, but she is hardly ever at home. She is always everywhere. Audrey Minot has opened a school, and Lumumba, who is eleven, and Zenzi, who is eight, enroll as students.

My youngest grandson, Themba, has just turned three years old. We have a birthday party for him, and I ask all the kids his size to come. Themba dances all day with this one little girl. He won't leave her alone. We give him a conga drum, and he plays it just like his father, Papa. He is really making music! He even makes the same gestures as his father. It is amazing to see. Everyone is impressed by Themba's intelligence. Already he can speak English, French, and Sousou.

I have a friend from the Ivory Coast who is staying with me. I will not forget the day he leaves. It is one of those days that burns itself into your memory. When my friend has to return to Abidjan, I take him to the airport. Long ago I gave up my Volvo for a Mercedes, but the German car has broken down, and it sits rusting in the yard while we wait for parts. Themba is sleeping in his room when we walk up the road to find a taxi. In Conakry, every car you see is a taxi. People are happy to give you a lift for a fee. People stand alongside the road and stick out their hands. This is what we do.

When I return from the airport, I ask young Ousmane, "Where's Themba?"

"He's still sleeping, Mazi."

I do some cleaning. It is hot, and I go to sit in the shade of the mango tree with Ousmane and Anna, a South African girl who is living with us. Lumumba and Zenzi come home from Mrs. Minot's school.

"Where's Themba?" Lumumba asks. He is growing tall and skinny, and his hair is all over like a bush. But he is not bad-looking, this grandson.

"He's sleeping," I tell Lumumba. "But he's been sleeping for a long time. Please check in on him."

Lumumba shares his room with Themba. He goes in, but he goes to the mirror, first. Lumumba loves to look at himself in the mirror, and he pantomimes that he is playing the guitar. After a while, he notices Themba in the reflection, asleep. He goes over to the bed.

"Hey, wake up!"

In the yard, I look up all at once when Lumumba comes running out of the house. He is frightened. "Granny! Granny! Themba is foaming!"

I run into the house. Themba is lying on his side in the bed. From his mouth foaming saliva covers the side of his face. I pick him up and wrap a towel around him. Ousmane comes and grabs the baby, and we run up to the road. We stop a car. The man takes us to the hospital. Our neighbor, Mrs. Berete, comes home in time to see us leave in a hurry. She is the wife of the former ambassador to Mozambique. When she learns that we are going to the hospital, she follows us in her car.

This is a Guinean hospital, and I am afraid because in Conakry everyone goes home at three o'clock. It is five o'clock when we arrive. We are told that the emergency room is on the *fifth* floor. There is no elevator. Ousmane has Themba in his arms and he takes the steps three at a time. I run behind him.

I am right: The regular staff has gone home. There is not a doctor or a nurse here, just a skinny young girl, a medical student who is full of herself. She thinks she is so important that she acts annoyed when we run up in a panic.

"What is it?" She does not recognize me. I am dirty from the housecleaning, and I am also sweating and panting from the run. Ousmane shows her Themba. She points to a bed beside the desk. Her voice is cold. "Put him down there."

She drags her feet over to the bed. She touches the child. I am so scared that my insides hurt. She gives Themba an injection. This makes no sense to me. I ask, "What is that?"

The girl ignores me. She sits down, puts her chin on her hand, and looks bored. She points toward Themba as if he is a piece of garbage that is offending her, and she says to Ousmane, "Take this back home."

I do not understand. But at this moment Mrs. Berete comes up the stairs. She goes to Themba and touches him. She cannot look at me. To Ousmane, she says in a low voice, "Please tell Miriam that the child is dead."

Ousmane picks up Themba. He is crying. I cannot cry, because I am in shock.

There are no autopsies in Guinea. I am not to know why my grandson died. This is a Muslim country, and by custom if you die in the morning you are buried by evening. If you die in the night you are buried by dawn. We take Themba back to the house. I have never handled a dead body before in my life. At home, it is the older people—your mother, your grandmother— who take care of these things. I know nothing. I feel so far from home, and this place really seems like a foreign country. We put the corpse on the bed and I must turn to my sponsor once more. President Touré always answers his own phone when he is at home. If he is not in it just rings and rings.

I hear his voice, *"Oui?"* I start crying.

"What is it, Miriam?" He gives me an order, "Stop crying and tell me."

"My grandson is dead."

"Which one?"

"The little one. And I don't know what to do."

"Where is the child?"

"He's here."

"I will send you somebody."

A Muslim woman comes. Her name is Hadja Ngame. She decides that Themba will have to go to the mosque near the paternal grandmother's house. Themba's father, Papa, is sent for. Nobody knows where Bongi is. I send out people to search for her. I do not know what condition she is in, but I am frightened what the news will do to her.

About midnight she comes home on her own. When she learns what has happened she yells all night. Sékou Touré's wife, Andrée, comes. She is very fond of Bongi, and Bongi is very fond of her. My daughter visits Madame Touré often. Madame Touré likes to tell me that Bongi sings better than I do. We laugh, and she says, "Oh, Bongi will be bigger than you!" She now sits with my daughter for an hour and calms her. Then her doctor gives Bongi some tranquilizers.

I go to the mosque the next day with my friends, Audrey and Gilbert Minot. The child is laid out. I cry when I see him. They are going to bury little Themba their way, which is very shocking to me. They do not bury people in coffins. They wrap the body in a white poplin shroud and place it in the ground. I feel so alone. At home a dead person is brought to a mortuary and there is always an autopsy to find out the cause of death. Also, because I am a woman in Guinea, I cannot even go to my grandchild's funeral.

Gilbert Minot goes to the funeral for me. Late in the afternoon he comes and shows me where the child is buried. I buy cement and tiles and give these to the father, Papa, so he can make a tombstone for Themba. He takes the things and I don't know what he does with them, because he never fixes a marker.

Themba lies in an unmarked grave for a long time. I go to visit him. It is the custom to make a special visit six months after a person's death. But when I arrive I cannot find my grandson. They have buried someone on top of him! Where Themba lies they put the father of a government minister, right on top of our child.

As I stand and weep it hits me hard that I am a stranger here. People are nice to me. I am grateful to have a sponsor like President Touré. But friendship stops where acceptance begins.

I should not complain, because unlike a lot of people, I know for certain where my home is. Yes, I know. But the hurt won't go away, because knowing is not the same thing as being there.

ON STAGE, I WEAR THE ROBE
that belonged to my mother, the *isangoma*. The colors swirl
and come together on this robe; they are the dark brown of the
earth, and the deep blue of the sky. I do not wear this heirloom
from my mother all the time, only every so often. And every so
often, a strange thing happens when I sing. I do a song, but I
am not conscious of it. After we leave the stage, I ask my
musicians, "Did I sing such-and-such song?"

"Oh, yes," they tell me.

But I have no memory of it. When I see films of the show or
listen to tapes, there I am, dancing with all the life that is in me,
and there is my voice and no other's. I cannot explain why I
should "black out." And no one can explain it to me.

I used the expression, "dancing with all the life that is in me."
During a trip to Swaziland in 1980, it is first suggested that the
life that is in me may be more than just my own.

I meet my niece Yvorne, who lives here in Swaziland. Yvorne,
whose African name is Nonsikelelo, is very dear to me. I thank
my ancestors and the Superior Being and anyone else who has
favored me with her, because Yvorne is the only one of my
family I can see and touch in my exile. When I left South Africa,
it was she who did what I once did and assisted my mother
when the *amadlozi* came and my mother went into one of her
trances. Yvorne knows all about *isangomas*. She takes me to
consult with one. This is a task that all my people must do if

they are ill, or if they want word of their ancestors, or if strange things are bothering them.

The *isangoma*, a young woman, talks to me in her hut. She doesn't know me at all, but she asks, "Don't you sometimes feel that you didn't sing this or that song when you perform?"

I am amazed. She then tells me what others have suggested over the years: that I, like my mother, am possessed by *amadlozi*. I have always wondered about this. My mother's spirits almost destroyed her before she went through *ukuthwasa*. If a person who is a channel for spirits suppresses them, they can make that person ill, or even kill them. If I am a channel for some spirits, like my mother was, why don't they make themselves known to me by causing illnesses or misfortune?

But they have made themselves known, the *isangoma* says. My spirits are stealing the show! *Amadlozi* are show-offs. This is why they made my mother dress in their clothes and carry on when she was in their spell. I sing before the public, and the spirits get a chance to steal my mind and present themselves. That is why to this day I have been excused, and I may still be excused from going through the hard ordeal of *ukuthwasa* and becoming an *isangoma*.

If my mother is possessed by spirits, and they say that I am, also, then what about my daughter? Bongi's behavior is so unnatural that I see the signs within her. And I am scared, because I know what the *amadlozi* can do. My daughter must also consult with an *isangoma*. This must be done as soon as possible. But even finding Bongi is difficult. She disappears for long periods. When she returns, I am so happy to see her, even though I know that in a few days she will be screaming and abusing us. Then she will disappear again. This time when she leaves she does not come back at all. I learn that she is no longer in Guinea, that she is somewhere in Europe. But beyond this, I am in ignorance. The long waiting begins for Bongi's return. Months go by, and I pray for her safety.

▼▼▼▼▼

In South Africa, my niece is stabbed to death. Her boyfriend kills her in a fight. Because one black person has killed another black person, the crime is not taken seriously by the white authorities. The young man who murdered my niece is given a three-year suspended sentence.

Within a year, my last sister in South Africa, Mizpah, dies. I have had differences with Mizpah. She is the one I discovered with Gooli, and this ended my first marriage. But we got over that, because we were sisters. I had not seen her since I left home. I cannot go to her at the time of her death. Even getting news to me about her is difficult. Because I am who I am, I cannot allow my relatives to write me directly or phone me. This would put them in jeopardy. With Mizpah gone, Joseph is my only brother, and I am his only sister. Once we were six children. Four lived beyond infancy. Now we are two. And the last two are separated by—what? The Berlin Wall? A hundred thousand miles? No, by that system in South Africa. That hateful system.

I cannot stop thinking about these things, even though my life seems a conspiracy to keep me from staying in one place long enough to brood. This traveling does not make me forget and does not erase the hurt. But instead of making me tired, all the motion makes me realize that I have a job to do, a purpose. I am not running away from anything, but toward something: toward a day when the world realizes, through voices like mine, that there is a terrible evil among all people that is dragging us down and must be stopped. I am not a vengeful person, but I know there is a political system that must answer for the murders of my relatives and ancestors. My message is my concerts. This is how, days after the death of my grandson or hours after a divorce has gone through, I am on stage, and all that people see is the good feeling I have being there to sing to them.

I am always rushing to somewhere. The jets are always flying; the spotlights are always picking me out on some new stage in a foreign place. Or if I am not performing, I am on some diplomatic mission with the Guineans. One time I use my "pull" with president Touré. I hear that he is going to China on a state visit with Madame Touré, and I ask to come along. I sit with the president and his wife on the plane.

"Miriam," he says to me sternly, "an unmarried woman is not respectable. Particularly a woman your age."

If anybody else said this I would laugh. But President Touré is not joking, and I am respectful of this. "But Mr. President, who would I marry?"

"I'll give you one of my ministers!"

He is serious.

As the father of his country, Sékou Touré can act like a stern parent to everyone. Many people are afraid of him because of the way he acts, which is sometimes very lofty.

Petitioning the president at his office is not a pleasant experience. People line the hall until we hear his voice say, "Call everyone in." All the people who have appointments to see President Touré enter the office at the same time and sit around the room. One by one, the petitioners step forward, completely intimidated. All eyes are on them.

President Touré looks up, and with his powerful smile and deep voice he says one word, "*Oui?*" As soon as he asks this he looks down and writes on a paper while the person talks. He never looks up. It takes much courage to make a request under conditions like this. As for challenging the president or offering criticism about anything, I never see a display of courage as great as this. If Sékou Touré agrees to a request, he says, "Have such and such minister call me." That minister calls immediately.

So, I have no doubts that he would order a minister to be my husband. On the plane trip to Peking, as we stop in Pakistan to refuel, I thank him for his offer, but I must decline. I do not tell him that there is a Guinean man that I am seeing.

In China we visit Mao's grave, and there he is in a glass case, preserved and looking just like he is sleeping. We visit the Old Palace in Peking, and a day-care center where the mothers at the factory leave their children. We attend a state banquet. But a trip to see the Great Wall never happens. The news comes that President Tito of Yugoslavia has died. Both President Touré and the prime minister of China must leave for the state funeral.

The rest of us return to Guinea, where, for me, there is much to do. The best dance club in Conakry is opening. I know it is the best, because I am the owner. Like my baby boutique, the club is named Zambezi. The name is dear to me. When I open an appliance store in another part of town, I call this shop Zambezi also. No one gets confused. The people of Conakry know where everything is. There are no street addresses in this oversized village. You ask a person for directions and he says, "It's beside the post office," or "It's down from the state radio station."

I work hard to open the Zambezi disco. The building is not far from my house. I must build an access road and have it tarred. Two hundred people can easily fit into the space. They dance to the records the D.J. plays. I am hostess, but I do not sing. We open at nine; people start coming in at ten-thirty and dance until four in the morning. Sometimes I cook for the club, making shish kebab, which are called brochets here. I braise fish and chicken on charcoal. It's exhausting but fun for me, and the people enjoy themselves at "Miriam's place." The Fullah tribesmen of Guinea dance with elaborate hand motions. It is interesting to see them add African movements to Western steps when English-language songs are played. "Night Fever." "Another One Bites the Dust." "My Sharona." Guineans also love Cuban music. The rhythms really make them come alive. My D.J. alternates between Western, African, and Cuban music.

Soon the club is known all over Africa, and as far away as Paris. Visitors to Guinea always make it a point of stopping by. I have no bouncer, because discipline is good. Every club in Conakry has what is called a co-director. This is a man who works directly for the Ministry of the Interior. Anyone who causes trouble knows who they will have to answer to.

One of the Guineans who always comes to Zambezi is a man in his thirties named Bageot Bah. Bageot works for the Belgian airline. He is young and good-looking, with even features and a dark-brown complexion, but I cannot say that I am really attracted to him at first. Also, he does strange things, like showing off with his BMW and acting upset when I do not notice him.

He chases me, and I make excuses and dodge him. But this Bageot is persistent. He is always scheming that I should go out with him. Finally, he wears me down. We go to the reservoir east of town and have a picnic. To my surprise, I enjoy myself.

There are other dates. We go up to my country house in Dalaba together. In the car on our way back, I am in front with Bageot, and Yvorne, my niece, is in back with Bageot's nephew. The BMW was not built for these crude, winding mountain roads. The car slips over the side, rolls over twice, and ends up on its wheels. We are shaken up and surprised, but no one hurt. The car is beat-up, but it can still drive. There is a voice from the road, "Well, hello, Bageot!"

It is a friend of his. Bageot declines his help, and we go back into town. All the way home he worries that his friend will tell everyone that he saw me with Bageot. As soon as he drops me off he drives south to Sierra Leone to have the car repaired, so no one will ask questions. This is a man, I have learned, who is very concerned about what people think of him.

But I am not concerned because I do not take our love seriously. Bageot is a Muslim, and like the other people in this land he believes in multiple wives. I do not. I have been living in Guinea for over ten years and this is one thing I cannot get used to. When Bageot asks me to come to his home, I say, "No! Do you know why I got divorced? I'm not going to any woman's house. At least have that much respect for her."

Seeing Bageot becomes a habit. He calls me up, and if I don't have any plans, we go out. He comes to my house, stays until two in the morning, and goes home. This goes on for a year. I am preparing to do my first dramatic role in a film. The protests of the Africans and the oppression they face in South Africa is the backdrop for a film by Souheil Ben Barka called *Amok!* I play a prostitute who is the sister of the main character. I have only a few scenes, but I do it because the project is worthwhile. My twelve-year-old grandson has a small role in the movie. He can be seen with blood running out of his nose as he holds the prison bars and shouts along with other men and boys jailed during the riots. Zenzi, my granddaughter, who is nine, has a bigger part. She opens and closes the film. Zenzi is seen running, running, as those of us in exile are condemned to do. The director thinks Zenzi shows promise as a young actress. He invites my grandchildren to come to Morocco to stay with him while they go to school. But when they arrive, his wife objects. I must drop everything to find someone to take care of them. Bongi cannot; she has gone.

While I am on the road, I receive a letter from Bageot asking me to marry him. I cannot take the proposal seriously, and I think: Is he joking? Then he phones me, repeating the offer. "Please don't tell anyone," he asks.

I laugh. "But you know, you are calling from Conakry, and you know those ladies are listening to everything you say. So, it's not secret anymore."

This is true: The operators are gossips. When I come back to Guinea, people are talking about us. I have to become concerned when I begin to see how serious Bageot really is. His mother comes to visit, along with a sister who translates her Fullah tongue for me.

"My son has told me that he loves you. I would like to make his intentions known, and I came to do just that."

I thank her sincerely for her visit, because this is an important Fullah custom for a mother to make this call.

I am truly troubled. To me, I cannot believe that someone who loves a person can share that person with someone else. If a man is in love and happy with his wife, he might go out once in a while, but if he loves his girlfriend enough to make her his second wife, then this means his first marriage is no longer any good. How can a person be in love with two people? When I hear Bageot's proposal, it means to me that his first marriage is finished.

I say to him, "Do you really want to marry me?"

"Yes."

"But you're already married."

"That doesn't matter. I can have a second wife. I can have a third or a fourth wife if I want."

I think this over carefully. I admit some truths to myself: I am not lonely with Bageot in my life. He is fun and considerate, and somehow I have fallen in love with him. But he will not get a divorce and if I want him I cannot get him this way. Divorces are very rare in this country, where a man can have multiple wives. Also, Bageot would never ask for one. He is afraid what people will say. If I want him, I must be his second wife. But I do not think of it as sharing him. The first wife, Irene, who pronounces her name "Iran," is no longer on his mind. I remember how I gave up Stokely when he fell in love with someone else. But the first wife is from this culture, and she thinks differently.

"Bageot," I say. "I am not comfortable with your arrangements in this country. I would like to make new ones of our own."

He is interested, because he wants me very much. I tell him that I am my own woman and I have my own house. If he wants to be married to me, he has got to come live with me. When I am in town, he is mine. When I am on the road, he can go to his other family.

What I propose is quite a test, but he agrees to it. I go to President Touré, and tell him what is on my mind.

"I am opposed," my sponsor says. "Polygamy has been abolished in Guinea."

This is legally true. In 1968 some advanced women in the congress pushed through a law that put an end to multiple wives. But it is other women who continue to break this law. They marry in secret religious ceremonies, and they just never go to sign the papers in civil court.

"But you told me to get married. Who is going to marry me who hasn't been married before?" I say this to convince a stubborn man, although I do not believe it myself.

"You were my responsibility yesterday, when you were married to an American," President Touré says. "Now that you are to marry a Guinean, I have a double responsibility."

I tell him that I recognize his sense of duty. He says, "Bring me this man."

Bageot is scared. It is not everybody who meets with the president in a private conference. He wants me to come, too. I would rather not, but he insists, so I sit on one side of the room during the interrogation.

"Who are you, and what do you do?" the President demands of Bageot. He is acting like a stern father who must judge the man who is asking for his daughter's hand.

He says, "Do you know what you're doing? Because Miriam travels. She is an artist. You will not interfere with her work?"

Bageot tells President Touré that he respects me and my singing. After some more questions, the president says he will agree to the marriage, but he puts a hard obstacle in our way. "You may marry, if you can get the first wife to sign a paper that says she agrees to it."

When we leave, we do not know what will happen. Bageot's mother likes me, and so do his children. He has two girls and a boy from Irene, and one girl from an earlier experience. But Bageot's brother and uncles do not care for me. They say: "She's too old for him. Why would he get involved with her? She is under the president. He's going to get into trouble."

Sékou Touré's obstacle is very big. This lady, Bageot's first wife, is not going to sign anything. Everybody talks to her, but she says, "No!"

Finally, Bageot says to her, "I am going to pack my bags and leave you!"

When I hear this, I am surprised. "What?"

"She's not going to sign. She's not going to do it. We're through."

I ask him to think. "Are you sure this is what you want?"

But Bageot is sure. He goes to his house and begins to pack. The wife stays in the other room and won't say a thing. He packs and packs. Finally, when he is moving his things out the door, she shouts, "I'll sign!"

At first she is so angry that she will not let Bageot's children see me. I bring them toys from my travels, but she will not let them come and thank me. This does not go on for long. After a while, she permits them to visit. The first wife and I are strangers to each other. But we are not enemies. When I am in Guinea, I have Bageot. When I am away, he is hers. It is hard for me to have enemies. Stokely and I are friends. He marries his Guinean girlfriend shortly after our divorce, and they had a child right away. Stokely is always stopping by. And when his mother comes into town, it is Bageot who picks her up.

Bageot and I are wed in a Muslim religious ceremony. I am not permitted to attend. The imam prays over two kola nuts at the mosque. And then he ties these together. When this is done, and the knot is literally tied, the marriage is a fact.

▼▼▼▼▼

For many years they have called me "The Empress of African Song." But when Swiss television comes to do a documentary about my life, they choose the title *Mama Africa*.

In Europe there is a film competition among the French-speaking nations teaming with French-speaking African nations. Switzerland chooses Guinea instead of the Ivory Coast, Gabon, Senegal, or the other former French colonies because I live here and they want to use me as their subject.

To the filmmakers I represent the continent and its music to the Western world. African music, though very old, is always being rediscovered in the West. Then it becomes new, and very hip. Just recently I was in Nuremberg, Germany. My new manager, Willie Leiser, booked me into a rock festival. I did not know why. The main group was The Who, and the other groups were also rock 'n' roll. When *I* came on, the young people in the audience did not know what to make of me. They suddenly became the most hostile audience I ever had. And for the first time in my life things were thrown at me: beer cans, paper airplanes. I almost walked off stage. But something told me I should continue. But I was angry! My anger must have gone into the force of my singing, because the audience was silent before I could finish the song. When I was done they were just standing there. And by the end of my set, they were screaming. When my musicians and I left the stage, the screaming went on and on for so long, I had to be called back.

The fascination of Africa: You cannot escape it. This is what the Swiss filmmakers had in mind when they join their Guinean fellows and come to record my life as it now is. They shoot in the garden of my new house in Hamdalaye, a neighborhood east of town. They shoot at my country house in Dalaba where the mountains are so beautiful and I love to hear the birds sing in the morning, and they shoot inside my Club Zambezi. When they finish *Mama Africa* and submit it, the film wins the competition.

It is shown on Guinean television. We gather around the set—Bageot, the children, the South African students who are staying with me—and we watch myself singing, buying vegetables in the market, and driving around in my taxi. The filmmakers loved my taxi.

When I left South Africa and visited London for the very first time, I admired the taxis of London. "One day, I would like to have that car." Later, when I saw how all other types of cars seem to break down in Guinea, I thought how practical one of the sturdy, high cars would be here. I was traveling to London to do a commercial for Toyota of Africa, and I asked a cabdriver where his car was made. He told me, and I went straight to the Austin factory in Coventry. I talked them in to selling me one, and paid cash. When it arrived, it became the only car of its kind in the country. Everybody knows when Miriam is coming down the street! The passenger compartment in back is behind a glass partition. There is a tall ceiling, a plush seat, and folding stools. It feels very elegant.

Bageot and I are traveling this way from Dalaba when we encounter a snake in the road. Once again I am reminded how Africa treats the unbeliever. Stokely had his misfortune when he killed a snake on the road. Now it is Bageot's turn.

The driver swerves the car to avoid hitting the big snake. But a tire runs over a portion of the long body. We look back. The snake is not dead. It is wiggling in the sun. Bageot tells the driver to reverse. When we return to where the snake is, my husband gets out of the car and pulls his hunting gun out of the trunk.

"Don't do that," I tell him. "Leave it alone. It's not doing anything to you."

"Bah!" In Guinea, they have no worries about bothering snakes. Bageot takes aim at the head and shoots. He is happy that he has killed the snake.

When he gets back into the car, I tell him, "You shouldn't have done that. At home they say that you should leave a snake alone or something will happen."

"Nonsense."

I can only sit back when we continue our drive and wait. We do not even go five miles before—blam!—a tire blows. The jolt is so great that if we had been going fast, the car would have overturned.

It is a small thing, and maybe not worth mentioning. But it reminds me that a person must respect Africa's mysteries. I am always being reminded. The white man calls Africa the Dark Continent not because of the color of our skin, but because he cannot understand it. But I do not have all the answers, either. Especially when things go very wrong, and we are thrown into tragedy—at times like these I feel very much in the dark. There comes now a time that seems nothing but darkness.

18

FOR TWO YEARS MY DAUGH-
ter has been in France, never writing home, and leaving me to
check with friends to see if she is all right. During this time my
husband Bageot is sent by his airline to a management program
in Brussels. I go along and rent an apartment for the month so I
can be with him and cook. I do not take any concert dates
during this time. Another reason I go is that I hear Bongi is also
in Brussels.

When I arrive, I hear that she is back in Paris. I ask some
friends to tell her to call us. On Christmas Day she shows up at
the door. For three days it is like old times. She talks about the
album she has recorded for a German company, and how happy
she is to be singing and doing her own concerts here and there.

But after only three days, she is gone. All the hope I had that
her mind has overcome those things that make her act so strangely
disappear along with Bongi. I go back to Guinea, and a year
passes before I see her again. President Touré has known of my
daughter's behavior, and I talk to him when the worry gets to be
too much. He agrees with me that Bongi should consult an
isangoma. There are some in Guinea, and, unlike the ones in
South Africa, these tribal medicine men and women are respected by the authorities. President Touré even has one attached to a Conakry hospital. This *isangoma* cures broken bones
and such. People come to him who do not care for the Western
methods.

But bringing Bongi home is a problem. I continue to write to her, and inquire about her through friends. Sometimes I just sit and cry: "I wonder where she is? I wonder if she's eaten, wherever she is? She's so thin . . ."

And I feel guilty. I wonder how many of her problems are my fault. In 1960 I made the decision to bring Bongi to the West. I wanted my daughter. But she was just nine years old and she was used to life at home: the one big family where her aunt or cousin or even neighbor lady is her mother. She had to do without this type of nurturing, which was so dear to me. And even though she was living with her real mother, I was away so often. Bongi couldn't be with me all the time; she had to go to school. I always had girls and students from South Africa around to look after her, so she had a touch of home and she never forgot her native tongue, but it wasn't the same thing. And then the marriages. Bongi never forgave me for divorcing Hugh Masekela. She knew Hughie in South Africa, and she was so happy when we were all together. And after Hugh, when I married Stokely, Bongi's friends taunted her: "Your mother is marrying a crazy man!" Bongi is such a sensitive girl. I know the way I have lived my life has hurt her. I feel badly, and now I am scared for her.

Bongi comes back to Guinea, and I get a surprise: My daughter says she wants to stay here for good.

She gets a job with the Ministry of Geology as a translator, French to English. She makes hospital visits all the time. Since there is no food service, she brings meals to the poor patients noon and night.

But it is a tense time for me, waiting for something to happen. I remember when I brought Bongi with me to Angola a few years ago. She was herself. I had a conference to attend, and she worked as a translator. For four days she was all right. And then she snapped. If she wasn't screaming and yelling at me, it was at somebody else. Then she got mad and disappeared. I always fear that this will happen again.

Now is the time for her to consult with the *isangoma*. If it is *amadlozi* who are tormenting her, she must go through *ukuthwasa*, or things will only get worse. The people of Guinea have different practices than we do at home, but they can still help. There is no way for us to go to South Africa. We make the arrangements for Bongi to travel far into the countryside, where there is an *isangoma* of great reputation. Bongi agrees to the trip. But when the time comes for her to leave, she disappears again. My friends tell me to be patient, but I am really hurting with worry.

▼▼▼▼▼

After three years in which my club gives many people a good time, Zambezi closes. My ten-year lease is not honored by the owner, who wants to raise the rent beyond reason. I do not want to sue a Guinean. I am a guest in this country. So, the disco disappears, and the few places of entertainment in Conakry become less by one. I am not much of a businesswoman, anyway. Leave me alone, and I will give away everything in the store. It is a miracle that my appliance store, also called Zambezi, is still open.

My business is singing, anyway. Concert promoters who want me contact my manager, Willie Leiser, in Switzerland, and he telexes me in Conakry. There is no telephone service in my neighborhood of Hamdalaye. Willie rounds up my musicians. They are no longer Guineans. I guess because my old Guinea musicians were paid by the government whether they worked or not, they just never felt like showing up for rehearsals. I found some fine African players in Europe. The girls who are my backup singers live in London. When we all get together the sound is fantastic. I am very happy with my group.

I sing songs that are written by South Africans like my friends Philemon Hou, Caiphus Semenya, Hugh Masekela. Some of these songs protest the treatment of our people. Bongi writes songs for me. I do "Pata, Pata" and some of my standards. I speak a little, too. Not much, and never loudly, but my words make their point. Sometimes I think I must sound like a revolutionary when I say we must rise up against the criminal regime of Pretoria. Afterward, I get scared of the things I say on stage. I say to myself, "My goodness, next time maybe I shouldn't say that." But the next time comes and I don't care. If I die on stage I guess I'll be the happiest person, because I will be dying like a soldier on the battlefield.

In the eight years since the Soweto uprising, my people have not been lying down. They have been organizing and protesting as never before. And also as never before, the outside world has shown that it wants Pretoria to make reforms. But the rulers are

not going to give up their power. The "reforms" they dream up
are phony attempts to fool world opinion. Among the oppressed
minorities, the Indians and Coloreds are given their own, second-
class "parliaments." These have no power, and they can only
"advise" the white parliament. But the idea is to give Indians
and Coloreds the illusion that they are part of things. The black
majority of the country is given no such illusion. Even in some
meaningless setup, the whites cannot stomach the idea of giving
blacks a say in their own lives. As for the Indians and Coloreds,
not everyone participates. Only the opportunists go. In my opinion, the Coloreds who attend their "parliament" are traitors,
because if you have one white parent and one black parent, how
can you choose one over the other? But a great majority of
Indians and Coloreds show that they want real reform. They will
not be divided from the black majority, like the government is
trying to do.

▼▼▼▼▼

President Touré is one of those strong people who do not
seem to age. He stands before his people at the rallies in the
stadium, dressed all in white, and he commands them.

"For the Revolution!"

I cheer with the people: *"Ready!"*

"Imperialism?"

"Down!"

"Honor?"

"To the People!"

"Glory?"

"To the People!"

It seems as if this ritual in the stadium, with all the people in
white, and everyone shouting and waving their arms in the sun,
it seems as if it will go on forever. Papa Sékou, the father of his
country, he does not get old.

But he gets sick. The man who came to visit Stokely and all
the others who were hospitalized during the malaria and cholera
epidemics but who was never affected himself, this is the one
who now comes down with an illness. We are not told what the
trouble is. We only know that he has gone to a hospital in the
U.S. And then we hear, just as suddenly, that he is dead.

The people are stunned; the nation is paralyzed. My grief is
very deep: This man was my sponsor in this land. He played

such a part in my marriage to Stokely and in my marriage to Bageot. He was there to advise me when Bongi was at her worst and when little Themba was taken from us. This was the man who sent me to the United Nations as a delegate and who twice asked me to address the General Assembly—great moments for myself and wonderful platforms from which I could speak about the plight of my people. It is true what they say about power corrupting, and the president could be arrogant and make people cringe. But he was much loved by his people. He was much loved by me.

The day President Touré's body arrives in Guinea, the road from the airport to the People's Palace, where he will lie in state, is a riot of emotion. The people have gotten over their shock, and a hysterical sadness has set in. Mourners throw themselves on the ground, weeping. They are packed along the roadside. I cannot help crying myself, out of my own grief and out of pity for these people who have lost their father.

The president is buried with full military honors. Thirty-nine heads of state attend the funeral, including Vice-President Bush from the U.S., the prime minister of France, President Zia from Pakistan, and President Houphouët-Boigny of the Ivory Coast. They speak of Sékou Touré as the man who led the African nationalist movement. They speak of him as the man who brought great pride to his people.

Before I leave I look at the widow, Andrée Touré, and her children. They are in mourning. It is the last time I will see them. It is the last time that any of us will see them.

▼▼▼▼▼

Three days later, the dignitaries and heads of state return home, and we go to bed understanding that the prime minister, the man who Sékou Touré picked to be his successor, is now in charge. We sleep little this night. There is machine gun fire all over town. The radio tells us nothing. The electricity is off, but this is not unusual in Conakry. Bageot and I lie in the dark and listen to the gunfire. I think of the invasion fourteen years ago, when the mercenaries came by our house, and I get scared. At least I know where my daughter is. Bongi has come home to spend the night in her room. The children are in Morocco at their school.

It is a rare morning when I do not get up very early. I do not need much sleep. The sky is just beginning to get gray when I start breakfast in the kitchen. A young girl knocks on Bongi's bedroom window. Her voice is full of the frightening news: "Bongi! Bongi! Tell your mother that there has been a coup!"

In Yimbaya, where I now live, there sometimes is no need for a telephone, because no news can travel faster than it can through the neighbors' own voices. We are all concerned, but what can we do? I have never been in a coup before. Under the stable leadership of President Touré, Guinea has not known one.

The girl who brought us the news comes back a few minutes later. Again, she taps on my daughter's window. Her voice is full of fright. "Bongi! Tell your mother to hide!"

Bongi is shocked. "Why?"

"Soldiers are coming!"

Bongi runs to tell me. I say, "Hide? Where am I going to hide?"

I do not have time to sort anything out before five soldiers with machine guns drive up in a fine car with no plates. They burst into the house. We all stare at the guns and at the man who is in charge. I know him. His name is Pierre Camara, and until yesterday he was a civilian. He worked for Air Guinea.

"We are looking for ministers!"

So, they think because Sékou Touré was my sponsor, I am hiding his cabinet in my house! They search all the rooms. I know what they are truly seeking: a way to scare me as they must scare everyone, so that we will obey them. Bageot, who works for another airline and knows Camara, talks to him. I listen to the names of all the ministers who have been rounded up and put in prison.

When the first group of soldiers leave, a communiqué comes over the radio: No one is permitted to leave their homes. The borders have been closed. We cannot even go to the market for food.

The day is hot, and we spend it sitting under the mango tree, watching the patrols of soldiers go up and down the road. A group of them see my London taxi parked in front of the house, and they come in to make threats.

"Is that from the presidency?"

They think that my car was a gift from President Touré, and they mean to take it. But I stand firm, because it is hard to find a car that won't be destroyed by the Guinea roads. "Look for yourself! Does it have 1-A on the plates? Then how can it be from the presidency?"

They leave, and soon Sergeant Sylla comes. At first I am happy to see him, because I have been paying this big, broad man to look after the house. We have become friends. But I become scared when I see that he is a different person from the one I know. He has his machine gun, and he starts shooting it off into the air. The noise is terrible. He has a strange smile on his face.

I plead with him, "But Sergeant, why are you doing this?"

"*We* are the ones who are the power!"

He goes away, and soon other soldiers arrive. But they are friendly. I have hired other military men to guard the house in the past, and any time they feel like coming by, they know I will feed them. They stop by now, to see how I am. I tell them that I am fine. And this is true: No one in my family has been hurt.

I am not hurt, but I am scared. No one who was close to the president feels safe. After two days, we are permitted to leave our homes. On the coup's third day, the airport is reopened. I have a six-week concert tour in Europe, and I must hurry to Morocco to make it in time. I am sure that people of the outside world are concerned about what is happening here in Guinea. I want to show them that I am all right.

The airport is a madhouse. All the journalists, diplomats, and Guinean ambassadors from all over the world who have been caught in the coup must go back to their posts. Bageot always leaves the airline office in town to help me here, where everyone knows him and he can speed things along. This is very helpful on a day like this.

I watch my bags go away. I get my ticket stamped, and I give my passport to Bageot so he can take care of the formalities. He returns, and I join the joyful people happy to get out of the country.

I never get on that plane. A policeman comes up to me. He is stern and abrupt. "The commissioner wants your passport."

I can feel that something is wrong. Why would the airport commissioner want my passport? I say with surprise, "But I've completed all the formalities."

The policeman shouts at me, *"The commissioner wants your passport!"*

Heads turn my way. I give up my passport and go to find my husband. I explain to Bageot why I am not on the plane. He tells me to go sit in the cafeteria while he goes off to investigate.

I sit and sit, wondering if I am being kept in the country as a prisoner of the coup, but not knowing why, and not knowing what will happen to me. Bageot comes to me. He looks worried. "Listen, just stay here."

I look out and watch the door close on the Royal Air Maroc plane. The jet pulls away. I watch it taxi onto the runway. It flies; it is gone. I feel that my safety is going away with that plane.

Bageot returns and says quietly, "I think we should go home."

When I get to the car, I weep. When I get home I really cry. I don't know what is going on, but I can guess. The radio and television are full of people who are condemning President Touré as an evil man. Just three days ago at the funeral they were crying like babies and calling him a hero. I guess they were just acting when they were crying. So how can anyone believe anything now?

I must find out if I am in trouble because of my friendship with the president. And I must get out of the country, if this is possible, for the concert tour. But if I leave I must be able to come back. My family is here.

In the morning I go with Bageot to see the new prime minister to ask what happened and why? I am told a mistake was made on the part of the Ministry of the Interior. We go to the Ministry of the Interior, and I am directed to the Ministry of Foreign Affairs. We go there. The minister tells us that he is traveling and that I should see his chief of the cabinet the next day.

I fear that I may never get out of the country. "Please, sir," I say to the foreign minister. "They tell me a mistake has been made. If you leave and don't give the word, I may never get my passport."

He is kind enough to sign a card giving orders that I should be taken care of, and I receive my first passport from the Second Guinea Republic. So, they will still allow me to stay as a guest.

▼▼▼▼▼

I make it to Morocco, and then to Europe for the concert tour that lasts one month and a half. Everyone was afraid that something might have happened to me in the coup, and they are happy to see me. And I am very happy to be performing.

Going on stage to sing is like stepping into a perfect world. The past means nothing. Worries about the future do not exist. All that matters is the music. I live for this. The love I have for my music, and my audience, is what makes this a perfect world: under the lights, with my pretty singers and good-looking musicians! And the message, the few heartfelt words that I say to plead for my people, this makes it even more perfect. My voice is heard by the people when I speak about the evils that are strangling South Africa. Every day there is more and more to say—there is more urgency and more tragedy.

The concert stage: This is one place where I am most at home, where there is no exile.

DOWN THE ROAD FROM MY house in Yimbaya, there is a river. The current is slow, and sometimes the surface of the water is like a mirror. The full moon reflects on it, without a single ripple to make a distortion. During the rainy season, when the water is high, the tops of trees look like bunches of parsley stuck in a mirror. Some clay huts line the river's edge, and the fishermen in their dugouts carved out of big logs paddle along with almost no noise. But every night you can hear the people banging their gum mallets on their bellaphones, the wooden xylophones the Guineans play.

My daughter walks down the road and sits along the river's edge for hours. She writes her poems and thinks her thoughts. She may think about our dear friend from South Africa, Philemon Hou. Philemon's death, coming so close to Sékou Touré's, was a real blow to me. We all loved him. *"We are an African people!"* he taught the children to chant. *"And don't you forget it!"*

My daughter is not singing much anymore. For the moment, she seems happy to just be here in Guinea. I find out one reason for her happiness when she tells me that she is pregnant.

Bongi has been seeing a young man, a Guinean named Sanousi. He is young, only twenty-two years old. Her son Lumumba is already sixteen, and Bongi is thirty-four.

Sanousi is a quiet and good-looking boy, and he is very attached to Bongi. This does not please his parents, because their son is still in school. But once we learn that Bongi is pregnant, Sanousi's mother does the honorable thing and comes to see me.

In this situation, it is our custom that the young man's parents ask the young woman's parents for pardon. I receive the mother, Hadja, in my living room, and we have our talk. She is a broad woman with a happy smile and small eyes that are almost lost beneath her cheeks when she smiles. But today we are serious. What Hadja does not know, and what I do not know, is that while we are speaking, Bongi and Sanousi are secretly getting married. First they have the ceremony at the mosque, and then they go sign the papers at the mayor's office.

It hurts me that I am again made no part of my daughter's wedding. But, I think, she is with a young man who loves her and she is as happy as if she is a kid, again. So, I am quiet. I give her my blessing.

▼▼▼▼▼

At least Bongi has an easier time of her romance than a cousin of mine back home. My cousin is living with a white man in Hillbrow, right next to Number Four, the biggest prison in Johannesburg. Every day and night they see this prison, and it is a reminder to them what their future will be if they are caught. It is "immoral" and illegal for a black and a white to live together. My cousin has to be careful. She disguises herself as her boyfriend's maid. It is not unusual for a bachelor to have a maid, but she must live elsewhere, usually in some little house in back. If she lives in the master's house, the neighbors will talk and sooner or later there will be a raid. These raids happen in the middle of the night. The police come when my cousin is with her boyfriend, but she hides in an attic that nobody knows about. It is a horrible way to live, but people do what their hearts tell them to do.

Back when I was a teenager, the Immorality Act was passed to outlaw interracial relations and make certain that the white minority would not disappear. But in 1985, Pretoria abolishes this act, which seems as much a part of South Africa as a springbok on a Krugerrand. The action is taken because black unrest at home will not cease, and worldwide condemnation of apartheid needs to be appeased.

We know the Pretoria regime. We know what its "reforms" are like. So we are not surprised when we learn the true reality of this change. The new law says that blacks and whites can marry, but they cannot live together. How can an interracial couple live together when the whites are in one part of town and blacks are segregated in another? Where is the couple supposed to meet? On a bench in the park? No, what this new law is saying to blacks and whites who fall in love is this: Go ahead and get married, then get out of the country.

We laugh at these "reforms." We laugh while we cry.

There is a new phrase in the air, and it hurts my ear like a sour note: "constructive engagement." This is Washington's way of saying, "Speak softly and do not even carry a stick, and maybe everything will get better." The U.S. is the one country that can do the most to pressure Pretoria into making honest reforms before our land is pushed into disaster. The United States is rich. The United States is powerful. And its people are concerned about evil things. Just this spring they go out and buy a record by a group called "U.S.A. for Africa." All the top singers raise funds to help the starving in Ethiopia. I see the video and there is Big Brother singing, and Stevie Wonder, Dionne Warwick, and so many others. Everyone in Africa is thankful for this aid. But we listen to the lyrics, and we wonder: What is this? "We are the world," the stars from America sing. But who is the world? Where are the singers from Africa, Europe, the East, the Third World? They are all Americans singing "We are the world." Oh, truly, we say, "America" is the world!

And in Washington, Mr. Reagan's government also says, "We are the world," and there is no suffering that is as important as American interests. Otherwise, why waste time bombing Libya when the number one terrorist government in the world is South Africa? You pick up the paper and you read: forty killed, eight hundred homeless. Tomorrow it is six dead, two thousand homeless. Every day. Every single day. We ask, what good is this "constructive engagement"? Why can it not stop the killing of our people? Why can it not help stop the poverty that we live in, the shanties that you see on TV? I do not have a home in those shanties, but I suffer, because when I look at that I hurt inside. And I don't know how many of my relatives are dying every day in Johannesburg, in the Cape, in Port Elizabeth. All over the country we are in one big prison. I mean whipped every day. I mean shot at every day. I mean chased from here to there every day. My mother died, and I cannot visit her grave. I could not locate my father's grave now if you asked me. And I ask myself: What did I do? Did I kill anybody?

And the homelands. People are taken from where they were born and sent to some barren land where nothing can grow. They are just parked there and told, "This is your homeland." And the people who stay behind work as servants, or work in the mines. We work for meager salaries while we dig for the most important minerals that go overseas so other people can live better while we live worse. We work to allow our rulers to live with their privileges. But in Washington and London they do not want to lose the uranium from South Africa. Warplanes have got to be built, and the raw material for these comes from our country. We are the labor force—the slaves. We die. Our children have no education. And we remain this way because someone has told the West that if we are free there will be no uranium, there will be no warplanes. And the West believes this, and we are in chains.

Hey, we *understand* what "constructive engagement" means. We are slaves, but we are not stupid.

▼▼▼▼▼

I am in London for my fifty-third birthday. The last time I was here was for a concert in 1971, fourteen years ago. My sponsor is an organization that receives government funding to help black-run businesses and to promote black culture in Great Britain. They invite me to sing at the Royal Festival Hall.

I am scared to go. Fourteen years? Young people who are now twenty won't even remember me. But I arrive and the place is packed. Mostly young people, too. They whistle and stomp. When I come out, the sound that I hear is what people mean when they say a performer "brings the house down." Afterward, the reviews are very generous. There is one article in particular that strikes my fancy because it is in the London *Financial Times*. Who would expect to be reviewed in the London *Financial Times*? But there it is, and the gentleman who wrote it is so enthusiastic I bet the readers wished I was a bond or something they could invest in.

After the success of my London concert I go to Morocco to see my grandchildren, Lumumba and Zenzi. I am feeling hopeful about things, and I want to convince them to let their mother come up and take care of them. They feel nervous about Bongi, the way she goes into her sudden rages. I decide to spend a few days here with them.

It must be the love of the Superior Being or my ancestors, but something enters my head to keep this decision from being—by just a hairbreadth—the most tragic of my life.

▼▼▼▼▼

When I left Guinea, Bongi was seven months pregnant. While I am gone, she suddenly goes into premature labor and she is taken to the hospital. In case this might happen, I had left instructions with my husband to take Bongi to a particular hospital. Instead, a friend takes her to another: a rundown old place left over from the colonial days. Here she is put into a filthy, hot little room with no ventilation. No food is served, and the bed linens have to come from the person's home. But Bongi is in such great pain when she is brought in on Monday that she does not notice these discomforts. Bageot, who is never at my house when I am away, does not check up on Bongi.

The doctors make their examination, and they decide to operate. No one phones me in Morocco. I do not know that my daughter is in danger. I know how troubled she is, and how little things can set her off. Big things like an operation and a troubled delivery, these can cause her great harm. Bongi needs me to be with her.

Tuesday is the day of the operation. A caesarian is performed to remove the baby. Bongi is told that the child, a boy, is very sick. She is sedated, and for a long time she sleeps alone without anyone who loves her around.

And alone she awakens. The two girls who share her room are asleep. The doors of the hospital rooms with their thin wooden slats for windows all open onto a long balcony.

It is night, and the moon through the window slats makes white stripes on the dark wood floor. A nurse comes by, going along the long balcony. She is a big woman who would be more at home as a matron for criminals in a prison than as an attendant for the sick in a hospital.

Bongi is weak, but she gets this woman's attention. "I want to see my baby. Will you bring him?"

"No. I can't."

"But why not?"

The nurse says, "It's against the rules."

In her weariness and emotional state, Bongi's mood quickly turns sour. "You bring me my baby now!"

The nurse explodes. She will not have someone ordering her around. "Shut up! I said it's against the rules. Stop making a nuisance. You think you're special because you're Miriam Makeba's daughter. You had the protection of Sékou Touré. Well, Sékou Touré's dead!"

"Bitch!" Bongi screams. "Bring me my baby!"

The nurse shouts back, "You don't have a baby! Your baby was born dead! It was *deformed*!"

Bongi is scared into silence. The big nurse leaves. For a long time Bongi sits up in her bed, and those things that destroy her mind come and take possession of her. She is sick and weak from the operation, but she stands up. She goes to the wooden doors and pushes them aside.

She says, "I've got to find my baby."

By the light of the moon she walks along the balcony. In silence she goes, and no one sees her. No one is there to stop her when she leaves the hospital and wanders the empty streets. For miles she walks, in her white hospital gown, like a ghost in the moonlight. The electricity is off in this part of town. The houses are like tombs. She walks by them, looking for her baby through the tears that run from her big eyes. Dogs bark at her from the alleys. The cats run by her feet, afraid.

She passes the mud-brown beaches where the sand has been taken and garbage is dumped in its place. She passes the rusty hulks of cars and the compost heaps of rotting mangos. She does not find her baby here. She does not find her baby anywhere. She has no name to cry out, because she never named the boy. She can only beg that someone show her where he is, where her baby has gone. But there is no one on the streets to join her in the pale moonlight.

There are some lights, and she goes toward them. It is a military base. The sentries see her coming toward them: this dazed, crazy woman in the short gown. They laugh at Bongi. The walking has caused the scars from her operation to tear. The soldiers point to the blood dripping between her legs, spotting her bare feet.

"*A mato ana kike wali!*" they say. "Look, she is having her period!"

They force her to stop, and put an end to her wanderings. The police are called, and they come to take her back to the hospital.

The staff is angry. Bongi is a troublemaker to them. They wipe her torn scars and give her sedatives so she will not bother them again this night.

▼▼▼▼▼

In Morocco, something tells me I must go home. The children say, "Don't leave. Wait until Monday and take the direct flight on Royal Air Maroc."

"No," I say, "I don't think I should wait."

Another flight takes me north to Brussels. I leave on Thursday and arrive on Friday to wait another day for the flight to Guinea. During this time, Bongi is visited by her husband's mother, Hadja. Sanousi himself is not permitted to see his wife. He does not know why this is, and he is sick with worry.

Hadja does not know what to do. Bongi nearly killed herself with her midnight walk. The mother-in-law wants to spare her more distress. So she consults with Bageot, and they invent a story. They tell Bongi that her baby boy is alive and well. Then they go out and find another baby. They bring him to the hospital, and tell Bongi it is hers. She is so relieved and happy. She holds it and cries, and then boasts to everyone about her beautiful son.

Bageot picks me up at the airport when my flight arrives on Saturday. My handsome young husband is in a serious mood, and he does not say much. We get in the car, but he does not take me home. I ask him where we are going.

"We have to go to the hospital, first."

"What's in the hospital?"

He tells me it is Bongi. I am surprised, excited, hopeful, and nervous, all at once. "What? She delivered?"

"Yes," Bageot tells me. "But the baby died. She was operated on."

The terrible news hits me hard. It is so unexpected. "And you didn't let me know? You didn't phone, or at least cable?"

Without taking his eyes from the road, Bageot says, "I didn't think it was important."

Sometimes in a marriage a husband or a wife will do something so terrible or so thoughtlessly cruel that it shakes that marriage to its roots. It changes the way the other person thinks about his or her mate, and years of work must go into getting the lost trust back, if it can be gotten back. This is what I feel

now with Bageot, who knows that my daughter means everything to me, and I call him the worst name I know.

At the hospital, Bongi is very happy to see me. I am shocked
when I see how pale she is. She has lost a lot of weight. And
just looking at the room where she is hurts; it is so dirty, small,
and hot. And though I tell myself to be strong and brave for my
daughter, I cannot help it, I start to cry, thinking about the baby
she lost.

Bongi looks at me with concern. "Don't cry, Mazi. I'm all
right. Did they show you my baby?"

"What?" I look at her and I don't know what she is talking
about. Bageot did not tell me about the deception.

"Oh, it's a beautiful baby," Bongi says.

I cover my face with my hands. Oh, my daughter is mad!
"No, I haven't seen the baby yet," I tell her.

Bongi looks at me and she is alarmed. "My mama is crying.
What's wrong? Is my baby dead?"

Hadja is in the room with us. She speaks up, smiling, "No.
Oh, no."

I stare at Sanousi's mother. What is happening? A large
woman, a nurse, comes in. She has a needle, and she is going to
give an injection. Bongi is frightened. She grabs my arm.

"Mazi, don't let that woman touch me! She is the one who
said my baby was dead. She said it was deformed! But she lied,
because they've been showing me my baby!"

I think that I am losing my mind. The nurse says to Bongi,
"You can talk all you want, but I'm going to give you this
injection."

Bongi screams. I must put an end to this. I ask Bageot to
request of this nurse that someone else give the injection. She
leaves, and a man comes back to do the job. Before Bongi goes
to sleep, I give her some perfume that I bought her in Morocco.
Then we go home.

I cannot sleep this night. Bageot and Hadja have dreamed up
the scheme about the baby boy, but they want me to tell Bongi
the truth: that her real child is dead. During the night I prepare
some soup that she likes, and I try to think. The first thing
Sunday morning, I go to her. I am at her side all day. Only at
five o'clock do I leave, when I must go get some food for her.
Hadja stays behind.

At ten o'clock, Bongi says to me, "You know, it's late. I think you should go."

To Bageot, she says, "Tomorrow, when you come, you should wear your white grand boubou."

She looks at me. Though she is weak, her eyes are bright. "You, too, Mazi. You wear your white grand boubou. And don't forget to bring one for me. Because tomorrow you'll be taking me out of the hospital. I want to thank all the people here, even the ones who were not so nice to me. Tomorrow, I go home with my baby!"

Bageot says, "Bongi, I will come in my white grand boubou."

We leave. A half hour later, Bongi says to Hadja, "You should go, now. It will be hard to find a taxi."

Hadja leaves, and Bongi closes her eyes to sleep. Ever since she went for her walk, she has complained of terrible cramps and pains deep inside of her. But the hospital staff does not want to hear these complaints. They ignore them, and her.

And so Bongi closes her eyes against this pain once more. There is no one to keep her company but two girls asleep and the white slats of moonlight on the floor. Does she see this light? Does she think about things? Maybe about the times she has spent with her mother? Or Nelson? Her children? Her music? She will never tell me. I will never know. Because a half hour after Hadja leaves the room, my daughter takes her last breath in this world, and she dies.

Her *amadlozi* will bother her no more. The tears of madness will no longer flow from her eyes. Ugly cries of rage will not tear from her throat. She cannot be bothered any longer. She cannot be touched; she has found her peace.

▼▼▼▼▼

I am up early Monday morning, boiling water, making breakfast, and preparing the grand boubous that we will wear. I iron the one I will take to Bongi. My happiness at having my daughter home is darkened by my fear: What am I going to tell her about the baby?

Bageot leaves early to pick up his kids and take them to school. He will come back for me so we can go get Bongi.

But he does not return right away. I grow furious. "Now where can he be?" Nine o'clock goes by. Ten o'clock. I have no telephone, so I cannot call anyone to check.

Hadja has a telephone, but when Bongi dies, the hospital never calls her. She learns what has happened when she goes to the hospital at seven in the morning. But she does not send anyone to me. She is scared. When she tells Bageot, he is scared. No one wants to be the one to break the news to me.

I wait and wait. It is eleven o'clock. In my impatience I go outside. I see my neighbors up the street. They walk away, quickly. They act like they are trying to avoid me. I look around. The neighborhood seems to be empty. Where has everyone gone?

They know. Everybody knows, except me. And then, at eleven-thirty, I hear cars. I come outside. My friend Gilbert Minot is in the car in front. Bageot's big brother is in the next car. And then Bageot is behind him.

Gilbert steps onto the veranda. His beard has grown gray from the days I knew him as a cinema student in Los Angeles. His face looks drawn. He is the one who will tell me. "You know," he says, "things didn't turn out very well with Bongi."

"What's the matter? You mean she's very sick?"

He does not answer. I see his face. I see all their faces.

I never hear anything after this, because I scream. I just scream.

▼▼▼▼▼

The afternoon passes, and the evening. I am not aware. My tears feel like poison, and they burn my cheeks. I fall to the floor, and there I am seized by a fit. My husband tries to hold me. But he cannot. I tear at my hair—my short hair that is impossible to grasp.

Quickly, the house fills up with people. The whole of Yimbaya tries to get in. Word has spread: a death at Makeba's. The neighbors know that when a house is visited by death, that house is open to all so they might come and mourn. And they come—old men and children, cripples and little babies.

No one takes notice I am insensible in my grief. I cry out: "Bongi! Bongi!" The cancer has eaten my womb, and you will be my only child! I see you running toward me in the morning. You are a little girl and you are crying. "They called me *boesman*! They called me *boesman*!" I say, "You tell the children that, yes, you are light, but you are pretty!" You run away, happy. "I am light, but I am pretty!"

When I think of the hurt I saved you from then, and the other times I was a good mother to you, it cuts me deep to think that in the end I might have failed you. You were consumed by *amadlozi* as surely as I was consumed by cancer. I knew this, and I tried to help you. My guilt is that I failed. The spirits destroy anyone whom they possess but who defies them. In my grief for my daughter there is fear for myself. I, too, fear *ukuthwasa*. Have my spirits, displeased, taken Bongi from me? First it would be Bongi, and then . . .

But my thoughts are like quick little fish that swim out of my grasp. I lie on the floor, crying out my daughter's name. There is noise in the house. A great confusion. People jam the rooms. They mob the veranda and the doors. There are crashes. Things break. I see nothing.

And then I see Bongi's husband, Sanousi. He is so very young. He stands very still. His eyes are large, and as red as the star of Mars in the sky. He will be quiet from this moment on, and never talk much to anyone again. I think, oh, Sanousi, you poor child! I love you and I want to help you. But how can I help you when I cannot help myself, and I lie screaming as midnight passes, and three o'clock, and five o'clock? No one can stop me as I scream and cry and fight against sympathetic hands. I want my family! But they are not here. They are imprisoned in the iron cage of apartheid, and they cannot travel to me, nor I to them. I cry out for my mother, for my grandmother. I cry out to Jesus and to our gods to save me from this terrible pain and this terrible fear.

A needle pierces my skin. Lights seem to flare and go out. The drug steals my senses, but it is as water against my grief.

▼▼▼▼▼

I take the children to their mother's grave. Zenzi lost her passport, and they missed the funeral. It was a Protestant ceremony. When the children arrived and met all the people who had gathered, they seemed confused and disturbed. The reality of Bongi's death does not set in until they come to the grave. The shade of the tall jungle trees, packed close together, makes this a dark place.

Lumumba is seventeen. He is tall, and he is becoming a fine-looking young man. Zenzi is fourteen, slim and pretty. They are shocked when they see the purple tiles of the grave.

The mother's death is now real. Lumumba begins to shake. He cries. Zenzi cries. We hold tight to each other, just us three. Oh, why can't we be at home?

If not for the great evil, none of us would have had to suffer the years of wandering through foreign lands. We would have been surrounded by the familiar, and by people we love and who love us. Instead, a hateful system has robbed us of all this, and cast us out. My daughter dies, her children are confused, and I am not free for a day from the longing and the hurt. And what did we do? What crimes did we commit? We are not the only ones. I look at the South African students who stay with me. I listen to the ones I meet all around. It is like their lives have been severed, and they are dangling in midair, their feet unable to touch the security of the earth. It is a strong one who does not become an alcoholic or give in to despair.

I begin to lose things. I become forgetful. This year I start wearing glasses, but I can never find them. I drink, which is new to me. And I begin to smoke too much. I am getting fat. Bageot and I fight over things large and small. At night, when the electricity is out, I take out Bongi's picture, which is transparent and mounted on a glass. I put a candle behind this glass and I look at it. Bongi looks like a fashion model. She is wearing a sleeveless red dress. Her teeth shine between her red lips as she smiles at something to one side. I drink—beer, palm nut wine, pineapple brew—it doesn't matter. I drink, and I mourn, and I feel my insides slipping away, all the strength that has brought me this far. Your death, Bongi, after all the things that have happened, and all the things that continue to happen, it is more than I can stand.

Oh, yes, this evil that has done so much to my people, it is destroying me, too. Don't you see, it is beating me?

20

THERE HAS BEEN A BIRTH, a special birth. I have come on my own to a place known to the local Guinea people as the Source. I am here to leave my baptismal sacrifice.

Africa has her mysteries, and even a wise man cannot understand them. But a wise man respects them.

This place called the Source is in Yimbaya. Ground water comes up, and this spring is the source of a tributary that flows into the river, which flows into the sea. But there is more here than a tiny stream and some green plants in a brown dirt field. There is mystery, here. There is magic. Because here is where the forces from the other side have chosen to settle. Things happen here. It is a place where the living and the dead come to terms. One must respect the Source, or there will be misfortune. We know this. In the West, the Theory of Evolution has not been proven one hundred percent. But if a person chooses to believe Darwin, he is not considered superstitious. He is considered the opposite, in fact. In Guinea, we have no scientific explanation for the power of the Source, or for the power of any of the many such places known to Africa. But even so, we believe, and we are not superstitious to do so.

I walk toward the spring and I remember the first time I was here, with my friend from South Africa, Philemon Hou. He died in December 1984, so that visit was two years ago, now. He stopped his car along the road and pointed here.

"There it is."

"Let's go," I said.

He shook his head. "No."

I was eager. "Why not, man? It's looks simple."

"No, I just wanted to show you that this is the place I was telling you about. Where we had the troubles."

He tells me that I must not disturb the spring without reason. People come here to leave sacrifice. They come to pray. But they do not come idly, like tourists. So, we continue on our way.

Philemon had been working on a movie with the Ballet Africaine. He worked on the musical arrangements for these beautiful artists and their beautiful work. They wanted to begin their film at the Source. But when they showed up, many negative forces worked against them. The sun would never shine right, camera parts were missing, the dancers hurt themselves doing simple things. They finally gave up and went to the mountains. But at least they were unharmed. One hears stories of people who come here with thoughts of mischief, and they die of accidents, if not here then shortly after.

There is a food one brings to make sacrifice. It is called "white bread," but it is made from casaba melon, not wheat. The local women make it, and they made the loaf I carry in my hands.

It is the rainy season now, and the sky is bright white, like a sheet of fluorescent light. Soon it will turn black, and the showers will come. I am still afraid of lightning after all the years that have passed since my little playmate was struck along the roadside. In my home I always put blankets over my mirrors when it storms. We were taught that mirrors attract lightning.

After Bongi's death, I did not always remove the blankets right away after the storms passed. I did not want to be bothered with what I would see in the reflections. I did not care to see what was happening to me.

Four days after Bongi's funeral, I had a concert to do. I did it. The audience had no idea that a part of my life had been taken from me, that I was not whole, that I was discouraged and beaten down. I sang and moved, and urged them to do so also. I think the *amadlozi* within me must have taken over. But the concert was a success. My schedule continued without interruption.

I asked myself why, when I was so tired and so discouraged?

It was because singing seemed the only way to keep the pain and the numbness away for a little while. But more than the happiness of performing was involved. My daughter died because she lost her mind in exile, and to avenge her death and the deaths of so many of my family and my people I must continue to speak out against the racism and murder that makes bloody and foul my home. I say very, very little on stage, just a few words at most. The people come to have a good time and enjoy themselves with African music. They do not come to be lectured, which is good, because I am not a speaker. Mostly, just the fact that I am there at all, that I have survived, is testimony enough that there is resistance toward Pretoria. Maybe a thousand people at a time see me and learn things. It is not much, but it is the best I can do. This is the way I will defeat the great evil, and this is the way I will save myself.

There is a young man who is staying with me this summer. He is writing my life's story, and this book will let me speak to many. We sit in the garden in the moonlight, while the neighbors play their bellaphones and the mosquitoes buzz outside the safety of our insect repellent, and I tell him many things. I tell him things that I have never told anyone, all the sad stories. We cry. I do not know, but I think this man may be *isangoma* like me, which is unusual, because he is white and he is from California. He tells me that people will find courage from my story. It embarrasses me to hear this; in my heart I know I am nobody special. I am just me, Miriam, and I sing—but I sing *good*.

But the funny thing is, I am finding courage just speaking of the past. I am sorting things out, and it leaves me feeling clean. And as my inner house gets in order, it shows on the outside. I am losing weight. I feel better. I look at the world the way I once did, and I say, "Hey, watch out! You ain't seen nothin', yet."

I think of the misery of my country, and I get angry; and when I get angry I come alive! The Botha regime promised two years ago to stop the forced settlement of my people into the hated "homelands." But this was public relations for the Krugerrand buyers. The promise was not kept. The homes of my people are still being destroyed, and we are being driven away like cattle. Pretoria said last year that it wanted to negotiate the participation at long last of my people in the government of our country. But this was a lie: Our leaders who must do the negotiating remain in jail. Pretoria promised to grant independence to Namibia. A lie. Pretoria signed the Nkomati Accord that says it will not interfere with Mozambique and other independent South African states. A lie.

But people are waking up. The West is realizing that if they associate with criminals and murderers, they will get dirty themselves. Sanctions are being applied. The big corporations are moving out.

And at home, the students will not be silent. The people defy the state of emergency and take to the streets, where we are shot at, gassed, beaten. Little children are jailed. This is nothing new, but what is new is the direction, the purpose. We grow stronger. Each hit on the head is like a vaccination: It immunizes us against the next. We have been jailed for nonsense in the past, for no reason at all, but just to keep us down. So what is so terrible about being jailed for demanding our rights as human beings? It is not terrible. It is honorable.

All this also brings me back from Bongi's death, when I thought I was beaten. Seeing all these things, and knowing I am alive to see them, and to be a part of them, it lifts me up.

▼▼▼▼▼

Ahead of me is the spring that the people here call the Source. The water is colorless now beneath the white sky. This place really is nothing special: just some stones and a few jungle trees and bushes. But you feel something here. You feel, not other people, but presences. I stop and stand at the little stream. The water gurgles at my feet. Water: where all life comes from. Africa: where all men come from. The Source: where I come now with my offering that is a gift to the past and to the future.

They are always knocking at your door: the past and the future.

When I first visited the United Nations with Jane and Mburumba Kerina in 1960, Dag Hammarskjöld was the Secretary General. This year I traveled to Brussels, where I was given the 1986 Dag Hammarskjöld Peace Prize. And there was another achievement award this summer from the French government, which once banned me when I was with Stokely. I think, I am happy now because my years of performing are helping to awaken the world to the plight of my people.

When I left Hugh Masekela, he wanted to go to California to be a star. Well, he did "Grazin' in the Grass," and he became one. I saw him in Washington a few weeks ago. I sat in his audience during a performance of his at the Kennedy Center, where I have also performed. When he introduced me, the audience gave me such an ovation that later backstage Hughie joked that he stole his own applause by pointing me out. We are friends. He writes for me.

When I last talked to Stokely a few days ago, it was after his recent trouble. Stokely was arrested by the Guinean officials and he spent three days in jail. They thought he was somehow connected with a coup that was attempted last year against the people who led the original coup after President Touré died. Stokely tells me that it was a mistake. That is all I want to know, just so he is safe.

When I last saw my adopted daughter, Muntu, she was pregnant. Miriam is going to be a grandmother, again. Muntu is married to a man from Zimbabwe, and she has started a life with him there.

I think of them all as I stand by the shallow stream with the offering in my hand. They are many, these faces that crowd my thoughts.

A friend called me from Johannesburg when I was in New York. He told me, "Winnie Mandela wants to talk to you."

I was surprised. It must be important, since so many things are happening to her. She is Nelson's connection to the outside world, his eyes and ears and voice. He has been in prison for twenty-three years, now. The world clamors for his release. But the authorities are deaf. First they told Winnie that she could not return to her home, and then they wouldn't let her leave it. When she did go, someone burned it down!

"How can I talk to her?" I asked. It must be difficult, I thought. Her life is always in danger. She has to be very careful always. My friend gave me a number and a time to call.

When I called, a man's voice answered. He was mysterious. "She has traveled. Try on Monday."

I thought of Nelson Mandela. When I met him it was 1954. I was just a girl. And I was so shy I could not look him in the face.

Monday came and I dialed the number. The same man's voice answered. "Who's calling?"

"Miriam." This was all I said. This was what I had been told to say.

"Hold on."

I heard her voice. It was full of happiness.

"Zenzi!"

"Oh, Winnie!"

"I wanted to talk to you, Zenzi." She grew serious. "I wanted to express to you from me and our father . . ."

We always referred to Nelson as "our father."

" . . . we wanted to express how deeply hurt we are that you lost your child in exile. Your only child. We just want you to know that we always think of you."

I started to cry. I could not help myself. I told her that I was proud of her, and that we watch and follow what is happening to her. We know that she is strong. The strength that she has she gives to us, too.

She said, "You mustn't cry, Zenzi. Because when we *do* get our land back we will bring all our children—and also our dead—back to their own country. Just be strong and continue."

"I will, Winnie." I apologized for crying. "I will continue."

"We all will."

"You must go now, Winnie?"

"I must. But before I do let me tell you what Nelson said I should tell you."

"Yes?"

"He said, 'When I looked at that little girl, I always knew that she was going to be someone!' "

▼▼▼▼▼

I put my baptismal offering on the ground: the "white bread" and a handful of kola nuts. They are for a little girl who has just been born by the name of Bongi. This is the baby of the sister of my daughter's husband, Sanousi. When the sister was pregnant, Sanousi's mother, Hadja, came and asked me if a girl was born, could she be named Bongi? I was very happy. When I returned from a concert in Senegal and saw the baby for the first time, I swore that for a moment she was my Bongi reborn. I wonder if such things can happen? I am here at this place to ask.

I kneel down onto the pebbly ground. God is everywhere, and I know he is here to hear me. I thank the Superior Being for making Hadja's wish come true. I thank my ancestors. I pray, and because I am only human, I ask for things. I ask that I and the people on the outside can be freed from our exile. I ask that my people at home be freed from our bondage. I ask that I may never forget those who have helped me, and to whom I am grateful.

I arrange the kola nuts around the white casaba loaf. I stand up and look at my work: an offering of remembrance for my Bongi, an offering of baptism for a new Bongi. An offering of hope. There are three things, I have said, that I will have until the day I die: hope, determination, and song. I am not dead, yet, and I still have these things.

I turn and walk away. I am told that if a person goes a short distance and looks back, the offering they left will be gone. This is strange, because there is nobody around. The offering would just have to be swallowed up into the ground. I walk away and I am scared to look back. If the offering is still there, then I would think that it is not accepted. I blame myself for feeling this way, because what is truly important is the prayers one gives. Still, my curiosity is powerful. I know Africa and its magic. What has my life been but an exercise in African magic? My will says, "Don't look back."

But all I have been doing these past weeks is looking back, back over my life. And I have not turned to salt. I have become stronger. No, my will says, continue to the road. Don't blaspheme. But my offering means so much. And I am too weak. I cannot help myself. I look back.

The offering is gone.